"Not only has Ed Olkovich made the complex, confusing, and often-neglected topic of estate planning easy to understand, but he has provided Canadians with a step-by-step guide to actually implementing it."
— Jamie Golombek, Vice-President, Tax & Estate Planning, AIM Trimark Investments

"Not only does Ed Olkovich provide simple steps, but he also removes the fear and dread. In his hands, estate planning is transformed into a welcome, even enjoyable responsibility."
— Ellen Roseman, Business columnist, TORONTO STAR

## Don't put off estate planning — think of your loved ones today

Many people believe planning their estate is a daunting task, but the truth is, it's easier than you think (and we don't mean by using will kits!). Making those big decisions in your lifetime will save your loved ones money and future stress, giving you peace of mind knowing you've provided for them.

How easy is it? Try six simple steps. Estates expert Ed Olkovich outlines strategies on how to put your affairs in order and plan your estate. Using sample documents, checklists, and worksheets, you will learn how to

- create, change, and bulletproof your will
- reduce taxes and protect assets
- designate powers of attorney and ___ ___ ___ directives
- avoid probate (the right way)
- prepare trusts to protect your children
- ___ ___ right executor

Most important, you will discover how to make the best investment of all — protecting your loved ones.

Edward Olkovich is "Mr. Wills" — a nationally recognized expert in estate planning. Author of three other books, he is an Ontario specialist in Estates and Trusts Law with 25 years of practical legal experience. He is a regular guest on television and radio where he offers advice about personal finance.

ECW Press • $19.95 CDN

Distributed in Canada by Jaguar Books

Business/Personal Finance

www.ecwpress.com

ISBN 1-55022-693-2

9 781550 226935

# Estate

## Planning in

## Six **Simple** Steps

Published by ECW Press
2120 Queen Street East, Suite 200, Toronto, Ontario, Canada M4E 1E2

LIBRARY AND ARCHIVES CANADA CATALOGUING IN PUBLICATION
Olkovich, Edward, 1951–
Estate planning in six simple steps / Edward Olkovich.

Previous ed. published under title: The complete idiot's guide to estate
planning in six simple steps for Canadians.
ISBN 1-55022-693-2

1. Estate planning—Canada—Popular works. I. Olkovich, Edward,
1951– . Complete idiot's guide to estate planning in six simple steps for
Canadians. II. Title.

KE5974.Z82O43 2005     343.7105'3     C2004-907043-6
KF750.Z9O43 2005

Editor: Dallas Harrison
Cover and Text Design: Tania Craan
Author Photo: David Hawe
Production and Typesetting: Mary Bowness
Printing: Transcontinental

This book is set in Joanna and Akzidenz Grotesk.

The publication of Estate Planning in Six Simple Steps has been generously
supported by the Canada Council, the Ontario Arts Council, the Ontario Media
Development Corporation, and the Government of Canada through the Book
Publishing Industry Development Program. Canada

DISTRIBUTION
CANADA: Jaguar Book Group, 100 Armstrong Avenue, Georgetown, ON, L7G 5S4

PRINTED AND BOUND IN CANADA

ECW PRESS
ecwpress.com

# Estate
## Planning in
## Six **Simple** Steps

Edward Olkovich

ECW Press

# Acknowledgments

A number of people must be acknowledged for their help in producing this book. First, thank you to Donald Bastian for his help and for introducing me to my publisher, Jack David. Thank you also to Mary L. MacGregor, chair of the Ontario Law Society's Estates & Trusts Law Specialization Committee, for her comments. And thanks to J. Howard Lane, CA, CPA who is always helpful with tax issues. All omissions and errors or inconsistencies in the text are, of course, solely my responsibility.

The dedication of my office assistants, Darlene Jukes and Eletra Lasci, makes everything possible. Patricia Standello and Tania Morgado helped prepare this manuscript. My editor, Dallas Harrison, helped to improve the manuscript. Thank you. Individual chapters were also reviewed by lawyers Frank Mendicino, Kimberly T. Morris, M. Jasmine Sweatman, and Teresa Lee of CIBC Legal Division. Finally, my family provided invaluable support and humour throughout.

# Contents

To Krystyna, a wonderful wife.

For thirty years, you have been the sunshine and sparkle in my life.

# Introduction

## Scandal Rocks Town

Yesterday police discovered the body of someone who mysteriously had no will.

Yes, it's not really news, because it happens every day. People, without an estate plan, die. It's too common a problem to make the papers. No one bothers to interview the family members who have to cope with headaches, bills, and pain. But I have to help relatives and friends when they come into my law office looking for answers. They are shocked that someone had not taken the time to plan.

As a lawyer, author, and speaker, I have shown thousands of Canadians how to handle their estate planning. In this book, you'll find a simple approach to wills, estate plans, and more. I have created a six-step process you can use to protect yourself and your loved ones. You can use it to create, review, or revise your estate wish list.

## Avoid These Twelve Estate Blunders

You'll probably never see headlines like these in the papers, but here are the problems I can help you prevent.

- "Couple Orphans Children with No Plan"
- "Widow without Life Insurance Loses Home"
- "Taxes Ate My Parents' Estate"
- "Disappointed Beneficiary Sues Estate"
- "Disgruntled Spouse Sues Stepchildren"
- "Surviving Spouse Begs to Keep Lifestyle"
- "Inheritance Gone with the Wind"
- "Homemade Will Costs a Fortune"
- "Executor Couldn't Save Business"
- "Siblings Steal Inheritance"
- "Millionaire Incapable of Accessing Money"
- "Homeless Shelters Filled with Incapacitated Parents"

## Stop Struggling

Your days of struggling with estate planning are over. You picked up this book because you want answers and to learn the six basic steps everyone needs to follow. Use them to start or update your estate plan and documents. I can't promise to make it exciting, but what you'll learn can save a fortune in costs and prevent delays and tears of disappointment.

## Estate Planning in Six Simple Steps

Will your loved ones suffer and pay more taxes than necessary? Without estate planning, that's what will happen.

Estate planning can save money and protect you, your assets, and your loved ones. I'll show you the basics in six building-block steps. You'll learn what it takes to make wills, choose executors, and provide for your beneficiaries. Some people fall into expensive traps — but you can avoid them with the help of this book.

I hear you saying "I'm still too young to make a will" or "I don't know where to start." I can get you started with my simple process. You'll educate yourself and get rewards you can enjoy today regardless of your age. You'll take care of yourself and the people who care about you. I'll explain how powers of attorney give you security and peace of mind today.

Everyone needs to do it, not just the rich. Whatever your age or financial situation, you must protect yourself and your estate. Whether you're single, married, or in a common-law or same-sex relationship, you must plan. Failing to arrange your affairs can lead to horrendous results.

## How You Benefit

This book will help simplify your life. I'll use stories and examples to explain the steps. You'll look at some sample legal documents, including

- wills;
- trust agreements;
- powers of attorney;
- marriage contracts;
- codicils to amend wills; and
- personal property memos.

My forms and checklists will finally get you organized. You'll learn to shield yourself and your heirs from tax grabs and legal battles. Here's a chart with some things estate planning can do for you. You'll learn how

| To Save | To Protect | To Understand |
|---|---|---|
| income and probate taxes | yourself from bad advice | wills and estate law |
| worry and time | your estate from legal claims | beneficiaries' needs |
| legal costs | your own inheritance | choices for executors |

As a lawyer, I have gained valuable experience about estate matters. I go to court to solve estate problems that could have been avoided. You can benefit from my experience teaching lawyers, financial planners, and clients about estate solutions.

## How This Book Is Organized

I'll identify and take you through each of the six simple steps to estate planning. Here's what you'll have done by the time you finish the book.

**Step 1: Get Started.** It's easy and rewarding to make a wish list for your plan. If you don't, you'll fail to protect yourself and your loved ones. I'll explain what you do with insurance, investments, and your business. You will learn what assets make up an estate and how to slice it up "easy as pie." I'll explain how ownership of your assets affects what you can do with your property. You'll learn how to preview your estate to cover your wish list.

**Step 2: Avoid the Big Tax Bite.** Paying taxes can eat up your estate's spare cash and destroy your dreams. Plan now to give those you love more and the government less. I'll answer the tax questions you're dying to ask and show you easy tax-saving tips. New rules make giving to charity more rewarding so you can keep on giving. You'll understand how to avoid probate costs properly without risking your estate.

**Step 3: Make Your Will.** Without a will, your estate is handed out regardless of your wishes. Wills let you choose who is in charge, who gets what, and who guards your minor children. Your will is your most important estate planning tool. It protects assets from costly court cases and your loved ones from uncertainty and hardship. You'll understand why lawyer-prepared wills work best. Checklists highlight the top ten mistakes you must avoid when making a will. Learn how to bulletproof your will so it stays out of court.

**Step 4: Choose Your Executors.** Who controls your estate and ensures your heirs get their entitlements? I'll explain how to pick the best executors. If you are asked to be an executor or trustee, you'll gain greater understanding of your responsibilities. I'll answer questions on estate administration and the skills executors must have. Among family, friend, professional, or trust company, you must choose wisely, or you'll pay for it. Use my checklist to help you find a trustworthy executor.

**Step 5: Benefit Your Beneficiaries.** I'll show you simple ways to give to your children and spouses. Who should benefit from your assets to avoid lawsuits? How will they handle your gifts? Can you protect minors and control your wealth from the grave? What about cutting someone out of your will? I'll show you the best way to avoid conflict, grief, and trips to the courthouse.

**Step 6: Protect Yourself Now.** Powers of attorney can keep you in control. Every estate plan can be destroyed without these documents. Do you know at what age you should have a power of attorney or a living will? I'll explain why you must treat your original will like gold. Learn how and when you must revise a will and estate plans. And, finally, you'll get organized with a brief estate inventory of important information.

## Six Steps to Successful Estate Planning

If you don't take the time to plan your estate, the government does. It has no choice but to write a will for you. You can't reduce taxes, costs, or grief for the ones you have left behind. Assets can go to the wrong people — not the ones you intended to benefit. Exercise your prerogative and make a plan for yourself and your loved ones. It's your responsibility, after all.

Now is the time to start, no matter how modest your estate. Whatever your circumstances, age, health, or wealth, you and your loved ones benefit from preparing for the future.

## Extras

I have included summaries of key points for you to remember at the end of each chapter. Items of amusement and interest are also included in every section. I have included a glossary at the end of the book to help you with terminology. I'll introduce new terms in each step or section of the book and explain them.

### Help Line

Inquiring minds will want to read these questions and answers.

### Bulletins

These are warnings, tips, and traps to avoid.

### Legal Lingo

This is legal jargon translated for the rest of us.

### Time Machine

This is intriguing information from the past.

### It's Been Said

These are sayings from famous people.

### It's Been Said
. . . . . . . . . . . . . . . . . . . . . . . . . . . . . . . . . . . . . . . . .

"Nothing is so fatiguing as the eternal hanging on of an uncompleted task."

— William James, 1842–1910, letter to Carl Stumph, January 1, 1896

Now turn the page and I'll show you how easy it is to get started.

# Get Started

My six-step process to estate planning uses your assets to satisfy your wish list. It's more than just dealing with property; estate planning is about taking care of people, the ones you love. Estate plans distribute all your assets. Even a simple estate plan must consider your legal options. I'll describe how to make this "easy as pie." Then you can follow my step-by-step process to preview your estate's worth.

Your legacy, what you leave behind, determines how you will be remembered. Rich or poor, we leave it all behind when we die. Yours may be a substantial wealth or collection of collectibles. But how you leave that property to your loved ones affects your legacy and their memory of you. An up-to-date estate plan can relieve your anxiety as well as your loved ones'. Estate planning is also about getting started — so let's begin. I'll show you how simple it is to take your first step.

# Chapter 1

# It's Easy to Start

In this chapter:

- Take your first step.
- What's it all about?
- Take a quiz to set goals.
- Visualize your rewards.

*It's a Wonderful Life.* A classic movie. Remembering the climax gives me a warm feeling. Everyone comes to the rescue of George Bailey, played by Jimmy Stewart, a great man who doesn't know how valuable a life he's led. Clarence, his guardian angel, tells George he's been given a remarkable gift. He shows George what would have happened if he hadn't been born. Sharing this gift saves George and helps Clarence get his "first-class" angel wings.

Corny as it sounds, I feel a little like Clarence (though I'm no angel!). I tell people they too have a remarkable gift. And you can leave this gift to your loved ones when you pass on. The gift is a properly planned estate that takes care of their needs.

But there's a catch — you can choose to make a plan or do nothing at all. To make this gift, you must take action. Think about it. If you died tomorrow, who would take care of your family, your friends, your alma mater? Would everyone raise a glass to toast your life? Or would everyone ask questions such as "Why did you leave a mess behind? Why didn't you just find the time to make a will"?

## Why People Hate to Plan

You may believe it's too difficult, too time consuming, and easier to do nothing. Yet the evidence is that you plan all the time. You plan dinner, which movie to see, and where to go on vacation next summer or on the weekend. So why not your estate? Is it too morbid or too complex a topic?

Well, not anymore. My six-step program will help you understand and benefit from estate planning. Like you never thought possible, you'll grasp, in concrete terms, how you can protect yourself and loved ones.

You'll understand estate planning as a *save* and *protect* system. Here's what I mean. Most people are familiar with security and alarm systems at home or work. Passwords, codes, and alarms prevent unauthorized entry to provide security. Estate planning is also a save and protect system, but you won't set off any alarm bells — except perhaps one inside your head warning you to get started.

You know planning is important for just about everything in life. Estate planning is no different. Good intentions and desires don't accomplish anything. You need something more tangible, but it doesn't have to be complex. Everyone needs, as a minimum, to make a will, establish powers of attorney, and use tax- and probate-saving techniques.

## What Does Estate Planning Do for You?

You've accumulated all kinds of things during your life. When you die, these assets will make up your estate. Everyone, whether rich or poor, has an estate. What would be left if everything you had was sold and turned into cash? Maybe it would be enough to fill a small paper bag. Or perhaps your cash would fill a suitcase or trunk. Now think about who will have their hands out to take your cash:

- the tax department for income taxes;
- estate courts for probate taxes;
- lawyers for estate legal fees;
- funeral directors (no explanation needed);
- executors for estate administration; and
- creditors for outstanding debts.

So subtract enough to cover all these demands if you can figure out what they will be. What's left is your net estate. That's all you have to cover the needs of your loved ones. Is there enough to carry out your last wishes? Make a list of whom you'd rather give your hard-earned cash to:

- your spouse, children, or stepchildren;
- your parents, brothers, and sisters; or
- your friends, favourite causes, and charities.

**Bulletin**

Imagine estate essentials as a toolbox where you keep your estate planning tools such as a will and powers of attorney. You'd store originals "off-site" in a safe deposit box. Keep copies for your own estate toolbox at home. Include copies of your deeds and insurance policies and an inventory of valuables. You can review them when needed.

### What's Your Recipe?

All those people with their hands out waiting to be paid — visualizing this scene may cause you to ask an important estate planning question. How can I save money and have more to protect my loved ones? My answer is to follow the six simple steps.

Your estate plan must meet your unique personal needs and objectives. No one plan works for everyone. Think of some possible variations and combinations in just three areas.

- **Employment:** you could be self-employed, earn a salary, retired, or at home.
- **Children:** yours could be feuding, estranged, challenged, or divorcing.
- **Spouse:** your spouse could be common-law, separated, dying, or incapacitated.

Don't think a one-size-fits-all approach to estate planning will work for you. Tailoring is required to reflect your needs at a particular stage of your life. Are you buying a home, investing, marrying, having a baby, or fighting a serious illness? At each point, your needs and wishes will be different. Only you can make the decision about what should happen to your estate. Your will should express your final wishes about your property and loved ones.

## Step by Step: Steps 1 through 6

If everyone's needs are different, the tools they use will be different too. In your own estate toolbox, you'll need essentials such as a will. Wills are legal documents that set out your wishes in black and white. A will lets you take care of people and controls who gets everything. You'll also need powers of attorney, another set of documents to sign. They legally authorize someone to act on your behalf if you become incapacitated.

You may also need a trust to manage assets while you're alive or after your death. Various tax, probate, and gifting strategies can also help you. You'll learn about them as you progress through the six simple steps of estate planning.

Whatever stage you are at in your life, you can get these advantages. Here's what we'll do together.

**Step 1:** Assess your assets to preview and identify estate needs and solutions.

**Step 2:** Save money with income tax, probate, and charitable gift techniques.

**Step 3:** Make a will that is bulletproof and covers all your requirements.

**Step 4:** Choose the best legal representative to manage your estate.

**Step 5:** Take care of your spouse, children, and beneficiaries' needs.

**Step 6:** Protect yourself today with powers of attorney and regular plan revisions.

## Surprising Statistics

Only forty-six percent of Canadians have a will, according to a 1999 Decima Research survey conducted for the Canadian Bar Association — Ontario for its Make a Will Month™ project. That's the number way back when I wrote the first version of this book. All the ads you see for will and estate kits suggest the subject still has people looking for answers. Why don't more people take steps to protect their loved ones? Perhaps difficult decisions scare people who are afraid to make a mistake. For some, procrastination is the way to deal with a sea of choices.

Take Michelle, who could never get started on her will. "You've got to help me," she pleaded. She walked into my law office with a briefcase of newspaper clippings. "I have saved every newspaper article about wills and probate," she said cheerfully.

I smiled as I glanced through her collection of colour-coded folders, each labelled by subject.

"I have a couple of university degrees, and I still don't know what to do," she admitted. "I don't want to sound silly, but I feel like a complete idiot. Where do I start? Should I see my financial planner, my tax advisor, or my lawyer first?"

"You're educating yourself. That's perfect, but now you must get good advice to make your own decisions."

Her story is not unusual. Michelle had questions about estates, wills, tax, probate, and powers of attorney. She wanted answers from someone she could trust.

## Loved Ones Need Your Vision

Estate planning is your vision — it's how you wish to care for your loved ones if something happens to you. Filling those needs is a good place to start. Look at Carol, who wants to take care of Hank, her elderly husband. Carol's money is to be used for Hank's nursing care if something happens to her. But Carol wants to know who will take care of her business. She wants to pay as little in taxes as possible so she'll leave more for Hank's care. She already has a will and doesn't know why she needs an estate plan.

An estate plan would help Carol deal with her property while she is alive. A will may only cover a portion of her assets, and it's effective only upon her death. Wills are key estate tools, but they're not enough by themselves. Carol needs to identify and make an overall estate wish list. Perhaps she needs life insurance, a tax strategy, and advice. Once she investigates these options, she can talk with Hank about their joint needs. They will be reassured they are on the right course with their planning.

---

**Legal Lingo**

*Jointly owned property* is a legally recognized form of ownership. All joint owners have an equal right to deal with the asset while they're alive. If one joint owner dies, that person's interest is automatically inherited by the other joint owner under what's called right of survivorship.

---

**It's Been Said**

"I do nothing but go about persuading you all, old and young alike, not to take thought for your persons or your properties, but first and chiefly to care about the greatest improvement of the soul."
– Socrates, in Plato's *Apology*

Wills deal only with assets that are solely in your name. Jointly owned property or insurance and pensions with designated beneficiaries are not affected by them. These items are transferred directly to your beneficiaries at death without a will. However, they can create income tax liabilities, which must then be paid by your estate. Assets you've promised under your will may need to be sold to pay those taxes. An overall estate plan deals with all assets and tax issues to avoid disappointment.

## Estate Plan Illustration

Look at André, who has a home where he lives with his daughter. His stock portfolio is $200,000, the same value as his home. André changed the ownership of his home to be joint with his daughter. She will inherit it as a joint owner when her father dies.

André's will states his son and daughter are to share all his wealth. But André didn't consider his income tax liabilities.

On his death, André's stock portfolio carries an $80,000 income tax bill. Yes, his daughter will receive a $200,000 home. She and her brother will share the stocks, but they're worth much less after the taxes are paid.

Paying an $80,000 income tax bill leaves $120,000 from the stocks. This amount is to be divided between the children. The result is the daughter gets $260,000 in assets. The son gets only half of the net stock value by his father's will. That's only $60,000 — and a bad case of bitterness. This is not really the fair split that André wanted to achieve. His estate plan should have anticipated taxes, and he should have revised his plan, including his will.

### Is That All There Is?

We all go from school to a first job, first car, and first big investment. Most people in their mid-twenties do not think about estate planning. They don't have a lot of property. They don't suddenly pass away in large numbers either. But that doesn't mean they can't benefit from understanding estate planning basics such as wills and powers of attorney. Even before you have substantial assets, marry, or have children, you can benefit from these tools as sound investments.

You need estate goals that are both short and long term. Estate planning is not something that can wait until you're retired; it's just part of your financial-planning picture. If you have children, you have to plan. What if you were not there tomorrow (definitely short term, but perhaps not a goal)?

. . . . . . . . . . . . . . . . . . . . . . . . . . . . . . . . . . . . . . . . . . . . . . . . . . . . .

### An Estate Planning Quiz

Here is a quick quiz you should take to help show you what estate planning is about. Don't worry if some of the questions seem strange now; they won't by the time you finish this book.

Answer each question to help you identify your estate planning needs.

| | Yes | No |
|---|---|---|
| I know what my loved ones will get when my estate is divided. | ❑ | ❑ |
| I've planned to transfer my assets, business, and investments. | ❑ | ❑ |
| I know how to reduce my income tax bill at death. | ❑ | ❑ |
| I have taken the proper steps to reduce probate taxes. | ❑ | ❑ |
| I have a current will that has people named as backups. | ❑ | ❑ |
| I have the right person to handle my estate when I'm gone. | ❑ | ❑ |
| I have provided for my dependants and guardians for my children. | ❑ | ❑ |
| I have appointed someone legally to make financial and health care decisions for me if I am incapacitated. | ❑ | ❑ |
| I understand the six-step process of estate planning that will help me make the best decisions. | ❑ | ❑ |
| I review my estate plan regularly to keep it up to date. | ❑ | ❑ |

The correct answer to each question is yes. You'll learn why as you go through this book.

---

**Legal Lingo**

A *will* is effective after your death and is a revocable written document. You sign it to set out your last wishes for your property after your death. Your will names beneficiaries, persons you trust to be your executors, and a guardian for minors. Wills must comply with each province's legal requirements to be valid.

---

You can write in your personal targets if you want right now. To help you, I'll show you what I did. My wish list is general at this stage. As you read this book, you'll be more specific. Right now here's what I targeted:

- to secure my spouse's and children's future;
- to pay the least in taxes; and
- to avoid problems, delays, and legal expenses.

Now fill in your top three estate planning wishes. Be specific if you can.

**My Top Three Estate Planning Wishes**

1. _____

2. _____

3. _____

Don't forget to get your partner to make up a list as well.

You'll refer to this wish list as you go through the six steps. It's valuable for you to set some priorities at this stage.

## Assemble Your Team

You need professional help to create a plan. Here's a list of people you may want on your team of advisors.

**Life insurance representative:** young families and those paying support or mortgages need a life insurance advisor to help pay taxes and/or support and to cover business interests.

**Financial planner:** he or she will consider your investments and financial goals and help you develop a plan.

**Tax advisor or accountant:** a tax advisor or accountant will know the intricate details of your tax returns and plans and provide valuable information to estimate and reduce taxes.

**Estate lawyer:** he or she can draw up legal documents, including wills, trusts, and powers of attorney, and can help you with probate and estate work for a loved one.

**Trust officer:** experts at a trust company can set up an asset trust or administer estates and explain services and fees as professional estate or trust administrators.

**Business succession expert:** this person will design a transfer plan for your business interests.

> **Legal Lingo**
>
> A *living will* sets out your medical treatment wishes. Living wills can't deal with property and are not really valid wills. Don't be fooled thinking you are protected with just a living will. You must have a legally valid will so you won't die intestate.

Some or all of these people can be part of your estate team at different stages, and, believe me, there are different stages to estate planning. It's not something you do just when you're sixty-five. If you marry, have children, buy a home, start a business, divorce, remarry, or simply age, you'll have a different wish list. You need a custom plan to reflect your situation through life's journey.

One constant need is to have an up-to-date will and powers of attorney. These are the tools you'll fall back upon. Each member of your team will always ask or assume that you have these estate essentials in place. Don't worry, you won't generate bad luck by getting them into your toolkit. Get over your fear and think of the good you'll do. Besides, it's no different from having a spare tire in your trunk; you don't expect ever to have to use it, but it's there in case of an emergency.

## Visualize Your Estate Planning Rewards

I have told you the benefits of estate planning are to save and protect your assets. Here are some of the rewards of taking the six simple steps.

- You leave a legacy of peace, wealth, and happiness.
- You reduce income and probate taxes before something happens to you.
- You leave more for your loved ones and less for the government.
- You control your financial and health care decisions as long as possible.
- You choose a substitute decision maker as your attorney to protect you.
- You select a person you trust to be your executor or attorney.
- You spare your family costly legal proceedings to handle your estate.
- You fulfil your moral and legal obligations, leaving no broken promises.
- You express your last wishes in a will to avoid family feuds and conflicts.
- You enjoy peace of mind knowing you have taken care of your family.

"He who has begun has half done. Dare to be wise; Begin!"

– Horace, *Epistles*

## Dying Intestate

If you die intestate, it means you've died without a will. This means the government writes a will for you. You have no say in who gets your property, how it is divided, and who is in charge. Your estate must be distributed according to a government formula. Each province has different rules for this process. They are arbitrary and can't be altered. Your intentions must be in a will, or they're worthless.

On the other hand, dying testate means you have a will. That means you can make three important decisions. First, who gets your estate, when, and how? Second, who is in charge of the process? And third, who will be your children's guardians and backups in case the first persons you chose are not available?

You want to plan to die testate with a current will, which sets out your choices for these three decisions and more.

## You're on the Way

Now you've set some simple yet specific goals for your estate plan. You'll want to revise or make a will so you can die testate. Remember Michelle from earlier in the chapter? After she started, she said, "It was so much easier to get started than I ever dreamed. I should have done it sooner. I now know I have taken care of everything that is important to me."

As a lawyer, I have seen the consequences of bad planning. I handle court cases in which judges attempt to resolve estate problems. I see the pain of grieving families and friends after a death. It's worse when loved ones fail to plan. They have no road map and no place to begin their recovery. Estate planning is your positive alternative for them.

In the next chapter, you'll see what is at the centre of every estate plan.

............................................
## The Least You Need to Know

- Estate planning benefits everyone, regardless of age or economic status.
- Planning saves taxes and legal expenses to protect you and your loved ones.
- You need a will as an essential in your estate toolbox.
- Keep control with powers of attorney as part of your estate plan.

# Chapter 2

# What Makes Every Estate Plan Tick?

In this chapter:

- What do you care about?
- How big is your pie?
- Create an estate inventory.
- Become familiar with restrictions.

People are at the heart of estate planning. That's what estate planning is — caring for the people you love. You plan to share your wealth with your family, friends, and causes. Planning lets you satisfy their present and future needs. Don't worry, I won't forget to cover your own needs.

Let's take stock of what's included in your estate. You may own assets or property jointly, alone, in partnership, or otherwise. How you own things controls what you can do with your estate. I'll cover the laws that restrict the use of your private property. You just can't do whatever you want with it — surprise, surprise!

## What's This Estate Business?

Estates consist of assets and liabilities. I'll focus on the assets for the time being. Your possessions (furniture, home, and cash) are assets. When you die, what you leave behind is your estate.

The first step is to prepare an asset inventory. Without it, you can't make a will to meet your objectives.

When you die, assets can go to your estate or directly to your beneficiaries, and this obviously makes a difference to your estate planning goals. You'll also have no control over some assets on death except through your will.

## Giving It Away Now Is No Solution

Marsha told me she was just too old and too tired to plan. "I just want to transfer my home to my son. He's going to get it eventually. I'll just make everything joint with me." She was taking estate planning to its extreme — just get rid of everything early so you don't have an estate. Well, a lot depends on whether you are fifty-five or eighty-five years of age.

Marsha has to remember that, if her son dies first, she has no plan for her assets. Her son's bankruptcy, divorce, or incapacity could create even larger headaches. Problems could develop that she doesn't anticipate. Giving it away now doesn't avoid taxes or family squabbles.

### Bulletin

If you are making a will, you have to know how you own your assets. It's not safe to think you own your home jointly or with a partner. You have to check your deed, transfer, or ownership records. Don't trust your memory.

Marsha's case points out how estate planning balances competing interests. Marsha must consider her present and future goals. She must weigh her own personal needs with those of her beneficiaries. What will she need when she retires, becomes disabled, or dies? She's confused about what she'll have to give away when she dies and doesn't know how to plan.

I had to simplify things for Marsha so she could take her first step. I told her to look at what she owned since her assets were probably controlled in three different ways.

## Three Things that Control Everyone's Assets

Your property rights are based on what you own and how you own it. If you own a car by yourself, you'll have rights as the sole owner. Your method of ownership, joint or in partnership, for example, will give you different rights. Especially important is the right to transfer ownership on death.

Do your assets pass by your will, by law, or by contract? How you answer these questions will identify what lies at the heart of your estate planning. How to give away your property?

> **Legal Lingo**
>
> *Joint tenancy* is a way to own property with a record of ownership like a deed or bank account. You're really the owner, not a "tenant." Joint tenants own things with a survivorship right. The share of the first to die goes to the survivors, even without a will.

## How Your Estate Assets Are Controlled

Remember, your assets are controlled by laws, contracts, and wills. In a moment, I'll show you how this affects everything in your estate.

| Laws | Contracts | Wills |
|------|-----------|-------|
| e.g., joint assets | e.g., life insurance | e.g., sole assets |

If assets are in your name alone, they must be distributed by your will. If someone inherits assets not covered by your will, then it's because of a legal or contractual right. For example, life insurance or jointly owned assets are transferred only after death. These assets are part of your estate but are controlled by contract or law.

Tom and Janet's home is jointly owned and worth $250,000. The surviving spouse inherits the home automatically. This is because by law they own it jointly with a right of survivorship. This form of ownership saves probate taxes and legal fees.

### What Makes up Your Estate Asset Pie?

How large a pie will you leave when you die? Nobody knows. But whatever is left of the pie makes up your estate. You can decide now how you want to slice it.

Let's look at your estate asset pie. Each slice may be a different size. Bill Gates has a much larger pie than you or me. No matter — the principle is the same. All of his assets are controlled by his will, by contract, or by law. Let's look at these three slices of the pie in more detail.

**Your Estate Asset Pie**

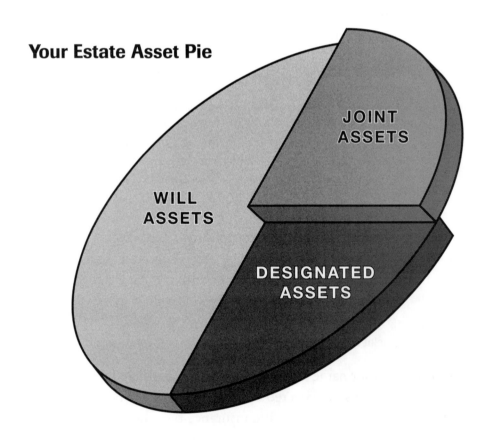

"Man's natural right of possessing and transmitting property by inheritance must remain intact and cannot be taken away by the state."

— Pius XI, 1931

## 1. Joint Assets Slice

Jointly owned property can be real estate or bank accounts, for instance. Each joint owner is considered to hold an undivided interest in the entire asset. Joan opens a joint bank account with her boyfriend to save for a vacation. She makes the deposits from her payroll. Her boyfriend then removes all the money in the account, but Joan can't complain. According to bank records, her boyfriend owns the money just as much as she does.

Joint ownership as a registered ownership looks like this: *joint tenants* — Joel and Jillian as joint owners with a right of survivorship and not as tenants-in-common.

Compare that with ownership that isn't joint: *tenants-in-common* — Fred as to an eighty percent interest, Ted as to a twenty percent interest, as tenants-in-common with no right of survivorship.

What's the principal difference between these examples? In the first example, the property goes automatically to the surviving joint owner. So, if Joel dies, Jillian automatically inherits. Nothing really needs to be done for Jillian to become the sole property owner. In the second example, when Ted or Fred dies, there are no automatic survivorship rights. An owner's interest in the property must be transferred by will or provincial intestacy laws if he or she dies without one.

Be sure you understand this. Joint ownership of assets is a key estate planning concept. It saves probate taxes and transfer costs. You don't need to probate a will to transfer joint ownership. However, transferring joint ownership doesn't avoid any income tax consequences, which need to be considered every time an asset or property is transferred as part of your estate.

When we discuss probate in Chapter 8, "Reduce Probate Taxes Properly," you'll get more details. I'll explain the weaknesses of having only jointly owned assets as a planning device. Joint ownership is no substitute for estate planning or having a will.

## 2. Designated Assets Slice

Most people have some form of employment pensions, RRSPs, RRIFs, segregated funds, and life insurance policies. By contract, you designate a beneficiary to inherit the asset or its benefits on your death. Life insurance policies on your house mortgage, for example, pay a benefit on your death. The insurance proceeds are payable to the lending institution; you can't give these proceeds to your wife or children by your will.

**It's Been Said**

"There is a written and an unwritten law. The one by which we regulate our constitutions in our cities is the written law, that which arises from custom is the unwritten law."

– Diogenes Laertius, circa A.D. 200

Designated assets aren't controlled by wills because they're already spoken for. The exception to this is if you have made the designated beneficiary your estate. How do you do that? Sometimes just by forgetting to designate a beneficiary. A policy would be paid to the estate of Joel Thomas if Joel forgot to designate someone.

## 3. Will Assets Slice

This piece of the pie contains property in your name alone, such as your car, the contents of your home, and bank accounts or stocks in your name. Here's a rule to remember what goes into the third slice. Whatever you own that's not joint or designated is controlled by your will. If you have no will, it passes on by intestacy. You'll read about will advantages in Chapter 9, "Valuable Advantages."

## Summing Up

All your assets fit into one or more of these three slices of your estate. You must plan to deal with all of them to provide for your loved ones. Before you start, you need to be aware of some legal restrictions, which limit your choices and can't be ignored without serious consequences.

---

**Legal Lingo**

*Spousal elections* mean that spouses receive property rights when they marry. You can't ignore these rights when you plan your estate; they take precedence over your will. Your married spouse can elect to take his or her entitlement under family property laws instead of the will.

---

## You Can't Do Whatever You Want

Now you understand the three kinds of assets that make up your estate pie. Can you do anything you want with your property while you are alive? No, even while you're alive, there are limits set by law. Why would it be different when you are dead? Laws control what occurs after your death. They exist to protect the innocent and to prevent abuse. There are three limits on your right to give away any part of your estate: legal restrictions, contractual restrictions, and public policy restrictions.

### 1. Legal Restrictions

Ignoring these major legal factors can result in a court battle to upset even your best intentions.

**Family property laws:** each province gives spouses different rights to claim against an estate. Some give only married spouses a right to share automatically in your estate. Spouses who are treated as married have a right to share in your estate. Unless you have a marriage contract, you can't leave such a spouse out of your estate plans. Surviving spouses have provincial property and support rights, which must be respected.

**Foreign legal restrictions:** laws where your real estate assets are situated usually control transfers on death. Consult a foreign lawyer to advise you on each country's estate and income tax laws. Consider having a separate will in each jurisdiction where you have major assets so that each can cover that country's assets.

**Support obligations:** they can continue after your death for married, common-law, same-sex, or divorced spouses or children by contract or court order. Your estate's assets can be seized to pay support. This support limits what's available to beneficiaries, so you must allow for these responsibilities.

**Dependants:** children and adults entitled to support can be dependants. If you ignore these claims, your estate will be just asking for a lawsuit.

**Minors:** underage beneficiaries don't have direct access to any property under your will without a court order. A guardian must control and manage a minor's funds. If you have no guardian named, the gift must be paid into court and is held there until the child becomes of age. You can't just leave a business to an underage child.

**Accumulation rules:** income that accumulates in an estate must be paid out at least every twenty-one years. You don't have the right to hold and control gifts forever from the grave.

**Testamentary requirements:** each jurisdiction has laws regarding who can make a will. You must satisfy these conditions to be able to transfer assets with a valid will.

**Income taxes:** these taxes must be paid before you can give anything away. In some cases, you'll also have to consider probate taxes.

---

**Time Machine**

Testamentary refers to testaments, which in the old days were used for personal property. Wills were used only for real estate. Now, generally, a last will and testament applies to both real estate and personal property.

---

## 2. Contractual Restrictions

You can lose control over some of your assets by signing contracts. Restrictions by contract, deed, or agreement limit your ability to deal with property. Pre- or postnuptial agreements are legal contracts that can bind you and your estate. These contractual limitations include the following.

**Business agreements:** shareholders, franchise, and partnership agreements may contain a first right of refusal or buy/sell clauses. Business contracts may dictate who buys your share at your death and on what terms.

**Annuity or life contracts:** periodic payments to you may cease with your death. You may not be able to pass those periodic payments on to your family. Pensions with a death benefit can have designated beneficiaries.

**Contractual provisions:** insurance contracts, RRSPs, and RRIFs have designated beneficiaries for these assets. You have no control over these items unless they are payable to your estate after your death.

**Property deeds:** land ownership can be controlled by deed. Property passes to surviving joint tenants without reference to a will. Deeds must be registered as tenants-in-common to allow you to deal with real estate through a will.

**Joint bank accounts:** the survivor inherits these accounts; they are not part of your estate. Spouses can use joint bank accounts as an estate planning device to avoid probate taxes.

**Prenuptial agreements:** marriage contracts can give or take away rights to support and to property. They can be signed before or after the marriage.

## 3. Public Policy Restrictions

Public policies can also restrict estate plans. These restrictions prevent any unacceptable ethnic, racial, or sexual conduct. For example, a gift in your will cannot be conditional on a person divorcing his or her spouse. Court decisions on public policy issues are strange and make for humorous reading. In one case, a lawyer wished to establish a scholarship for a law graduate with the lowest marks. The law school believed this scholarship would reward a lack of achievement and dedication. It was not required to accept the gift for public policy reasons.

> **Bulletin**
>
> Oral promises? Get them in writing. Your aunt may say she'll give you her house when she dies. Get it in writing; you can't enforce this type of oral promise.

## Create an Asset Inventory

So let's start your asset inventory. What is included in your estate? Let's begin by looking at what most people have. Check off if the asset is jointly owned, designated, or otherwise. You will use this list later to help prepare a will.

# Estate Asset Inventory

| Asset | Joint | Designated | Will |
|---|:---:|:---:|:---:|
| 1. Personal property (cars, boats, art) | ❑ | ❑ | ❑ |
| 2. Life insurance | ❑ | ❑ | ❑ |
| 3. Private and government pensions | ❑ | ❑ | ❑ |
| 4. RRSPs, RRIFs, and annuities | ❑ | ❑ | ❑ |
| 5. Home or real estate | ❑ | ❑ | ❑ |
| 6. Bonds, stocks, and mutual funds | ❑ | ❑ | ❑ |
| 7. Bank accounts and certificates | ❑ | ❑ | ❑ |
| 8. Business interests | ❑ | ❑ | ❑ |

## 1. Personal Property

Personal property includes cars, boats, stock certificates, and everything other than real estate. On the other hand, *real property* is referred to as real estate or realty. Sometimes you must examine the registration for any personal property to determine ownership. If you are the registered owner of a car, it is also part of your will assets. Personal property without ownership registration, such as cash and furniture, is covered by your will.

## 2. Life Insurance

Life insurance policies may have an owner, a designated beneficiary, and someone else who pays the premiums. Check to see who the beneficiary is since this determines who gets the proceeds. You may not be able to change an insurance company's beneficiary if it's irrevocable. If the insurance policy is payable to your estate, it is covered by your will. If it's payable to your spouse, you can't deal with it by will unless you change the "designated" beneficiary.

"The money that men make lives after them."

— Samuel Butler, 1835–1902

---

**Bulletin**

Yes, it's possible to have more than one will. You can have a will in each jurisdiction (province or country) where you have valuable assets. It's necessary since tax, estate, and property ownership laws are different.

---

## 3. Private and Government Pensions

The pension plan may give surviving benefits to a spouse or partner if they are designated. Unless a death benefit is payable to your estate, pensions are not covered by your will.

## 4. Registered Retirement Savings Plans (RRSPs), Registered Retirement Income Funds (RRIFs), and Annuities

RRSPs and RRIFs generally pass by contract directly to a beneficiary outside your will. These assets are not part of your will plan. There are tax consequences to your estate with all designations for these assets. Keep designations current and on file with the plan holder. Annuities may be payable during your life or transferable — so find out.

## 5. Home or Real Estate

Your home is real estate, so it receives different treatment from personal property. Realty usually represents the biggest monetary investment for most people. Your principal residence is also the largest tax-free asset to deal with in an estate. Ownership of realty can be joint, in partnership, or a percentage interest as tenants-in-common. Each type of ownership will make a difference for your estate plan.

## 6. Bonds, Stocks, and Mutual Funds

Stocks and bonds may be jointly owned or designated in certain circumstances. You need to examine the investment itself. Some people buy bonds for their children and grandchildren. If they are registered in the minors' names, they won't form part of your estate and will be excluded from your will. Government bonds can have joint ownership with survivorship rights ensured by registration of ownership. If the bonds and stocks are not jointly owned, they will form part of the estate and be sold.

## 7. Bank Accounts and Certificates

Bank accounts and bank certificates, if they are on joint account, go to the survivor. This excludes them from the estate and consideration in your will. For many people, having a joint account is convenient. It's an easy way to support grieving loved ones after death. The funds are accessible without probate or delay and are not included as part of your estate.

## 8. Business Investments

They can be one of your largest assets or liabilities, as you will see in the next chapter.

After you have analyzed your personal inventory, you can determine which assets will be covered by your will. Now you can set your goals and preview your estate.

In the next chapter, I'll show you an example of a more advanced estate inventory. If you or a family member is self-employed, own a business, or hold investments, definitely read on.

### But What If?

Perhaps you already jointly own all your assets with your spouse. And now, after reading this chapter, you are going to designate all your other assets to each other. Well, you may be wondering, do you and your spouse still need wills?

Yes, trust me. You and your joint owner and designated beneficiary can die together in what is a common disaster. In such cases, your will takes over to deliver assets to your backup beneficiaries. If you have minor children, your will is where you appoint their guardians to protect them and their inheritance.

Do you know that life insurance can create an estate overnight? Keep reading.

## The Least You Need to Know

- You must know what happens to each asset at death to plan your estate.
- You have legal, contractual, and public policy restrictions on your assets.
- Wills deal with all property in your name or that you inherit.
- You can reduce probate costs by carefully using joint ownership and designations.

# Chapter 3

# Taking Care of Business

In this chapter:

- Understand buy/sell agreements.
- Determine life insurance benefits.
- Establish an investment checklist.
- Understand funding with insurance.

Do you have a business or unique investments in your asset portfolio? If so, you'll need a save-and-protect plan for your investments and your beneficiaries. Your estate plan can be affected by a family member in business. In either case, this chapter will be of interest.

How can life insurance help you? Why is a buy/sell agreement essential for successful business succession? We'll look at some of those areas and estate planning tips that can help with your investments. At any rate, check the investment inventory in this chapter for further reference.

## Taking Care of Business

Take Tony, my dry-cleaner, for example. Tony said that his wife, Ruth, had cancer and that she needed a will. He was so busy he never made it into the office with his wife to make a will. Everyone was surprised when it was Tony and not Ruth who died without warning.

## It's Been Said

"Joy is a partnership
Grief weeps alone . . ."
— Frederic Knowles, 1869–1905, *Grief and Joy*

Small business owners are like that; they take care of the business first. They hope it will take care of them later. Tony left his family without any means to protect the value of his business. When he died, his family couldn't cope, and things went from bad to worse.

Plan to take care of whatever kind of business interest you have. We'll look at the different forms businesses can take. You may start as a proprietorship, move through partnership, and end up a shareholder. Each stage has different planning considerations.

## Are You in Business for Yourself?

The sudden death of an owner can cause a business's value to plummet. Special steps are needed as part of your estate plan.

If yours is a part-time, home-based business, you may not need an elaborate plan. But you still need to consider what happens in the event of your death. I'll begin with sole proprietorships because they are the easiest form of business to start up.

Register a business name for a few dollars and, voilà, Mary is in business as Mary's Marvellous Web Sites. It's relatively simple, so people just register, get a business licence, and start selling. But this can severely impact your financial situation.

Because Tony's dry-cleaning business was a sole proprietorship, the bank had to freeze his business account when Tony died. He was the only person who could sign cheques. His estate needed a legal representative to operate his accounts and pay his bills. His wife was too ill to handle the business or estate matters. The couple's son, Sam, became the court-appointed administrator because Tony had no will. Sam needed a bond to ensure that all the bills were paid, which took months. The business withered and died without benefiting Tony's family.

## Sole Proprietors Need Wills

Had Tony made a will, he would have left something of value for his family. Events would have unfolded differently. His will would have given his executor power to operate the business. The business could have been able to pay creditors. As it was, Tony's Dry-Cleaner closed its doors. His family had to pay business bills from his personal assets. It's not that Tony's family inherited his debts (unless they had cosigned loans or guaranteed them) but that they couldn't distribute Tony's remaining assets without first paying his bills.

---

**Bulletin**

Partnership agreements are legal documents that protect you and your estate. It's best to have legal advice to prepare one. Most contracts contain a buy/sell provision in case a partner dies.

---

Business value can disappear overnight when customers cannot get deliveries, service, or parts. Someone has to write cheques and pay bills and employees. Wills empower your executor to operate and sell the business. This ability can maximize the business value without any personal risks to the executor.

---

**Legal Lingo**

*Buy/sell agreements* are legal contracts that partners and shareholders need. These agreements ensure a deceased's interest is bought out by the surviving party. A fixed price or formula is used to establish the amount.

---

## What if You Have a Partner?

Operating a business with someone else probably means you are partners, unless you're incorporated. Partnerships terminate on the death of a partner unless a written agreement specifies otherwise. When a partner dies, the partnership assets may have to be sold. Net proceeds are distributed to each of the partners personally. Profits and losses are divided equally unless you have a written *partnership agreement*. Agreements can cover management and a buyout if a partner dies or is disabled. The purchase price and payment terms for a deceased partner's interest can be set out.

Here's an example. Rick, Taylor, and Leah own a rental income property as partners. Each has the first right to purchase a deceased partner's interest. This right is in their partnership agreement. If, for example, Taylor dies, Rick and Leah, the surviving partners, have agreed to buy out Taylor's interest. One-third of the net value is paid to Taylor's estate. But what happens if neither of the surviving partners has any money? Keep reading, you'll see how life insurance can help.

Limited partnerships, a variation of a partnership, are becoming more common for professional firms. One partner may assume responsibility for the business operation, while others limit their liability. These types of partnerships also need a buy/sell agreement.

## Business through a Limited Liability Corporation

A business that is incorporated is a separate legal person or entity, with a separate legal name. By law, the corporation has rights and obligations. It can sue and be sued in the corporation's name. With other businesses, you must sue in the name of the individual business owner. For example, the business's bank account could be listed as Crystal Jones Limited. Using the word *Inc.*, *Corp.*, or *Ltd.* in a business name shows the public it's a limited liability business. This can be a significant advantage since business liabilities can't affect your estate.

### It's Been Said

. . . . . . . . . . . . . . . . . . . . . . . . . . . . . . . . . . . . . . . . . . . . . .

"A corporation is an artificial being, invisible, intangible, and existing only in the contemplation of the law. Being the mere creature of the law, it possesses only those properties which are the charter of its creation."

– John Marshall, *Dartmouth College* v. *Woodward*, 4 Wheaton (1819)

Help Line

Corporations have shareholders to elect directors and a president to manage the corporation. Frank is the sole shareholder of his corporation, Frank's Car Services Inc. He's elected himself president, secretary, and treasurer, and he does all the work. The corporation that runs the business pays Frank a salary. He gets a share of the business profits through a bonus or dividend.

Frank's personal assets have nothing to do with the business's assets. The corporation owns the assets of Frank's Car Services Inc. Frank's assets, such as his home, are in his name jointly owned with his wife. When Frank dies as a shareholder of a corporation, the business does not die. It must continue operating to keep its value. The business does not have to be wound up to pay creditors before Frank's estate gets anything.

## Incorporating Your Business Makes Estate Sense

If you incorporate your business, it will not negatively affect your estate. Shareholders' assets are distinct and separate from those of the corporation. Translating this into simple English, it means the corporation has limited liability. A company is liable only to the extent it covers its debts from its own assets.

For example, Roger owns a house worth $220,000 jointly with his wife. He is the sole shareholder of Roger's 3TX Corp., which has one asset, a bank account with $10,000. It owes suppliers $50,000. Since the liabilities exceed the business assets, the business is insolvent. Corporate suppliers can't come after Roger and try to take his home to pay themselves.

Unless Roger has personally guaranteed the supplier's account, he doesn't have to pay it. To keep the business afloat, Roger could loan his personal money to the corporation. This is possible because the corporation is a separate legal entity. It can contract, sue, and borrow independently.

**Q:** Are partnership and shareholder agreements the same thing?

**A:** Corporate law applies to shareholders, and partnership law covers partners. However, the mechanisms for a buy/sell can be very similar in each type of contract.

## Comparing Corporate Advantages with Other Businesses

If Roger is a sole proprietor and owes $50,000 to his suppliers, it's a whole different story. Suppliers can pursue his personal assets until he's exhausted physically and financially. You can see the impact this has in an estate planning context. If Roger dies, and his business liabilities exceed his business and personal assets, his estate would be bankrupt. What would his estate beneficiaries get? The business could rob his estate beneficiaries of any rewards. Roger can reduce this risk by incorporating his business. His own assets can't be touched unless he signed a personal guarantee.

Landlords and banks usually require personal guarantees to cover corporate insolvency. So why incorporate if the biggest debtors can still come after your estate? Peace of mind comes when you know the liability is not open ended. It's important to be able to tell a spouse and partner, "Whatever happens to the business, you'll still be protected." You can save your loved ones from this huge financial burden in one other way.

If bank lines of credit are personally guaranteed, offset this risk. Buy life insurance to cover major debts. If you die, you should have insurance to pay off any amount owed to the bank. How much insurance should you have or can you afford? You, your family, and your life insurance representative will need to discuss that. It's vital to give your family a feeling they are protected from risk. They won't have to sell assets to satisfy the bank. You'll see even more tax advantages to having your business incorporated in Chapter 6, "Tax Planning Tips."

## Write out Your Business Plan

Who will buy your business interests from your estate if you die? Deal with this issue while you can. Private corporations or a share in a partnership have a limited number of potential buyers. That's why shareholders enter into *shareholders agreements*, which are similar to partnership agreements in many ways. A shareholders agreement includes *buy/sell clauses* to deal with this contingency.

Surviving shareholders would agree to buy the deceased shareholder's interest in the business. They may express it as a first right of refusal or option. These agreements are called *buy/sell* for short.

Some shareholders may not be concerned by who is involved as a shareholder. So a surviving spouse's participation in the business won't bother anyone. Where shareholders must be involved in day-to-day operations, it's a different story. They may not accept an inexperienced spouse or children as new shareholders. Surviving shareholders or partners may benefit even more from a buy/sell agreement.

---

**Bulletin**

Entrepreneurs plan everything when they go into business. They shouldn't forget to plan to get out of business voluntarily or otherwise. Life insurance–funded buy/sell agreements can protect investments for estate planning purposes.

---

## What's This Buy or Sell About?

It means the surviving partner, shareholder, or corporation can or must buy a deceased's interest. You can buy or you can sell your interest on terms you'd incorporate into a legal contract. But you don't automatically get this contract when you incorporate or start a partnership business. You have to negotiate the details, including how the business will be operated and who can be a shareholder or partner. If the business requires more money, the contract can say how it will be obtained.

Jonathan and Jennifer are the two shareholders of J&J Inheritances Inc., an estate planning business. Both have put up $5,000 to get the business rolling. When they negotiated their buy/sell agreement, they hired separate lawyers to get independent advice. They agreed that if a shareholder died the survivor could buy out the other owner's interest on the terms in their agreement.

Deceased shareholder estates are then guaranteed to have a buyer for their interest. The corporation or surviving shareholders get the first rights before anyone else buys. Sometimes the price and terms of the buyout are negotiated in advance, or you can agree to a formula to calculate a price in the future.

## How You Benefit

Jennifer also benefits from the contract. She knows the terms under which she can buy without any surprises. Standard terms covered by the contract include:

- payment in instalments (over one year or more);
- price calculation method (by appraisals or formula); and
- how the option to purchase proceeds.

Jennifer's buy/sell gives her thirty days to make up her mind to buy out the other shares. Jennifer has a formula in her agreement. It states she is to obtain an appraisal and then subtract any debts and her own cash contribution to the business.

## Paying the Price

How can Jennifer raise money to buy out Jonathan's interest? If the market is slow, she could lose her profit and even her investment in the business. Jonathan's estate also needs money to pay his taxes. A way to take care of this is to purchase life insurance.

### Help Line

**Q:** Can life insurance provide money for a buy/sell agreement?

**A:** Yes, insurance can provide purchase money without draining the business of its cash. The tax rules for deducting the insurance premiums and who owns the policies are complex. You'll need expert tax and insurance advice to maximize benefits.

## Life Insurance and Your Business

Here are the options Jennifer has to purchase Jonathan's shares:

- use cash;
- sell assets;
- borrow money; or
- use life insurance.

Of these, life insurance is the easiest if it's in place. Jennifer purchased it at the time the buy/sell agreement was signed. That's why planning is vital.

Options such as life insurance paid for by the corporation or by the shareholders have different tax results. This is a complex area. You'll need professional advice from your tax advisor and life insurance representative.

The death of a business owner can trigger substantial financial consequences. You should have a plan in writing to deal with them. Life insurance can finance that plan if you're buying or selling.

## Let's Summarize

I've covered the typical business structures — sole proprietorships, partnerships, and corporations. You've learned how they need to be covered by your estate plan. This is important if you or a family member has business investments. Here's a summary in case you're starting a business.

- Sole proprietorships need wills to allow the business to operate after death.
- Partnerships also need a buy/sell agreement for a partner's death.
- Shareholders need buy/sell agreements to deal with changes caused by death.
- Life insurance can fund buy/sells. Premiums may be deductible.
- Protect loved ones with insurance to cover risks of death and debts.

## Nine Benefits from Life Insurance

Life insurance provides money that:

1. supports loved ones with income on a short- or long-term basis;
2. offers a tax-free benefit for your policy's beneficiaries;
3. gives immediate benefits on death;
4. bypasses the slow court process and probate taxes;
5. avoids creditors' claims if paid to someone other than your estate;
6. protects children from a prior marriage;
7. creates a pool of money to pay your estate liabilities on death;
8. funds a business buyout plan or gifts to charity; and
9. helps you save if there is a cash-value component.

## What Type of Insurance to Buy?

There are advantages and disadvantages with each type of life insurance you can purchase. Basically, you are looking at term or permanent insurance, and there are some differences.

You will deal with an insurance agent or broker who gets paid a commission. The amount varies according to type and amount of coverage. You may even buy directly from an insurance company.

Term insurance is for a specified term or number of years. It has no cash or investment value when you stop paying premiums. Premiums can increase based on your age and health over the term of the policy.

Life insurance is one of your designated assets in your estate. Make sure you always have the correct designated beneficiary named on the policy. Usually, they would be specified individuals who are not minors. If you wish to benefit a minor, set up a trust or name a trustee.

Permanent insurance is a more complex tax and estate planning tool. Basically, it comes in whole life, universal, or variable policies but provides guaranteed coverage. It is more expensive than term but may have some cash value if you cancel it.

How much insurance do you really need? That depends on what you can afford, your liabilities, and your loved ones' needs. You would normally get a number of insurance assessments that review your options and costs before purchasing insurance.

## Help Line

**Q:** What type of insurance do I need?

**A:** Term or permanent insurance are the two basic options. You can consider different variations within each of these categories. Your insurance representative should explain the pros and cons before you buy.

## Investment Checklists

Basically, you want to review your estate inventory to consider some other items. I've listed investments as an inventory separate from the asset inventory of the previous chapter. Some assets, which we'll cover before moving on, fall into these categories.

Use this checklist to complete your asset inventory. Keep them together in a safe place.

## Investment Inventory

| Investment | Check if applicable | My Plan to Transfer this Asset Is . . . |
|---|---|---|
| Sole proprietorship | ❏ | _____ |
| Partnership | ❏ | _____ |
| Shareholder | ❏ | _____ |
| Franchise agreements | ❏ | _____ |
| Family heirlooms | ❏ | _____ |
| Investment properties | ❏ | _____ |
| Family farms | ❏ | _____ |
| Debts owing to you | ❏ | _____ |
| Trust accounts | ❏ | _____ |
| Professional practices | ❏ | _____ |
| Dot.com ventures | ❏ | _____ |

**It's Been Said**
. . . . . . . . . . . . . . . . . . . . . . . . . . . . . . . . . . . . . . . . . . . . . .

The golden rule of business may be traced to this: "Do to others what you would have them do to you. . . ."
— Matthew 7:12

# Investments in Your Estate Inventory

## Franchise Agreements

If you own a franchise, beware. Franchise agreements with head office specify and restrict your planning. Franchisors must consent to any transfer of the franchise you own. Consent may be given only if the new franchisee agrees (a) to training to operate the franchise, (b) to pay franchise fees, and (c) to be bound by the terms of the franchise agreement. Is there a beneficiary who can operate the franchise? If not, and it's sold, you can deal with the proceeds. Cover this with a will.

## Family Heirlooms

These are investments of a sort. The things your grandmother told you must be passed down and kept in the family. They may have sentimental value, or they may be priceless. How do you give away valuable investments such as antiques or art collections? Even if your relatives know that the silver in your collection is to go as one set to your sister, it's not enough. It may require special treatment. List it here. Your will and your executor may need special clauses to deal with family heirlooms.

## Investment Properties

Picture in your mind a summer home by the lake or a rental income property. Now picture the income taxes on the property that have to be paid when you die. Most people do not see this liability when they deal with second properties. They enjoy their ownership but forget that on death such gifts carry tax consequences. The taxes must be dealt with by your estate and paid before any asset can be transferred. Leave your executor the information necessary to allow your tax advisor to claim all losses and improvements.

## Help Line

**Q:** Can I just name my estate as a beneficiary of my life insurance?

**A:** If you don't name a beneficiary, life insurance benefits will be paid to your estate. This amount will be subject to probate costs and creditors' claims. Normally, you would not make a policy payable to your estate. One exception is that it's really necessary to fund estate obligations.

## Family Farms

If you have a current active farming business, there are special rules to consider. You need a tailor-made plan to transfer these assets. Get proper advice from a tax specialist familiar with farm issues.

## Debts Owing to You

You may wish these to be paid or forgiven as part of your estate plan. You'll have to specify this in writing. Otherwise, the usual procedures will be followed to collect the loan or debt involving cousin Alex. Alex will have to prove that he had made all payments or that the loan was not to be repaid if you died.

## Trust Accounts

You may have set up "bare trust" accounts at the bank for children or grandchildren. As a rule, you cannot deal with these funds as part of your estate. You still need to answer questions such as who will be the new trustee when you die? Is the money to be paid out? What are the restrictions on the trust?

## Professional Practices

A professional practice usually can be sold to another member of your profession. Requirements of the professional governing bodies must be met. Some of the comments applicable to the sale of a business apply here as well; you cannot leave your dental practice to your daughter if she is not a dentist. Consider specifying that this particular asset has a specific executor, such as another dentist, for a sale.

---

**Bulletin**

Be careful if you have designated someone as an irrevocable beneficiary of your life insurance. You cannot change irrevocable designations without the beneficiary's written consent. But don't worry, designations are usually revocable, and you can change them unless you specifically state the designation is irrevocable.

---

## Dot.Com Ventures

You're super rich because you have a dot.com business worth millions. So now you have a responsibility to plan for its transfer. You never have to worry about needing money. Now you can think of how it can be used to benefit family, friends, and your community.

By now, you have an idea about what assets go into your estate. In the next chapter, I'll show you the debts you incur and the deductions you make when you plan.

············································································

## The Least You Need to Know

- When you're in business for yourself, it's vital to have a plan that includes a will.
- Business investments require professional advice to create an estate plan.
- Plan your way out of a partnership or a corporation, with a buy/sell agreement.
- Life insurance can protect loved ones with tax-free money and cover your risks.

# Chapter 4

# Preview Your Estate's Worth

In this chapter:

- Identify the Big Four expenses.
- Assess estate priorities.
- Cut up your pie.
- Don't sweat the small stuff.

*You have to plan.* Is that message getting through? There is no avoiding your own death. I know you're saying, "How can I plan to give anything away if I don't know what will be left over when I die?" One way is to preview your estate. You'll find out what to expect if you die tomorrow.

Do you have enough to satisfy your estate wish list? Calculate what's available for distribution after your estate expenses are paid. This figure will show you what's in your *distributable estate* or what you have to give away. The amount may surprise you. Then you can make adjustments if what you have to distribute won't support all your wishes. Is your plan hung up on how to give away all those small treasures you've collected? I'll clear a path for you to see your way out of this forest. You'll get tips to distribute your favourite knick-knacks.

## Why Estate Previews Are Essential

"Aren't you making this too complex?" Some of you may be saying this right about now. "I just wanted to have a simple will. I'm going to leave everything to my partner. They will do the same for me, so why bother with a preview?"

Let me answer these questions and remove any reservations you may have before I move on. Yes, your estate plan is simple when you leave everything you own to each other — especially after you've followed my ideas on how to divide your estate. But you have to take your planning to the next level to deal with the contingency of a common disaster, when both partners pass away at the same time.

Ask yourself, "What will I have to give away? Who will get what?" The only way to calculate or really estimate this is with an estate preview.

Want more reasons? Okay, what if you have children and both you and your spouse pass away? Will you leave enough behind to raise them? Will it put them through law school or something even more noble? You have to re-examine your loved ones' needs and how you can satisfy them, especially if they are vulnerable. Do you need to reduce debt, increase your insurance coverage, or get another job?

Perhaps you have no children to worry about. You still need to know what you can distribute, whether it's $100,000 or $500,000, and how you should divide it. I'll show you how to do this in some simple steps that follow.

### Help Line

**Q:** What's a distributable estate?

**A:** It's what's available in your estate after all expenses and taxes are paid. What's left of your assets is what gets distributed to your beneficiaries.

## Preview by Working Backward

Mrs. Quirk was a charming white-haired woman who wouldn't tell me her age. She walked gingerly with her cane and seated herself in my office. "What shall I do with my estate? How much do I give to each beneficiary? Can't I just spend it all on myself before I go?"

"Yes," I said to the last question. "But it sounds like you don't want to do that. Let's figure out what you want to do with your estate."

"I want to give $10,000 to each of my relatives."

I asked, "Do you have enough assets to meet those wishes?"

"That depends on how much I sell my house for and how long I live."

"No," I replied, "it depends on what you'll have left to distribute through your estate."

Mrs. Quirk didn't want to tell me exactly what she was worth. I had to work backward. I knew she had a house, life insurance, and money in the bank. On top of that, she needed to estimate her expenses or debts when she died. She was still puzzled. "How will I know what I will have left over five or ten years from now?"

"Estimate your estate costs to preview your estate," I told her. "Just assume your house has been sold."

She interrupted, "You and I come from two different schools. I am not prepared to assume anything."

"All right, then," I said, "let's start with the things that are certain. There are four things you'll have to pay whenever you go."

### The Big Four Bills (Everyone Pays)

Here is a short list I call the Big Four. Unless you're broke when you go, they must be paid before anything is distributed.

1. **Funeral costs:** if you prepay this expense, you won't need to consider it.
2. **Debts or loans:** list the major ones, not your current monthly bills.
3. **Estate expenses:** Executor fees, probate taxes, and legal costs should be estimated.
4. **Income taxes:** Consult professionals to estimate this bill if necessary. I don't expect you to be able to do this by yourself. You can try to estimate your bill after going through step two, in which you'll learn more about income taxes. For now, just follow through with my examples.

When you add up all four of the categories, you get a total of your estate's liabilities. You can use this estimate in a moment as part of the preview process. It will help you see what you have before you get into a lawyer's office.

> **Legal Lingo**
>
> *Executor* is the person you appoint by will. The executor pays your estate expenses, the Big Four, before distributing assets to beneficiaries.

"Many receive advice; few profit by it."

— Publilius Syrus, 85–43 B.C., *Maxims*

## Estimate Your Estate Liabilities

Let's figure out the costs of the Big Four.

**Funeral expenses:** this is a variable. Consider a range of $10,000–$15,000, with extras that you may want, such as airfare for relatives to attend the funeral or a wake at the pub.

**Major debts:** list mortgages, car loans, and other major personal debts or guarantees.

**Estate expenses:** let's introduce you to your executor. This person handles and distributes your estate. The law can allow him or her roughly five percent of your estate for the work. You'll also have to consider probate taxes and legal fees, which are another variable. I suggest clients budget a ballpark figure of ten percent of your gross estate for all these expenses. It may be high, but it's safe and easy to calculate.

**Income taxes:** at this stage, you need only an estimate. You'll need tax advice to estimate your liability for the sale of major investment assets, your business, or professional practices. I'll go into more detail later. For our exercise with Mrs. Quirk, she had no significant tax liabilities.

**Legal Lingo**

*Probate taxes* are paid to provincial governments through the estate court. You'll pay probate taxes whenever assets are passed through your estate whether you have a will or not.

### Picture This

Your entire estate is represented by this circle. Now imagine what your distributable estate will look like after the Big Four bills are deducted.

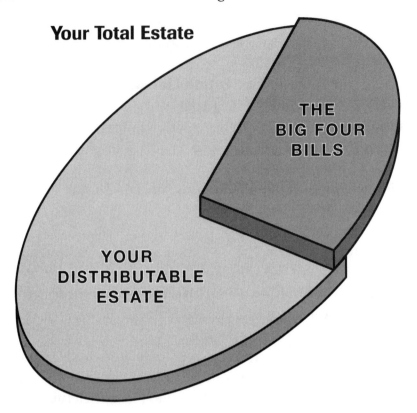

**Your Total Estate**

THE
BIG FOUR
BILLS

YOUR
DISTRIBUTABLE
ESTATE

### Divide It into Parts

Mrs. Quirk still wouldn't tell me how much she was worth. I told her to deduct the Big Four off the top: funeral costs, debts, estate expenses, and income taxes. Day-to-day bills really aren't that large, so I told her not to bother with telephone or utility bills.

After deducting expenses, Mrs. Quirk asked if she'd have enough. She wanted to pay $10,000 to each of ten nieces and nephews. I told her she needed $100,000 clear of all estate expenses. She wasn't satisfied it could be that simple.

"What if I want to make a donation to a charity?" Mrs. Quirk added. "How much can I afford to leave?" She hoped it would be a fifty-fifty split of the estate. "I want one-half for the charity and one-half for the family," she told me.

"Why, that's perfect," I told her. "Divide your estate into shares. That way you don't worry that you'll make a mistake."

Mrs. Quirk's preview of her estate showed she would have a total of $300,000. She couldn't gift $200,000 to charity and the same again to relatives; otherwise, she could have mistakenly left $200,000 to charity and the same to relatives and not had enough. She'd have needed an estate of $400,000. That's an easy mistake to make. To avoid it, preview your estate to see if you'll be able to cover every objective. Here's my three-part process that's simple to follow.

## Three-Part Estate Preview

Let's look at Barbara, who is a computer consultant, as she previews her estate. Barbara wants to give her house (which is worth $120,000) to her brother. She also wants her sister to get half of her estate. Can she accomplish these two objectives? Here is a three-part process that answers the question. Remember, start with the information you know today. That way you won't be guessing.

Since Barbara owns the real estate by herself, it will be controlled by a will. She has life insurance, which is payable to her estate. Identifying her assets, here's what her estate looks like:

### Step 1: Estimate Estate Assets

| | |
|---|---|
| Home | $120,000 |
| Life insurance | $80,000 |
| Bank deposits and investments | $100,000 |
| **(A) Estimate of estate assets** | **$300,000** |

### Step 2: Estimate Estate Liabilities

| | |
|---|---|
| 1. Funeral costs (estimate) | $10,000 |
| 2. Major debts (personal loans and bank mortgage) | $30,000 |
| 3. Estate expenses (estimate ten percent of estate) | $30,000 |
| 4. Income taxes (estimate) | $30,000 |
| **(B) Estimate for estate liabilities** | **$100,000** |

## Step 3: Estimate Your Distributable Estate

A (assets) – B (liabilities) = C (distributable estate)

($300,000 – $100,000 = $200,000)

**(C) Available to distribute**              **$200,000**

## What Have You Got to Give?

Barbara used my three-part process to preview her estate. Of course, she used today's values for her assets and liabilities. It's a good place to start to realistically assess your estate goals.

> **Legal Lingo**
>
> *Estate residue* is what's left over in your estate after expenses and specific gifts are made. In your will, it reads as what is left, as in "the residue of my estate goes to my spouse."

After previewing the distributable estate, Barbara changed her mind. She decided her estate would sell her house, not make a specific gift of it. The house sale proceeds would then form part of her estate residue. Barbara also set up a fund for her nieces for their university education. She hoped to leave $40,000 in her will for this purpose. The rest of her estate would be only $160,000 in today's dollars.

## Identify Your Estate Plan Priorities

After previewing her estate, Barbara reconsidered her options. Her first priority had changed, and she set up investments for the university fund with her financial planner.

Barbara's current estate plan no longer leaves her home to her brother. Instead, her brother and sister will equally share the residue of her estate.

## Another Way to Cut up the Pie

Larry is a high school teacher with a son from a previous marriage. He wants his son, for whom he is paying support, to benefit from his estate. Larry also has a common-law spouse, Sonia. He wants her to share what they have accumulated together.

Larry's assets include a life insurance policy, a townhouse, and stocks he has purchased through work. He has prepaid funeral arrangements and may inherit property from a cousin in Italy.

This is how Larry estimates his estate looks like using my three-part preview outlined above. He started by listing his estate assets and subtracting liabilities.

## Step 1: Estimate Estate Assets

| | |
|---|---|
| Life insurance payable to the estate | $100,000 |
| Townhouse (sole owner) | $160,000 |
| Stocks | $40,000 |
| Inheritance | (unknown)* |
| **(A) Total estate assets** | **$300,000*** |

## Step 2: Estimate Estate Liabilities

| | |
|---|---|
| Big Four Bills | $60,000 |
| Child support obligations | (unknown)* |
| **(B) Total estate liabilities** | **$60,000*** |

## Step 3: Estimate Your Distributable Estate

$300,000 – $60,000 = $240,000 (subject to unknowns)

Larry has two large unknowns in his plan. They are the inheritance and his ongoing support obligations. He wants Sonia to be able to live in their home. He says he can't plan his estate because of these variables.

## Let's Look at the Details

Here's a suggestion to meet Larry's estate plan objectives. It may show you how to deal with unknowns in your own plan.

**Townhouse:** Larry wants Sonia to live in his townhouse if he dies. After Sonia dies or sells it, Larry's will specifies what happens to the proceeds; the money goes to his son. Sonia will be responsible for the house's carrying costs while she lives there.

**Life insurance:** Larry makes the life insurance policy payable to Sonia. He has asked her to cover his support obligations with this money. Legally, she is not bound to do this. Larry feels her moral duty is good enough for him. He thinks this would reduce his probate taxes and estate expenses. Sonia would have the balance of the money after Larry's support obligations to his son are fulfilled.

**Stocks:** it's not possible to predict the value of this stock portfolio at death. Stocks may have tax liabilities. The net value may be inadequate to pay the child support. Larry should consider the stocks as part of the residue. He won't make specific gifts of them and would be free to sell them without changing his will.

**Future options:** Larry will review his plan if he marries Sonia. Her spousal claims would be considered in a *prenuptial agreement*. If Larry inherits real estate overseas, he will prepare a foreign will to appoint a local executor. Doing so can improve the management of his estate and minimize taxes.

## What if You're Going to Inherit?

Larry doesn't know how to deal with his future inheritance. Significant inheritances should be factored in on today's estate plan. You'll review your plan whenever significant or foreign assets are acquired. What if Larry hopes to inherit a painting before he dies, but he never receives it? Any gift of the painting in his own will won't apply. One way around this is for Larry not to make a specific gift of the painting. Inheritances can fall into his residue, which means that beneficiaries of the residue share them. Larry could also use my suggestion for the small stuff. These steps will keep you from going crazy, so keep reading!

## Don't Sweat the Small Stuff

Years of experience have taught me this: people don't know how to give their things away. They get stuck on the small things such as who will get grandfather's watch. One client gave me handwritten pages of instructions to divide up her china cabinet. She left my office and called to say that she had changed her mind by the time she had returned home; she was already preparing a new list of the "china beneficiaries." "Don't make up my will until the list is ready," she told me.

**It's Been Said**
..................................................................

"The great end of life is not knowledge but action."
Francis Bacon, 1561–1626

Sometimes people never get past the planning stage because their lists never get finished. Remember, you're only human. It's not possible to have a perfect will.

Financial factors also come into play when the knick-knacks are divided. Each time a will clause is changed, you need to see a lawyer. Save legal fees by avoiding unnecessary changes. Revising wills to keep them updated is a good idea. Changing wills so someone else gets the man-and-his-dog figurine isn't.

**Time Machine**

In the old days, legacies were just gifts of personal and not real property. Today you leave a legacy to dispose of any property through a will. The person who receives it is called a legatee. Persons who make wills can be legators, a term seldom used.

## Five Ways to Deal with the Small Stuff

**1. List key items in the will.** "My piano goes to Jerry." This method should be used for valuable items or treasured heirlooms to go to individuals or backup beneficiaries.

**2. Divide all items by a written memorandum.** This method allows you to dictate how certain objects can be gifted. However, you may not be able to keep secret what everyone gets. This document must be signed, dated, and referred to in your will. It's legally binding and must be complied with by the executor.

**3. Divide items by a nonbinding written memorandum.** This is a separate document that can be revised at your discretion. It gives you leeway in expressing your wishes. You won't have to revise your will each time a recipient dies, moves, or marries. Legally, this type of memo is not binding, but beneficiaries may honour your wishes. The ease in amending the document without a visit to a lawyer makes this a favourite option.

**4. Give your executor discretion.** This power is given by your will. You can specify that all the items be divided as the executor sees fit. He or she will have complete discretion.

**5. Give it away while you are alive.** Another way to deal with a personal item or artwork is to give it away with a warm hand rather than a cold one. The gift is made while you are living, and you can share in the enjoyment that the treasure may give.

### Help Line

**Q:** I just bought a house but made my will last year. Do I revise my will every time my assets change?

**A:** Wills speak from the date of your death. They dispose of all property owned by you on that date. Those assets acquired after the will is made are also included. If you want to deal specifically with an asset such as the house, you'll need to revise the will.

**It's Been Said**

••••••••••••••••••••••••••••••••••••••••••••••••••

"The fear of death is more to be dreaded than death itself."

– Publilius Syrus, 85–43 BC, *Maxims*

### Sample Memo for the Small Stuff

Here's a sample of a memo I use with clients to help them give away their small stuff. I prefer that you not handwrite the list in case someone claims it's a holograph will.

## Personal Property Memo for My Will

I, Jane Generous, give the following items of my personal property to the persons named (not including money, evidence of debt, documents of title, and securities)

Items of Personal Property
(clearly described)

Names and Current Addresses of
Beneficiaries

_____   _____

_____   _____

_____   _____

_____   _____

_____   _____

_____   _____

_____   _____

Date: _____

Jane Generous _____

To avoid being lost or misplaced, this memo should be kept with the original of your will. If you prepare a new writing to replace this one, to avoid confusion you should destroy the original writing and all copies.

Careful attention to these five methods can avoid bickering and disputes after you are gone. Remember, if you still want to leave the grand piano to relatives in California, the moving and insurance costs will come out of the estate unless you specify otherwise.

## Step 1: Wrap-Up

Congratulations! Your first step in estate planning is complete. You have learned how to

- make your estate wish list;
- visualize your goals and rewards;
- create your asset inventory;
- slice up your estate pie;
- take care of business and investments;
- use insurance to protect loved ones;
- deduct the Big Four bills on death;
- preview your estate; and
- deal with the small stuff.

So by now you may have conquered your fear of talking about your estate. But all this means nothing if you don't continue. That's right, you've started the journey with the first step. Splendid. But, as with any journey, you need to take the next step and the next. Go beyond planning to make or update your will.

I think it's time to bring out one of my strongest motivational tools — taxes. They're not really a secret weapon because we all know what they are. But how many of us know how to save taxes? The next few chapters will show you real-life income and probate tax stories. They'll alert you to the dangers of not putting your estate-saving plans into action. Step 2 will protect you from unnecessary tax grief.

· · · · · · · · · · · · · · · · · · · · · · · · · · · · · · · · · · · · · · · · · · · · · · · · · ·

## The Least You Need to Know

- Determine what's left in your estate after the Big Four bills are paid.
- Use an estate preview to assess your estate's worth and priorities.
- Refer to valuable personal items in wills or use a separate memo.
- Planning is no substitute for action, so go on to Step 2.

# Avoid the Big Tax Bite

Seems every day when I get home there are bills to pay. Of course, the biggest bills are always the tax bills. When we are gone, we'll have our personal bill payer or executor to take care of them.

You'll be surprised to learn which of your assets create the largest tax liabilities when you die. You can explore this topic, and I'll explain some strategies to reduce the tax bite on your estate. Giving to charity can be tax rewarding and make you feel good. I'll show you how to avoid some probate taxes. If your estate doesn't get eaten up by taxes, you'll have more to give away. Sounds simple! Careful planning is essential to keep your hard-earned dollars from the tax collector.

# Chapter 5

# Deadly Tax Bites

In this chapter:

- Be aware of tax deadlines.
- Take a dead man's approach to taxes.
- Report winners and losers.
- Understand terribly terminal returns.

Here's a large number: $4.1 trillion! That's the national net worth of all Canadians. It represents $127,500 per person, according to a report from Statistics Canada for the end of the first quarter of 2004. Is your own estate's value above or below that average? Net worth is what's left after liabilities, but I doubt the report factored in the tax liabilities triggered on death.

Step 2 of the six simple steps is determining how your estate will be taxed. Don't be discouraged. I'll also deal with simple tax-saving strategies in the next few chapters to help reduce the taxes your estate will pay. What I'll show you is so simple but successful you'll find it hard to believe. But it's true. Planning can save your loved ones a small fortune.

## Paying Your Final Dues

So you won't be around to have the personal pleasure of filing your last tax return. It's your estate's personal representative's job after you go. If you have a will, filing that return is your executor's job. If you die intestate (without a will), someone must apply to court to be appointed your estate administrator. Your executor, administrator, or representative will file your tax returns.

---

**Bulletin**

On December 12, 2003, our Ottawa tax partner became Canada Revenue Agency (CRA). Its Web site is www.cra-arc.gc.ca/agency

---

Your estate pays interest and late-filing penalties if returns (yes, there is possibly more than one) are not filed on time. I recommend professional income tax advice to file returns even within a simple estate. It's essential because of the complex rules that apply to your last or *terminal return*. Your representative can elect in some cases to reduce taxes by filing additional elective returns. Get advice to take advantage of all these tax options and possible tax savings.

## A Taxing Liability

So who is going to pay all of your estate's tax bills? You are. That's why you need to hire someone to do the job right away. Your executor can act immediately after your death. Otherwise, your relatives have to wait until one of them is appointed administrator by a judge.

Hopefully, you previewed your estate's tax liability as I suggested in Chapter 4, "Preview Your Estate's Worth." That way you can ensure enough money is available to pay your taxes. Cash or liquid assets such as life insurance will be good to use because they are readily accessed. Your estate's representative won't have to sell your assets to pay the taxes. Will the timing for a sale be right? Do you have money coming from the buy/sell agreement for your business interest? See how each step in the estate planning process is connected?

## Deadlines for Tax Returns

Now your representative can file returns and pay your taxes. The next step is to find out the deadlines for filing. There are more than a couple, so let's clarify what the important ones are.

- Income received and earned to the date of death is in your *terminal return.*
- Income received after death by your estate is in the *estate trust return.*

Now let's review the filing deadlines.

**The terminal return:** this covers all income earned from January 1 of the year of death to the date of death and taxable capital gains arising from deemed dispositions at the date of death. It also includes any remaining taxes payable, after instalment payments or taxes withheld at source. The terminal income tax return is due by April 30th of the following year. This is the usual deadline. If the date of death occurs after October, the terminal return is due six months from the date of death.

**The estate trust return:** this is a special one called a T3 trust return. It covers income earned by the estate from the date of death to estate distribution. Estates are usually wound up in a year or so. During that time, the estate's assets can generate some interest or other income. This estate return is due within ninety days of the year-end chosen by the estate's representative.

> **Legal Lingo**
>
> *Deemed disposition* means you're considered at death to have received the fair market value (FMV) for all capital property – yes, even if you give it away without getting any money in return. This deemed sale triggers tax liabilities for a deceased's estate. Capital assets include all capital property that results in a capital gain. Typically, capital properties include land, stocks, and art but not cash investments. Buildings are defined as depreciable capital property and will be subject to capital gains tax if the deemed proceeds exceed the asset's original cost.

### And That's Not All

The executor has still more responsibilities after your taxes are paid. He or she needs to have proof that no money is owed for income taxes. This proof is called a *clearance certificate* from the government to certify that all income taxes have been paid by the estate.

Two kinds of clearance certificates can be requested by an estate's representative. Once a terminal return is assessed, a final clearance certificate can be requested for the estate. It's fundamental to protect the executor before a final distribution. The reason is that the executor can be personally liable for unpaid taxes. A separate certificate is also available to cover a deceased's tax liability to the *date of death*. If an estate is distributed in stages, it may be helpful to get an interim clearance as well.

Sometimes executors and beneficiaries agree to an interim distribution of estate assets. This may happen when there's limited exposure or liabilities. For example, a deceased may have no creditors or claims outstanding. In such cases, a partial clearance can be requested for the amount to be paid out of estate trust funds. If capital is being distributed from a trust, a separate clearance can be obtained.

## Why Your Estate Representative Cares

Your executor or administrator really cares because the government makes him or her care. The responsibility to pay income taxes rests with your estate representative. It doesn't mean if you're broke he or she will have to take out a personal loan or sell his or her own assets — it's still your IOU to the tax department.

This liability extends only to the assets available to or under the executor's control. Here's an example. Say you die owing $75,000 in taxes. Assume you have $25,000 in assets after the funeral is paid. That's the extent of your representative's personal liability for your taxes. If $25,000 were accidentally distributed to a beneficiary, the representative would be liable even if the money can't be recovered from the beneficiary. The executor is liable for that mistake and owes the $25,000.

## Dying to Pay Taxes

There are tax rules and always tax exceptions. So let's start with the rules. Special tax rules come into play when Canadians die. These rules specify what extra items are included in your final tax return. Almost all income is caught, as when you're alive. But there is an added wrinkle. You're considered to have disposed of all capital assets for their fair market value. This is the *deemed disposition* rule. It generates tax liabilities even though your assets aren't sold and no cash is received. There are exceptions, which I'll get to in a moment, so don't stop reading.

## Small Things with Big Tax Consequences

You may think yours is a below-average estate according to Statistics Canada's findings. So why worry about taxes? Our tax system catches all kinds of income sources when you die. When you add them up, you'll be richer than you think. You'll also pay more taxes. It's a catch-22 situation. Dying can give you the largest income tax bill you've ever had. Let's break this down so I can explain the deemed disposition rule that comes into play just before death.

## Tax Winners, Deduct Losers

If you have real estate, stocks, or jewellery, for example, you have capital property. Capital property is deemed sold just before your death. You're taxed as if a sale had taken place at the property's fair market value. This rule allows the government to tax the unrealized asset appreciation.

Here's an example. Julie bought a high-tech stock in 1999 for $10,000. When she died, her shares were worth $40,000. Tax laws treated the stock as if it had been sold immediately before her death. This translated into a profit or capital gain of $30,000.

Even though she never sold the stock, the taxable capital gain must be reported. It's included in her income in the year of her death. The current inclusion percentage for capital gains is fifty percent. Since Julie died after February 27, 2005, one-half of her capital gain, or $15,000, would be included in her income on her terminal tax return. Julie's estate would now pay the tax on $15,000 of extra income. Assuming Julie has a combined federal and provincial tax rate of fifty percent, this would be $7,500.

Should Julie have anticipated this tax bill? Yes. Her estate now has to find enough money to pay her final tax bill.

## Help Line

**Q:** What's depreciable capital property?

**A:** It's capital property used to earn income so you can claim capital cost allowance (CCA). This is an expense deduction for tax depreciation claimed on tax returns. CCA is used to reduce income taxes, but it can possibly only be a deferral since it can be "recaptured" and included in income on a later disposition.

---

**Legal Lingo**

*Adjusted cost base* is the original cost of the property you acquire, adjusted as permitted by the tax laws, for allowable capital improvements.

---

## How to Calculate a Taxable Gain

Over the long haul, you're bound to have a taxable capital gain. So you might as well learn how the government would tax the appreciation in the value of any capital assets. It's the same method of calculation on death.

Briefly, it works like this. You bought a vacation property ten years ago for $30,000. When you died (after February 27, 2005), it was worth $90,000. You're deemed to have sold it at its fair market value (FMV) of $90,000.

Your estate calculates the gain on the property as follows:

$90,000 − $30,000 = $60,000.

Now take one-half of the increase of $60,000, which is included as a taxable capital gain. That one-half of the capital gain is reported as income in your terminal tax return.

Another way of looking at it is like this.

- FMV − cost = capital gain.
- $90,000 − $30,000 = $60,000 capital gain.
- Half of the capital gain is a taxable capital gain.
- Report as income $30,000.

Deemed dispositions also apply to *depreciable property*. These assets, buildings, and equipment, for example, are usually used to earn income. That's property on which you may have been claiming capital cost allowance. Death could trigger a recapture of CCA, which is also reported as income and is fully taxable.

## Keep Adjusting That Cost Base

One of the elements of the capital gains calculation is to determine the property's *adjusted cost base*. In most cases, the adjusted base is your actual cost of the property. But this cost can be adjusted in many ways — in other words, what you pay for the property plus any amounts you may have spent on the property. These expenditures and income tax rules allow you to add or deduct items to calculate the adjusted cost base.

The easiest example to understand would be the purchase of that vacation property. Annual maintenance and repairs to the property do not affect the adjusted cost base, but capital improvements are another story. The cost of renovating the vacation property and adding improvements can be added to the adjusted cost base.

Looking at the above example, if capital improvements cost $10,000, then the adjusted cost base would be added to the purchase price. This adjusted cost base would be $40,000, which is then subtracted from the fair market value to calculate the capital gain.

---

**Bulletin**

Rollovers are important tax advantages. They are the main exception to the deemed realization rule. Rollovers allow a postponement or deferral of capital gains. These are available to qualifying spouses, common-law or same-sex spouses, spousal trusts, and financially dependent children or grandchildren.

---

## Rolling over the Disposition Rules

These deemed sale rules apply to everything — capital assets such as real estate, jewellery, stocks, transferred by will or designation or even those jointly owned. The one exception to these tax rules occurs with a rollover to qualifying spouses, spousal trusts, or financially dependent children or grandchildren.

Whenever a rollover is applied, the deemed disposition rules do not apply. No taxes are paid until the new owner disposes of the asset. The taxpayer reports the taxable capital gain or allowable capital loss at that time, using the original cost to determine gains or losses. This leads to a deferral of tax until the next disposition of the property. You want to take advantage of rollovers to save taxes. If you don't, your loved ones could pay plenty. That's what happened to Gunther's wife.

Gunther converted his $90,000 severance package from work into a registered retirement savings plan (RRSP). He designated his sister to be the beneficiary of this plan. This investment doubled in value and before he died was sheltered from tax.

When Gunther passed away, the RRSP was transferred to his sister. His wife and executor had an accountant prepare his final tax returns. "I'm sorry to tell you this," the accountant said reluctantly. "Your husband's last tax return must include $90,000 as income from the RRSP. That puts your husband in the highest tax bracket. In round figures, it's approximately $45,000 in taxes."

Gunther's wife was in shock. She asked if there had been some kind of mistake.

"Yes," the accountant said, "and your husband made it. He should have designated you, his spouse, as the beneficiary of the RRSP. You would then transfer the amount into your own RRSP."

This story could have had a happier ending. The spousal rollover would have saved his estate $45,000. Simple steps can save a lot of money.

### It's Been Said
..............................................................

"Riches are gotten with pain, kept with care, and lost with grief."
– Proverb

## Forget Deferrals: Elect to Pay

Gunther's example shows the advantage of a rollover. If Gunther's wife didn't have to pay $45,000 in taxes on the RRSP income, she'd get a deferral. Taxes aren't magically eliminated but postponed or deferred until the wife draws on or collapses the RRSP. Think of the deferral advantages of investing an extra $45,000 for ten years or more, for example.

The rollover also applies to transfers to a spousal trust, which is held exclusively for the benefit of your spouse. This way, if you transfer assets to a "qualifying" spousal trust, you meet the requirements. We'll discuss trusts in more detail in Chapter 6, "Tax Planning Tips." The benefits of spousal rollovers are also covered in spouses as beneficiaries in Chapter 20, "Spouses: Good, Bad, and Divorced."

I know what you're saying: "Why should anyone want to pay taxes and not take the deferral?"

Well, with some assets, your estate's legal representative could take advantage of existing business or capital losses or deductions. Taxable capital gains may be offset by losses to reduce future taxes that would be due. The executor can elect out of the spousal rollover rules and recognize the taxable capital gain in the terminal return. A new adjusted cost base is thus established for the property. Your executor can file an election so the spousal rollover will not apply. That's another reason professional income tax advice is essential when completing your terminal tax return.

## Show Me the Particulars

Look at these tax rollovers more closely. Use Kathy, who died in 2004, as an example. Her assets include

- an RRSP worth $200,000 with her son Robert as a designated beneficiary;
- stocks worth $100,000 owned jointly with her sister Bernice;
- life insurance worth $100,000 payable to her daughter as the beneficiary; and
- a home worth $200,000 of which she is the sole owner.

After Kathy's death, her executor had an accountant prepare the final tax return. Following is how her property was treated for tax purposes.

**RRSPs worth $200,000:** these were transferred to Kathy's designated beneficiary, Robert, clear of tax liability. But there are tax consequences to Kathy's estate. Her executor must include on her final tax return all $200,000 of the RRSP as income. If Robert was an eligible financially dependent child, the estate may be entitled to escape tax due to the rollover rules.

**Public company stock worth $100,000, jointly owned with her sister:** assume Kathy paid for the stock when it was purchased for $40,000. She would have a capital gain of $60,000. One-half of this amount would be included in her income reported on her terminal return as a taxable capital gain.

> **Legal Lingo**
>
> *Terminal* means the end of a series, and for tax purposes a terminal return is the last personal return. It is filed to report all income and taxable capital gains to the date of a person's death.

**Q:** How many principal residences can you claim?

**A:** After 1981, a family can have only one home designated as a principal residence. Capital gains on this house may be fully or partially exempt from income tax.

**Life insurance benefits worth $100,000 with Kathy's daughter as the beneficiary:** good news here because there are no tax consequences on life insurance to either Kathy's estate or her beneficiary.

**Personal residence worth $200,000:** this was Kathy's *principal residence*, and — surprise — a rule makes it tax exempt. Kathy was entitled to have only one principal residence, however. This asset is transferred by her will on a tax-free basis.

Kathy's tax calculation could change dramatically. For example, Kathy would be entitled to tax credits if she donated her RRSP or life insurance through a direct beneficiary designation to a registered charity. You'll see this in more detail in Chapter 7, "Great Expectations."

## What's Included as Income? Almost Everything

I'll give you some idea of how complex an area this can be. Following is a partial list of the special income to be included in terminal returns.

**Registered retirement savings plans (RRSPs):** the full amount of your RRSP is included as income unless a rollover is available to a qualified beneficiary. A financially dependent child or grandchild can become a qualified beneficiary. Furthermore, federal laws can recognize common-law spouses — of the same or opposite sex — as legally married for income tax purposes.

**Registered retirement income funds (RRIFs):** if you have no surviving spouse as the designated beneficiary, the fair market value of the RRIF is included as income.

**Income received:** the general rule is that income, other than interest, is taxed when received. Interest income is subject to tax on the accrual basis or when earned. Business income or income from employment, interest, and taxable dividends from investments is included on your terminal return.

You may be able to file an additional elective tax return if certain income is earned and not received prior to death. That way your estate is entitled to claim an extra set of basic exemptions to lower your overall tax cost. This is referred to as a "rights and things" return. For example, eligible income includes declared and unpaid dividends or earned but unpaid employment income.

**Income accrued:** this income is from bonds, mortgages, and other interest-bearing investments. If there is accrued interest income at the date of your death, it must be included on the terminal return. Accrued interest income does not qualify to be reported on the "rights and things" elective return.

**Capital property:** there is a deemed disposal at fair market value at the date of death. The resulting taxable capital gain is included in income on the terminal tax return. This rule applies if the spousal rollover rules do not apply. Taxable capital gains arise if there was an increase in value over the original acquisition or purchase cost. Remember that recapture of capital cost allowance on depreciable property is also reported and is fully taxable.

---

**Bulletin**

If a death occurs prior to November, terminal returns are due by the following April 30th. If death occurs in November or December, a terminal return and the related income tax are due within six months of the date of death.

---

**Receivables:** these are amounts not received at the time of death that qualify for a separate elective return. These include dividends that are declared but not paid or unpaid salary.

**Annuity income:** this is treated as ordinary income unless there is a capital component that is nontaxable.

**Pension plan benefit:** in some cases, you receive a death benefit. When you have no spouse or designated beneficiary, there could be a taxable benefit that must be reported.

**Partnership or proprietorship income:** your income from a business up to the date of death has to be reported. A separate elective return may be filed for this income if the estate's representative chooses it.

## Use Your Deductions and Credits

From all of this income, you are entitled to get tax credits and certain deductions. They are beneficial in minimizing or reducing tax, so let's see what they can include.

**Medical expenses:** they can be pooled for up to twenty-four months prior to the date of death.

**Charitable donation credits:** these nonrefundable tax credits apply to the year of death. So, if you make an individual gift by your will, it's deemed to be made immediately before you die. That allows you, under special rules, to claim a tax credit up to 100 percent of your net income in your terminal return. If you can't use up all these credits, you can carry any excess credits back to the year prior to your death.

**Nonrefundable tax credits:** basic personal and other credits are claimed for the full year.

**Net capital losses:** these losses are carried over from prior years. Net capital losses have an indefinite carry-over period. Normally, they can only be used to reduce taxable income in a year if taxable capital gains have been realized. The deduction is limited to the amount of the taxable capital gain. In your terminal return, however, these net capital losses are deducted from all sources of income.

**RRSP contributions:** these are deductible prior to death in the year of death. Estate representatives for a deceased can contribute to a spousal RRSP within sixty days of the calendar year-end. This gives the deceased's estate a deduction used to calculate net income in the terminal return.

## How Big Is the Tax Bite?

Let's look at another illustration, using Murray as an example. You're his executor, and you need some basic tax advice. Murray's beneficiaries are already asking you, "When do we get our money?"

In Chapter 4, "Preview Your Estate's Worth," we talked about the Big Four, the bills that need to be paid on death. You read how important it is to get professional income tax advice to estimate the tax liabilities. Now we'll take a closer look at the tax liability as it relates to each estate asset.

> **Time Machine**
>
> In ancient Greece and Rome, taxes were a form of extortion or tribute from conquered foreigners. Force was required to collect taxes. Today taxpayers pay to support the governments they elect.

## Murray's Taxable Estate Inventory

| Property | Ownership | Fair Market Value | Tax Liability |
|---|---|---|---|
| Home | Murray alone | $200,000 | None – principal residence |
| Household contents | Joint with wife | $10,000 | None – spousal rollover |
| Savings, chequing | Joint with wife | $10,000 | Yes – share of interest income |
| Stocks and bonds | Murray alone | $200,000 | Yes – dividends, gain or loss |
| Recreational property | Murray alone | $80,000 | Yes – capital gain only |
| RRSPs | Designated spouse | $100,000 | None – spousal rollover |
| Pension | Designated survivor | $200,000 | None – unless income received |
| Life insurance | Designated beneficiary | $200,000 | None – tax-free proceeds |

The fair market value of the stocks, bonds, and recreational property is $280,000. The total gain on these three assets is $90,000, one-half of which, $45,000, is included in Murray's income as a taxable capital gain. Assuming there is no other income, the estate pays tax on $45,000 in the terminal return.

Since the RRSP is designated to a spouse, there is a spousal rollover, and the same applies to Murray's pension. There will be no income tax consequences to his estate because the rollover applies. We'll talk more about rollovers to spouses and spousal trusts in the next chapter. For the sake of illustration, what if the RRSP was not payable to a spouse or a qualified beneficiary? Then $100,000 of additional income would be included in the terminal return. Assuming a fifty percent combined tax bracket, this would have cost Murray's estate an extra $50,000.

"The hardest thing to understand in the world is the income tax."
Albert Einstein, 1879–1955

# Seven Deadly Tax Points to Remember

1. Estate representatives must file your final (terminal) and estate tax returns. They are personally liable to pay taxes from your estate. Final estate tax clearances should be obtained.

2. The terminal return and other elective returns can be filed to include all manner of income. Get professional income tax advice to decide if elective returns can be filed to save taxes.

3. Deemed disposition rules force deceased taxpayers to include all unrealized taxable capital gains as income.

4. Rollovers to qualified spouses, spousal trusts, and some financially dependent children and grandchildren allow you to avoid the deemed disposition rules.

5. Since 1981, only one principal residence is allowed per family.

6. Make sure you have enough cash available to pay your taxes on death; otherwise, estate assets may have to be sold.

7. Your estate can't be distributed until taxes are paid and a clearance certificate is obtained.

**It's Been Said**

"The seven deadly sins [are] . . . food, clothing, firing, rent, taxes, respectability, and children. Nothing can lift those seven millstones from man's neck but money; and the spirit cannot soar until the millstones are lifted."
— George Bernard Shaw, 1856–1950

### Estate Plan Your Taxes

When planning your estate and its distribution, take advantage of the tax rules. Maximize the benefits from the following items:

- principal residence exemption;
- registered retirement savings plan designations;
- rollovers to your spouse or a qualifying spousal trust; and
- tax-free life insurance proceeds.

Tax rules are complex and uncertain even for experts in the field. However, you can save money by using the six simple steps. For example, if you're a spouse, take advantage of the spousal rollover rules. They allow you to postpone payment of income taxes for taxable capital gains from RRSPs or RRIFs. Consider these spousal advantages as you plan your estate's distribution.

Use any tax-free life insurance that's available. It can provide support, pay taxes, avoid creditors, or generate charitable tax credits.

Understanding the tax rules can help you decide on the best way to handle your estate components. In the next chapter, we'll review tax planning techniques that you'll want to consider.

### The Least You Need to Know

- Your estate's legal representative must file your last tax return.
- On death, capital properties are deemed disposed of at fair market value.
- Taxable capital gains on capital property are reported in your final return.
- Tax planning lets you use rollovers to avoid deemed disposition rules.

# Chapter 6

# Tax Planning Tips

In this chapter:

- Learn gifting strategies.
- Understand trusts, trustees, and taxes.
- Review a simple trust.
- Consider special tax issues.

Want some tax tips to help you plan? In this chapter, you'll learn about trusts and special tax tips.

Taxes take a big bite out of your estate, but planning can reduce the size of that bite. The result is that you'll have more money for your favourite people and causes. You'll consider two techniques: gifting assets before death and using trusts. Both reduce the complexity and size of your estate for income tax purposes.

## Great Gifts Galore

Gifting is an important estate planning technique. It is a means of transferring ownership and reducing future tax liability and probate costs. Gifts can be made while you're alive, in anticipation of your death, or in your will. They have different names, but basically there are two types. *Inter vivos* gifts are made while you're alive, and testamentary ones are made after you're gone.

## What Is a Gift?

A gift is a legally defined way of transferring your assets. Gifts made during your lifetime contain three elements.

- The person making the gift (you, the donor) must intend to do so.
- The person receiving the gift (the donee) must accept it.
- The transfer of property (the gift) must be irrevocable.

## Gifts Have Tax Consequences

Unlike the United States, Canada has no specific gift tax laws. Canadian donors, not the person receiving the gift, pay the tax. We are, however, subject to income tax rules that apply to gifts, but they're not based on the size of the gift. The income tax laws deal with capital gains and income-splitting but not the gift itself. Because of this, you shouldn't try to gift away your entire estate before you go.

Here's an example to explain how the gift isn't taxed but the income is. Your wife wants to give you and your children something special at Christmas. Her favourite stock pick has made a profit, and it looks promising for the long term. Feeling generous, she gives 100 shares worth $20,000 to you. Your two children each receive gifts worth $10,000. At tax time, she deals with these gifts on her return as follows.

**A gift to a spouse:** the gift to you, as the husband, of capital property carries no income tax consequences. That's because the gift qualifies for the spousal rollover as explained in the previous chapter. When you sell the stock, the taxable capital gains calculated with reference to your wife's original costs must be reported by her. Also, any income from the transfer date would be reported in your wife's income.

**A gift to a child:** the children were under the age of eighteen when the stock was gifted. Your wife will pay tax on any capital gains triggered when the stocks are transferred. Purchased at four dollars per share, the stocks are now worth ten dollars each. This results in six dollars a share profit or capital gain. One-half of that amount is your wife's taxable capital gain and is included as her income. She'd then be taxed at her graduated tax rate.

## Help Line

**Q:** What's income-splitting?

**A:** Income-splitting strategies save taxes. You do so by shifting income from a family member in a higher bracket of tax to another family member who may pay less or no tax.

## Help Line

**Q:** I think I have found a way to income-split with my family. How can I determine if it is legal?

**A:** Consult an income tax professional. There are anti-avoidance rules that will attribute income if the transaction is simply to sprinkle income to reduce the overall family tax burden. You need a primary *bona fide* family business or investment purpose.

**Income attribution on gifts:** what if your wife transferred bonds instead of stocks? Again, any income earned on the bonds by you or your minor children would be attributed back to her. Your wife would have to report the income in her own return.

**Capital gains and minors:** capital gains on transferred property to minor children don't attribute back. This is beneficial since it lets the children pay the tax on future capital appreciation. When the children sell the stock, they report the taxable capital gain. This helps if the children are taxed at a lower rate than your wife.

> **Legal Lingo**
>
> *Income attribution rules* are tax rules that generally attribute any income or taxable capital gains realized from the gifted property back to the donor. There are exceptions if there is consideration equal to the fair market value of the property. If minors receive gifts, a subsequent taxable capital gain does not attribute.

## Income Attribution Rules

These rules limit the ability of families to income-split to reduce taxes. They are directed to transfers of property, cash, gifts, or loans to your spouse. All income from the property or capital gain on the disposition of such property is attributed back to you. The exception is the capital gain realized by minors, as explained above.

Say you give your spouse $10,000 in cash, which he or she puts in the bank. If your spouse is unemployed, his or her tax rate is likely to be much lower than yours. But if the money earns interest income of $500, it's attributed back to you and taxed as your income. If you are considered "spouses" for tax purposes, you will be subject to the attribution rules.

You need to consider income tax rules whenever a gift is made to a spouse or a related minor child. In Chapter 8, "Reduce Probate Taxes Properly," I'll also explain how you can reduce exposure for probate with gifts. Beware of the attribution rules since it is easy to get caught by them.

## Tax-Deferred Spousal Gifts

A gift between a husband and wife is technically taxable. The deemed disposition rules apply, but by using the spousal rollover rules such transfers are tax-deferred events. The taxable capital gain is deferred until the property is actually disposed of by your spouse. When that happens, the taxable capital gain will be attributed back to the donor spouse unless you are deceased.

> **Bulletin**
>
> Income-splitting can be done legally without invoking the income attribution rules. For example, pay your family a reasonable salary for work done if you have a business. Splitting income, if done properly, is good planning.

Let me now introduce a new concept. It's called a "trust."

The rollover rules also apply if a gift is made by a spouse to a qualifying spousal trust. These can be living trusts or those testamentary spousal trusts created by your will. Trusts can provide flexibility to distribute property and income. I'll explain how you can use trusts in your estate planning.

## Trusts: Flexible Planning Tools

Trusts can be used to reduce capital gains taxes on death. Through trusts, taxes can be deferred, and income can be split. A trust is a relationship created by law with useful estate planning purposes. Trusts have certain advantages and drawbacks, which I'll talk about as I go along.

Three essential legal ingredients are contained in every trust. The first, a settlor, which could be you, creates the trust. The second is the trustees who are appointed to manage trust property. Finally, the trust must have beneficiaries to receive the trust property. When Dermot's grandfather dies, his will sets up a trust for Dermot. The grandfather's stock portfolio was to be held by Dermot's mom as trustee. The stocks are the trust property. Dermot's mom controls the assets until Dermot, the beneficiary, turns twenty-one, as stipulated in the grandfather's will.

---

**Legal Lingo**

*Inter vivos trusts* are living trusts such as private, family, or personal trusts.

---

## What Type of Trust Do You Need?

You can set up a trust while you are alive. These are living, family, or personal trusts. Trusts can also be easily created by your will to be effective upon your death. Your privacy will be protected with a personal trust because it's not filed with any court. Once filed for probate, your wills and their contents are open to public inspection.

You can also use trusts to

- manage property if you become incapacitated;
- reduce taxes by income-splitting;
- enable confidential asset transfers to trust beneficiaries after death;
- avoid probate costs;
- prevent problems if a legal battle starts over your will; or
- keep control of assets away from trust beneficiaries.

## Why Use a Trust?

Trusts can be set up for a number of specific purposes, including the needs of

- spouses who require asset management help;
- disabled beneficiaries;
- minor children;
- spendthrift adult beneficiaries;
- retirement management;
- tax planning; and
- charitable benefits.

Setting up a living trust can be expensive, though, not something you'd consider while you are struggling to develop your asset base. If you are young and single, or just recently married, you need a will, but you can get by without a separate trust.

To set up a living trust, you'll pay at least $2,000 in legal fees for consultations and the legal work. This is more expensive than creating a will. Will fees start at several hundred dollars and go up from there. These costs, although they can vary, may intimidate you from considering a trust. There will also be trustee fees and ongoing responsibility for filing separate trust income tax returns.

Are you interested in getting more information about trusts? Contact a trust company, because it acts as a corporate trustee. You can get free information on trusts. If you hire a trust company, you'll sign its compensation agreement. It sets out fees for the management of the trust assets. You would probably consider a personal trust if you can place several hundred thousand dollars in excess assets into it. Are you over sixty-five years of age and in the top marginal income tax bracket? I'll explain some other living trust options in a moment. First I'll show you who is involved in a basic trust.

---

**Legal Lingo**

The *settlor* is the person who settles or transfers property into trust. The *beneficiary* receives benefits from trust property. *Trustees* manage the trust property, income, and capital.

---

Here is an example of a simple discretionary living trust called a Henson trust. Again, as with all my documents, it's intended not for use but for illustration.

---

### TRUST AGREEMENT

THIS TRUST AGREEMENT made as of the day of February 2005
BETWEEN:

FRANK, of the Province of Ontario
(hereinafter the "Settlor")
OF THE FIRST PART

ELI, of the Province of Ontario
(hereinafter the "Trustee")
OF THE SECOND PART
RECITALS

Frank wishes to benefit his nephew Johnny.

Johnny is the beneficiary of this trust. He is unable to work and receives government assistance.

Eli agrees to act as the Trustee and to hold the funds in trust for the benefit of Johnny on the terms set out in his trust agreement.

---

## 1. Duty of Trustee

Eli agrees to act as Trustee and shall hold and invest the sum of ONE HUN-DRED THOUSAND ($100,000.00) DOLLARS for Johnny. In the Trustee's absolute discretion, he may pay the whole or part of the income therefrom, together with the capital thereof to or for the benefit of Johnny, as the Trustee shall in the exercise of his absolute and unfettered discretion con-sider advisable from time to time.

## 2. Trust Income

Any income not so paid in any year shall be accumulated by the Trustee and added to the capital of the trust fund. If it becomes unlawful for the Trustee to continue such accumulation of income, then the income not so paid in any year shall be paid to Johnny's sister Elizabeth, as the Trustee in his absolute discretion deems advisable.

## 3. No Vesting of Trust Assets

No portion of the trust income shall vest in Johnny. He shall only be entitled to have the payments actually made to him, or on his behalf, and received by him or for his benefit. Without in any way limiting the Trustee's discretion, the Trustee may take such steps as will maximize the benefits which Johnny would receive from other sources if payments from the income and capital of the trust fund were not paid to him for his own benefit. The Trustee can make payments varying in amounts and times, as the Trustee in the exercise of his absolute discretion may consider in the best interests of Johnny.

## 4. When Trust Shall End

When Johnny dies, the remainder of this trust property shall go to his sister Elizabeth or her children if she is not alive. This trust shall end, and the trust property shall be distributed when any of the following events happens:
    a) Johnny dies;
    b) The trust property is used up or fully distributed; or
    c) The day before the twenty-first anniversary of the trust's commence-ment;

## 5. Trustee Replacement

If a trustee dies, has a conflict or is unable to continue, or fails to act in the best interest of Johnny, then my sister, Annie, shall act as my alternative trustee.

**IN WITNESS WHEREOF** the parties hereto have hereunto respectively set their hands and seals as of the date hereof.

**SIGNED, SEALED, AND DELIVERED** in the presence of:

**Dated:** _____

_____          _____
       **Witness**                                      **Settlor**

**Dated:** _____

_____          _____
       **Witness**                                      **Trustee**

## Guide to Trust Terms

**Settlor:** this is the person who sets up the trust, which in our example would be you. You would be the settlor, grantor, donor, or even the creator of the trust.

**Beneficiary:** this is the person who receives the benefit from the trust property. You can control how and when he or she receives trust property.

**Trustee:** this is the individual or institution that carries out the terms of the trust. Trustees manage assets and distribute income to beneficiaries. You could, for example, pick a relative or a trust company. In case you're wondering, you won't be around to act as trustee for your testamentary trusts. Don't worry, in Step 4 I'll cover all your alternative choices for executors.

**Backup trustee:** this person takes over as a surviving trustee. This occurs if the original or primary trustee is unable to act because of death or incapacity.

**Trust estate:** this is all the property legally transferred by the settlor for the benefit of beneficiaries.

**Trust deed or agreement:** this is a legal document typically prepared by a lawyer to set out all the terms of the living trust. It explains how trust property is to be administered. You'll need expert advice from people familiar with trusts to prepare it. Don't be tempted to use preprinted forms.

**Testamentary trust:** this type of trust is created by your will and becomes effective only when you die. Your will contains separate trust provisions to deal with trust assets, including distribution of income and capital to beneficiaries. For example, in my will I had a trust for my children, Nick and Adam, while they were minors. My trustees managed the investments until my children were old enough to inherit them.

> **Legal Lingo**
>
> A *Henson trust* is a fully discretionary trust, if recognized in your province, to benefit beneficiaries who receive government assistance. It is named after an Ontario court decision that approved of a specific type of trust with certain restrictions and income benefits for disabled beneficiaries.

## Taxing the Trust

You can set up or settle a trust by transferring just a dollar or a gold coin to get it started. Then you can arrange to transfer additional assets into the trust while you are alive. At the time of your death, extra assets can be obtained through your estate. Whatever the source of the funds, there will be taxes due unless you put in cash or claim a tax rollover.

Unlike corporations, trusts are treated as separate individuals for income tax purposes. Unlike individuals, though, the trust does not get any personal tax credits. Each year trustees file a T3 trust tax return and pay the tax on the trust's taxable income. The trust may allocate income to the beneficiary, in which case the beneficiary is taxed. There's a difference, however, in how trusts are taxed.

**Living trusts:** these are taxed at the highest marginal individual rate rather than at the graduated rates. This is the top combined federal and provincial rate. That means you may not have advantages from an income tax perspective.

**Testamentary trusts:** income in these "will-made" trusts is taxed at graduated individual rates. The rate can thus be lower than the highest rate.

You'll have to make decisions about how to find the right trustee. In Chapter 15, "Hold Something Back," I'll give you some options. Of course, if you are creating a living trust, you and your spouse can be the trustees. If you want a trust company to act on your behalf, you'll need to discuss its fees. There will be start-up costs and annual fees for management and services.

Not everyone needs a living trust on an *inter vivos* basis. You'll need testamentary trusts, however, if you have minor children, special needs beneficiaries, or an elderly spouse.

Trusts also give you an insight into another popular way of making gifts to charities. I'll show you how charitable trusts can provide tax credits and benefit your favourite charity.

## An Exception for Sixty-Five Year Olds

Exceptions have been created to Canada's trust law since 1999. If you are sixty-five or over, you might benefit from these new tax planning techniques. You'll be able to transfer or roll over assets into two new forms of living trusts on a tax-deferred basis. Doing so modifies the existing deemed disposition rules for putting assets into a trust. But this only applies, since 1999, to alter-ego or joint partner trusts, which I will describe one at a time.

**It's Been Said**
..............................................................

"Necessity never made a good bargain."
  – Benjamin Franklin, *Poor Richard's Almanac*, 1733

## Alter-Ego Trust for One

Here are some additional criteria for this living trust.

- The trust must be created after 1999.
- The person creating the trust (the settlor) must be at least sixty-five years of age.
- While alive, only the settlor can be entitled to receive all trust income and capital.

There's no change in how income in the trust is taxed. As with other living trusts, income earned and retained in the trust will be taxed at the highest marginal rates. Thus, alter-ego trusts would be of interest only to taxpayers who are already in the highest tax brackets.

What may make this trust attractive is that it can be used as a will substitute for the distribution of your estate. Because of the tax-free rollover of assets into the alter-ego trust, the normal deemed disposition rules do not apply until a settlor's death. That's when trustees distribute assets to the contingent trust beneficiaries named in the trust. This happens without having to probate your will and without the public disclosure normally available for wills. This trust allows for more personal control and management of trust assets.

## New Joint Partner Trusts for Two

Another living trust is a joint partner trust for couples sixty-five years of age or older. Similar to an alter-ego trust, this trust for "spouses" also qualifies for a tax deferral when assets are placed into a trust created by spouses. The trust must be created after 1999, and only the spouses can receive trust income and capital while alive.

On the death of the last surviving spouse, the joint partner trust dictates who are contingent beneficiaries to inherit the trust property. This process also avoids probate for those assets remaining in the trust.

These two forms of living trusts open new estate planning opportunities for those aged sixty-five or more. Again, the costs of preparing the necessary trust documents and transfer of assets have to be weighed against the overall benefits. Remember, the tax rollover applies only at the time the assets are transferred into the trust. There will still be the deemed dispositions on death as if there was no trust created. For the joint spousal trust, this would be on the death of the last surviving spouse.

## Recap of Senior Trusts

- Alter-ego and joint partner trusts are vehicles seniors can employ to bypass the probate process. This approach has benefits since the trustees already have legal ownership of trust assets.
- There is no delay, no probate cost, and no will contest or dispute that will create problems.

- A family business can be managed and transferred without fear of estate claims from creditors, former spouses, or disgruntled beneficiaries.
- For the elderly in the highest tax bracket, these trusts offer greater flexibility.
- You can better protect yourself from power of attorney abuse with assets in multiple jurisdictions.

Are you starting to enjoy your golden years? If you have substantial assets to protect or reason to bypass probate, talk to a trust expert. There will be costs and complex issues involved in setting up the trust, but you may find it worthwhile.

### Help Line

**Q:** I understand there is a Canada–U.S. tax treaty that prevents double taxation for Canadians.

**A:** You can still be subject to double taxation on American situs assets. If your worldwide assets exceed the exemption level, U.S. taxes can become an issue.

## A Potpourri of Special Tax Issues

Here are a few more rules and exceptions you need to watch out for.

### Uncle Sam's Long Tax Arm

Canadian taxpayers are taxed on their worldwide income. So the terminal return includes any rental income or taxable capital gains from your U.S. condo, for example. But did you know you can also be subject to U.S. estate taxes? If you own property in the United States, you need advice from experts in cross-border taxation. That's because you can be subject to U.S. estate tax on death on what's called situs assets. This can include holding real estate, debts, or shares in an American corporation normally located in the United States.

Avoiding the possibility of double taxation requires planning. Investigate some techniques, such as holding assets through a corporation, because the corporation does not die. You could also arrange loans to reduce asset values or take out life insurance to cover the liability. Snowbirds should take heed.

## Qualified Family Businesses

Don't forget that the fair market value of your business interests is included in your terminal return. There is some tax relief if you own shares in a qualifying small business corporation. This applies only to corporations, not to unincorporated businesses. Listen to this, because there's a capital gains exemption of up to $500,000 on the sale of qualified small business corporation shares.

There are special rules that must be met to qualify. If you own qualified small business corporation shares, consider taking advantage of this capital gains exemption without disposing of the shares to a third party. Also, there are other rollover rules that allow you to transfer business assets into a corporation on a tax-deferred basis. This may help with taking advantage of that $500,000 capital gains exemption.

## Don't Give up the Farm

Again, there's an exemption from tax for qualifying farm property. Those who meet the requirements can claim a $500,000 lifetime capital gains exemption. The farm must be actively used for the business of farming in Canada. This is really an intergenerational transfer rule. It applies only to transfers to a child, grandchild, or great-grandchild.

To qualify, you must be a Canadian resident owning and operating a farm. You would be disposing of shares in a family farm corporation or a farm partnership or farm property. Farm rollovers can be claimed during your lifetime or at death on a tax-free basis. That's provided you comply with the tax rules. At the same time, you pass control of the family farm business to the next generation.

## Freezing Your Estate

This has nothing to do with keeping you on ice. You use an estate freeze as a tool to "freeze" or fix the fair market value of an estate asset at its present value. Any future appreciation or growth will not be taxed on your death in your estate. Rather, your beneficiaries — normally your children — will be taxed. Consider this manoeuvre if you own shares of a corporation whose business has growth potential. Your children may or may not be involved in the business operations. You can, however, eliminate the uncertainty of taxes your estate would pay by using a freeze. Of course, you'll also want the children to own the asset after you're gone.

Complex rules and procedures are required to accomplish an estate freeze. You may have to set up a holding company or family trust or reorganize the corporation's capital to accomplish the freeze. Normally, you would want to trigger your accrued taxable capital gains so you can utilize the unused exemption of $500,000 of capital gains or $250,000 of taxable capital gains. You'll pay any capital gains tax on values above that amount, unless there is a method to defer it.

### It's Been Said
. . . . . . . . . . . . . . . . . . . . . . . . . . . . . . . . . . . . . . . . . . . . . . . . . . .

"He that dies pays all debts."
– William Shakespeare, 1564–1616, "The Tempest", Act 3, Scene 2

The simplest example of a corporate reorganization has you exchanging your common shares for preferred voting shares. You keep voting control over the corporation's business affairs. Normally, this is done without triggering any income tax on a rollover basis. The shares would be retractable, meaning at your option you can demand that the corporation buy back your shares.

Your children then purchase a new class of common shares from the corporation. They pay the nominal value of ten dollars per share. Since you can demand that the company pay you for your preference shares, the common shares have little or no value. However, as the value of the corporation increases through growth, the new common shares increase in value while your shares do not. The growth in the equity of the company would thus be in the children's hands. The children can then possibly dispose of their common shares with little or no tax, claiming their own $500,000 lifetime capital gains exemption.

## Beware of Your Tax Sources

Uncle Sam has another, perhaps indirect, impact on Canadians. Many of the books, Web sites, and sources of information on tax and estate planning are American resources. These foreign sources extol the virtues of "dying broke" to avoid U.S.-based inheritance and gift taxes. Worse still, they want you to consider revocable and bypass trusts to avoid going broke by paying for hospital care.

Canadian taxes, trusts, and television are different. You have to realize that when you do your reading and research. Even Canadian Web sites, articles, and material on wills are not accurate, up to date, or supervised, so beware.

You may benefit from a living trust, especially if you won the lottery, but you'll always need a will. I'll show you why in Step 3. In the next chapter, you'll see what millions of Canadians volunteer to do.

··············································································

## The Least You Need to Know

- Gifts to immediate family and other relatives may result in attribution problems.
- For income tax purposes, gifts of capital property are deemed to be made at fair market value.
- Gifts of appreciating property will reduce capital gains tax paid by your estate but could generate immediate adverse tax consequences.
- You can use living or testamentary trusts to separate property ownership from its benefits.

# Chapter 7

# Great Expectations

In this chapter:

- Plan charitable gifts.
- Use will bequests.
- Understand tax credit rewards.
- Donate RRSPs and stocks.

You may donate your time, energy, and money to one of 80,000 registered Canadian charities. But do you understand the tax and estate planning advantages of charitable donations? I'll take you through a host of options in this chapter. By the time you're finished it, you'll feel great and ready to be generous.

Let me tell you a story about Rita and her accountant, Bill.

Rita was in her accountant's office on April 30th, the last day to pay her taxes. She was waiting for Bill to tell her how much money to send to Ottawa. She could hardly wait to hear the bottom line.

## Personal Rewards versus Tax Rewards

Bill was trying to soften the blow. "Rita, did I miss any charitable receipts in your bundle of papers?"

"I made the same donations as last year," Rita replied.

Surprised by her answer, Bill asked, "Didn't you get a large raise last year?"

"You're right," Rita replied. "My income is up, and so are my taxes, but not my donations. I really do want to give more, but I don't know how to get started. So many people are asking me for something through my church, college, and hospitals. I don't know how to give or what to give. Believe me, there are people knocking on my door almost every day asking me to donate."

"You'll have to plan to give more, if that's what you want to do," said Bill. "You just can't wait until April 30th to find a tax saving with a charitable flavour. Determine what your charitable goals are so you can make a difference."

"So why," Rita wondered, "is this about taxes and not about charity?"

## Have Your Cake and Eat It

Bill started to explain the tax advantages of planned gifts.

Rita interrupted him and, with a puzzled look on her face, asked, "How can you combine tax credits with charitable donations? Isn't that like having your cake and eating it too?"

"There's nothing wrong with that notion," Bill exclaimed. "Especially if you can do it legally. You can help children in a hospital, find cures, and save taxes at the same time. Consider it a bonus," the accountant explained.

"No, it's a miracle," exclaimed Rita.

## Why You Want to Give

Your approach to charity can change through the various stages of your life. Tax savings may be just one factor. Rita was young and single. Her parents, however, were retired and well off. Their charitable objectives were different. However, they all wanted to make a difference. Let's get back to what estate planning has to do with this thing called *planned giving*.

Gift planning is part of your own estate planning process. Your favourite charity uses it as a key way to obtain funding. Government incentives encourage charitable giving as well. Most large charitable organizations have professional development staff who can create a personalized gifting proposal that can benefit your estate plan. Of course, you'd review the strategy with your own accountant or lawyer.

## Gift Benefits You'll Want

Here are some of the benefits of planned giving, which allow you to

- satisfy your charitable goals;
- receive nonrefundable tax credits;
- avoid capital gains on gifts of capital property;
- retain income rights on property you donate;
- supplement your retirement income;
- get professional asset management; and
- reduce the size of your probate estate.

I'll show you several methods you can use to make charitable gifts. You'll be amazed at all your choices.

Gifts can give a current benefit or a deferred one. For example, you could make a series of payments while you're alive. These gifts give a current benefit to the charity. Gifts with a deferred benefit can include transfer of a life insurance policy to a charity.

What can you do now? Make a cash contribution in one year or give

**Time Machine**

Historically, there were four areas the law recognized as charities. They were trusts for the relief of poverty, the advancement of education, religion, and community benefit. These classifications have been broadly interpreted to include health, social, recreational, animal welfare, and many more causes.

instalments over several years. Cash gifts are relatively simple. You have no ongoing obligations and can stop them at any time. Annual amounts in excess of $200 qualify for greater tax savings. But there are many more options, and we'll examine them in a moment.

## Some Tax Limits

I'll start with something you probably know already. Canadians like to be generous. And they can be especially generous when donations give tax credits. That's an "added value" to feeling good about a gift.

### It's Been Said

"A small gift is better than a great promise."

— German proverb

The government gives everyone a "nonrefundable tax credit" for donations to registered charities or the Crown. "Nonrefundable" means you can offset the credit only against taxes you owe.

Annual donations are limited to seventy-five percent of an individual's income in a year. You can carry forward excess amounts for up to five years. But there's a special treatment in the year of death, which can increase this percentage up to 100 percent of a donor's income that year. If necessary, you can go back to the preceding year's income to use up credits.

## An Overview

There are a number of ways to make these charitable gifts, which I'll outline before we move on to specific examples.

**Cash gifts:** you can easily make this type of donation. You get an immediate tax credit of up to seventy-five percent of your income. Amounts can be pledged over time, or you can pay them on a regular basis.

**Testamentary bequests:** you make these gifts of money or assets in your will. It gives tremendous flexibility in the type of gifts you can make. Bequests can be of specific assets, such as a piece of art, real estate, or percentage of your estate. You can leave a gift of all or a portion of the residue of your estate. A contingent gift can be conditional; if your primary wish can't be met, a charity can be your secondary beneficiary.

**Life insurance:** ultimately, it is used to pay a death benefit to a charity.

Several options exist on how to use life insurance to fund a charitable donation. You can purchase a new policy or transfer an existing policy or just name multiple charities as beneficiaries.

**RRSPs and RRIFs:** you can designate a registered charity as your beneficiary. You'll get a tax credit that can equal tax owing on the disposition of these assets.

**Charitable annuities:** if you're over the age of seventy, you are probably familiar with annuities. This is where you deposit capital in return for a steady stream of income. Monthly income payments combine capital and interest with little or no tax liability. When the annuity is purchased through a charity, there is a tax advantage. So you get an income stream as well as a tax receipt. The residue goes to your charity of choice.

**Charitable remainder trusts:** you know something about trusts from the previous chapter. These are living trusts set up so you can enjoy income and tax benefits during your lifetime. You set up the trust so that upon your death the remainder of the trust's assets goes to charity. Your gift is private and avoids probate.

**Publicly traded stocks:** donate publicly listed securities so that you can reduce your tax on the capital gains. This is an attractive option introduced in the 1997 federal budget. These gifts can save taxes and give you a nonrefundable tax credit.

> **Bulletin**
> _____
>
> You can get free information about charitable tax credits and rules from your favourite charity. As well, interpretation bulletins and guides are available from your local Canada Revenue Agency office and its Web site.

Now let's look at some specific gifts in more detail. I'll start with life insurance. '

## Life Insurance Benefits Are Great

New rules for life insurance have been in effect since February 28, 2000.

Life insurance can make a substantial deferred gift. Usually, it's a "whole life insurance policy," which has a cash surrender value. Your life insurance company can advise you if your existing policy qualifies by having a paid-up cash value.

You transfer existing policies by naming the charity as beneficiary and owner. Once you do so, the ownership of the policy can't be changed. This is unlike a bequest in your will, which is revocable at any time. Transferring an existing life insurance policy with a cash value is a taxable disposition. You will, however, receive a receipt for the cash-surrender value of the policy. For most people, this value will offset any income taxes payable.

If you purchase a new policy with the charity as owner and beneficiary, you will get a receipt based only on the premiums you pay. These annual payments are stretched out over several years. You can't change the beneficiary, though. The charity is guaranteed its money upon your death.

Here's another advantage when the charity is owner and beneficiary. Proceeds pass outside your estate and avoid any probate expense. And the charity receives the insurance proceeds directly.

You can also name a charity just as beneficiary. Doing so gives you control over ownership and the beneficiary until death. You still receive a tax credit even if the gift is made through your will for the amount of the proceeds.

> **Bulletin**
>
> Bequests in wills represent a significant portion of all donations received by charities.

## If You're Young and Healthy

Depending on your age and health, a small cash outlay could fund a very large insurance payment at your death.

Ian is in his early forties and would like to make a sizable donation to the building fund at his university. He has purchased a life insurance policy that will cost him approximately $3,000 a year in premiums. After approximately ten years of payments on the policy, it will likely be fully paid. Here are the relative costs and benefits:

Total insurance premiums Ian pays: $3,000 a year for ten years    $30,000

Tax credits Ian receives: $3,000 a year for ten years    $30,000

Value of gift to charity on death:  $150,000

After-tax cost to Ian of gift: fifty percent of $30,000    $15,000 (assuming a continued tax rate of fifty percent).

Ian's policy has provided a substantial gift of $150,000. The net cost, after tax credits, is $15,000. Bear in mind this example is for demonstration purposes only.

Small payments for insurance while you're alive can generate substantial proceeds at death. Other assets in your estate portfolio will not be affected. Of course, depending on your age and health, the cost of the insurance benefit premiums could be excessive.

## Will Bequests — Don't Forget Them

Making gifts through your will has its advantages — you can change your mind and your will. Wills, however, don't bypass the probate process. Creditors, a spouse, or other individuals can challenge your will. A challenge could affect your estate distribution and the bequest to a charity.

You can make gifts of your property as well. Examples include artwork, real estate, and "cultural" property donated to certain public authorities or museums. You will need to have certified that the cultural property is significant to Canada culturally. Gifts of property will need to be appraised to calculate their fair market value. The appraisal also determines your tax credit for the donation and any capital gain.

Do you want to leave a cash bequest in your will to your favourite charity? Are you struggling because you don't know how much you can leave? Here are some tips to consider.

- Give a percentage or share of your estate's residue.
- Gifts through your will can fail if the charity named does not survive you.
- Properly identify the charity by its legal name to avoid conflicting claims.
- Don't place conditions or restrictions on the gift that the charity can't meet.
- Consult the charity if your gift is sizable or involves unusual assets or conditions.

You may wish to explain your charitable intentions with a side letter to your beneficiaries. Although not legally binding, it may be comforting in explaining your reasons for sizable gifts. When bequests are made under your will, your estate is entitled to a tax credit. It can be applied toward all your income in the year of your death and the preceding years.

## Charitable Annuities

If you're over seventy and don't need capital to meet your spouse's or dependants' needs, consider a charitable annuity. Annuities can give you a worry-free cash flow worth investigating. You deposit some of your capital assets with the charity of your choice. The charity then secures the capital and administers it. You get an annual guaranteed return, a portion of which can be tax free, and an immediate tax credit. The amount of the receipt is based on factors such as your age and the amount used to establish the annuity.

## Charitable Remainder Trusts

You can transfer your home, for example, into a living trust and get a tax receipt. This gift saves probate and estate costs, and you receive the benefits or trust income from the property. Upon your death, the trust remainder goes to the charity. The size of donation depends on the value of the residual interest (after your death) that goes to the charity. These trusts, however, are irrevocable, complex, and private. In other words, you can't get any of the trust property back. There are costs involved in the setup and annual trust administration. So tax reduction may not be your principal concern; you may be more interested in funding medical research. The calculation of the tax credit is complicated, and you will still need independent financial advice.

You can also simply create testamentary trusts in your will and leave trust remainders to charity.

## It's Better to Donate Stocks Directly

Gifts prior to death can help you realize your philanthropic goals and help charities. Such gifts will give you a tax credit as well. But gifts of capital property will realize potential capital gains, which can be offset by the tax credits. Special rules introduced in 1997 provide further incentive for gifts of appreciated publicly listed securities. Shares of stocks and mutual funds are included.

Here's how it works.

You directly donate your securities instead of selling them and donating the cash proceeds.

You receive a tax receipt based on the fair market value of the securities on the day the transfer is made. Use the receipt to claim tax credits with the usual carry-forward provisions.

The taxable portion of the capital gain is decreased to twenty-five percent from the usual fifty percent. As a result, the tax credits will normally offset the capital gains and thus decrease taxes you owe.

You remove the gift assets during your lifetime from your estate. Doing so eliminates executor, probate, and legal costs to process the gift through your estate.

---

**Bulletin**

You will get a tax credit only if a charity has a registration number issued by Canada Revenue Agency. Call the agency toll free at 1-800-267-2384. You can also search the more than 80,000 registered charities at www.cra-arc.gc.ca/charities

---

## The Least You Need to Know

- Charitable gift giving can be planned to achieve maximum tax credits.
- Donate RRSPs, RRIFs, and life insurance once personal obligations are covered.
- Review your will to ensure your charity's proper legal name is used.
- Check with the charity if you wish to donate special assets such as art or real estate.

# Chapter 8

# Reduce Probate Taxes Properly

In this chapter:

- Ask the top three questions.
- Reduce your probate burdens.
- Don't make dangerous gifts.
- Keep yourself secure.

David was upset. His father had died, and he couldn't get access to his father's bank accounts. "I don't understand it," he said. "Why do I have to waste my father's money on probate? I just want to pay his bills." He was in a law office asking the top three probate questions. What's this going to cost? How long is it going to take? Why couldn't this be avoided?

Probate court fees or taxes have been around for centuries. And, for just as long, people have tried to escape from the probate process, with varying degrees of success. Today a new industry has arisen targeted mostly at the elderly. Its advice is to "avoid probate whatever the cost." Some of these techniques are ill-advised strategies based solely on a *probate-paying paranoia*. I'll show you various schemes and describe some you can safely use to save and protect your estate.

## Who Is Entitled to Your Estate?

Let's go back to David as he struggles with his questions. His father, Stephen, was divorced and died with a will. David has a brother, Michael, who is attending university in Australia. They equally share their father's estate. David said the bank refused to release his father's funds to him. "It all belongs to my brother and I, so why are there problems?"

David had shown the bank manager a note signed by his brother: "To whom it may concern, please deliver my half of my father's estate to my brother, David Jenkins." David was to wire Michael his share of the bank money for Michael's university tuition. "If just Michael and I are involved, why was the bank being so difficult?"

## Start with This Concept

Although David and Michael may be their father's heirs, the bank manager doesn't know that they are the only ones entitled to the money. The father's spouse or creditors could have claims as well. Such claims take precedence over a beneficiary's entitlement. Besides, who is to say the document David has is his father's last will and testament?

Anyone can walk into a bank with another will made by a person. That person can also claim the money. What would happen if the bank issued a cheque clearing out Stephen's bank account? Of course, David would be the first to start a lawsuit against the bank. Banks protect themselves from this kind of liability by requiring a court appointment or probate.

## Probate Has Benefits

David didn't understand the benefits of a probate court appointment; probate or estate courts validate his authority to act under his father's last will. David would then be confirmed as the executor of the estate. Banks can rely on this authorization to let him deal with his father's estate. But probate doesn't satisfy just the banks. Stephen's substantial assets probably can't be sold or transferred without it.

The probate process allows anyone who has an interest in the estate to come forward. For example, what if someone claimed the will David held is invalid? Probate applications give the court jurisdiction to deal with any competing claims against the estate. Such claims could come from disgruntled or dependent children, ex-spouses, and creditors.

What happens if a new wife materializes, one whom David didn't know about? Her marriage could revoke the will. The probate process allows all interested parties a venue to observe the estate's activities. If competing interests or disputes arise, the estate court is the forum for resolution.

---

**Time Machine**

In canon or church law, "probate" was proving the will (*probatio*). It gave the executor the judge's approval to the proof of the will.

---

## Smaller Is Better Sometimes

In a small estate with few assets, probate may be unnecessary. Banks have a limit on the sizes of assets they'll distribute without probate. In many cases, if the assets are under $5,000, the banks will release them with the death certificate and proof of entitlement. Most bankers, stockbrokers, and bullion traders will insist on probate for large amounts. It's a way of limiting their exposure to creditors and other claims.

David's father couldn't avoid probate by not making a will. His estate assets would go through probate even if he had no last will.

Each province has a surrogate, probate, or estate court to handle estates. These courts confirm an individual's authority to act on behalf of an estate with a will or not. Provincial governments (except in Quebec) levy a tax on the value of assets being administered. Because you may make a number of wills during your lifetime, it's important that only the last will be probated. But who's to know which one is the last one? This is another reason that financial institutions holding estate assets request the court's seal of approval to the most recent valid will.

## Is It a Fee or a Tax?

In 1999, a Supreme Court of Canada decision ruled on the legality of Ontario's probate fees. These filing fees bore little or no connection to the services provided by the courts. Court approval for a $50,000 estate was the same as for a $1 million estate. Canada's highest court declared that such fees are really a tax. The provinces were given time to legitimize the tax, and Ontario implemented an estate administration tax. The probate fee was changed to a probate tax retroactive to 1950. So don't expect a refund if you paid "fees." You'll still see it commonly referred to as a probate fee or tax.

Help Line

**Q:** How do you know if someone dies without a will?

**A:** Wills can be lost or misplaced by their owners. You'll want to check the usual places, such as bank deposit boxes, lawyer's offices, and personal files. A court will want to know you used every effort to locate a will.

## What's Worse — Lawyers or Probate?

No law says you need lawyers to probate an estate. David can get probate forms and file them with the court. He'll have to file an inventory of his father's assets whether there's a will or not. He may try to do it himself if the estate is small, say under $50,000. The paperwork can be filed in the county where his father resided before death. The court responsible for estates would process the application in a few weeks if everything was prepared properly. Even lawyers have difficulties, so expect several trips to the courthouse.

Here's what David would file:

- his father's original will;
- an *affidavit of execution* by witnesses to the will;
- a notice to beneficiaries under the will;
- an application for probate or certificate to appoint an executor/estate trustee;
- a declaration of the value of the estate;
- material to dispense with a bond; and
- a cheque for the probate tax.

If David's father hadn't made a will, his brother Michael would need to consent to his appointment as the estate's legal representative. Michael could agree that David doesn't have to file a bond, which is required at the court's discretion. Bonds ensure that an administrator or executor of an estate doesn't disappear with the money. The bond cost can be a few thousand dollars based on the size of the estate.

## Is It Probate if There's No Will?

Probate is a process that determines who is in charge of your estate and who shares in it. Probate is not just a tax. Depending on whether a deceased has a will or not, there are different steps to "probate" an estate.

*Letters probate* are court documents given to executors named under a will. Executors' authority comes from the will, not the court. The court confirms that the required proofs for the last will are satisfactory. The court document is referred to as letters probate or probate by the public and professionals. Ontario has adopted a new term: *certificate of appointment of estate trustee with a will.* It's really "a certificate with a will" and the longest title in the world. But then again estate trustee is a gender-neutral term.

*Letters of administration* are documents issued by estate courts whenever a will can't be found. Instead of an executor, the estate has an administrator appointed. Administrators have no authority until they are appointed. Executors, however, have authority given to them by the will immediately upon the deceased's death. So what is a letter of administration now called? In Ontario, it's a *certificate of appointment of estate trustee without a will.* Generally, it's referred to as "letters of administration" for an intestate estate.

---

**Legal Lingo**

*Affidavit* is a written statement signed by the person who wrote it. This person swears under oath that the contents of the affidavit are true from his or her personal knowledge. Affidavits can be affirmed and accepted by the courts.

---

## How to Search for a Will

Assume David's father died intestate (without a will). David still has to conduct a reasonable search for a will. He'd start by checking his father's files and bank deposit boxes. Any lawyers his father may have been in contact with would be approached as well. What if David found a will? He'd need affidavits of execution sworn under oath by the witnesses to the will. This procedure confirms the legal formalities for signing and witnessing a will were complied with. These and the other court forms would be filed with the provincial estate court.

In some cases, wills can also be filed or deposited with a province's estate court. David could search the court files in case an old will was deposited by his father. He could also search local banks for safe deposit boxes. Legal journals frequently have notices published asking lawyers for information about a will's whereabouts.

If a will wasn't prepared by a lawyer, there's often some issue that requires legal advice. David could retain a lawyer for this purpose. The lawyer could also deal with David's relatives if there are problems. Often no arguments arise until it's time to divide everything up.

## Keep Receipts and Records — or Else

It is critical to keep records before and immediately after a person's death. Look what happened between Marisa and her brothers. Marisa was a retired legal secretary who looked after her mother. Marisa was living in Mom's home when her mother died at the age of eighty. The mother's estate was relatively small, and there were no tax issues. But Marisa had renovated and repaired Mom's property using her own money.

Shortly after Mom passed away, Marisa's brothers asked for their share of the estate. Marisa hadn't kept proper accounting records from the start. She had mixed her money and bills with her mother's whenever she did their banking. Her brothers hired a lawyer. They were threatening legal action unless they saw all the bills and receipts for the renovations. Because Marisa had paid cash for the work, she was slow forwarding an explanation. Her brothers took this to mean she was hiding something.

Marisa should have got legal advice, especially after Mom died, about her duties as executor. Her legal advisors would have told her to keep receipts and separate records to substantiate all financial transactions. Such advice would have saved her a lot of grief. She didn't know she'd have to prepare an inventory of assets for probate.

## Help Line

**Q:** Are there two kinds of probate?

**A:** No, but probate can be obtained in two ways. The "common form" requires estate representatives only to file the necessary paperwork with an estate court. The "solemn form" requires witnesses and all parties affected by the proceedings to appear in court. This usually happens because there appears to be something wrong with the will.

---

**Legal Lingo**

*Letters probate* refers to the court certificate attached to the original will. It confirms that the court is satisfied the will has complied with the formalities of proof.

---

## What's It Going to Cost?

Canada, unlike the United States, doesn't have an estate or death tax, an added penalty your estate pays just because you died. Canadians have no inheritance tax on the overall size of an estate or gift taxes. Remember, though, all provinces except Quebec have legislated probate taxes. Many call this a form of death tax since it's based on the value of certain assets in your estate. In some provinces, there is no maximum amount payable for probate.

Large discrepancies exist between the provincial probate rates. Ontario is at fifteen dollars and British Columbia at fourteen dollars per thousand dollars of estate value. These two are the highest rates in the country. In previewing your estate, you should estimate this expense. If you have a substantial estate, you'll be looking at complex probate alternatives. Possible savings can justify the effort and costs if you add them all up.

## Prepare an Estate Inventory for Probate

David used a lawyer to apply for probate in his father's estate. He wanted to avoid any risks and delays in distributing the estate. David was also concerned about personal liability for his father's taxes and creditors.

His father's estate included a life insurance policy of $100,000 and an RRSP of $300,000. A townhouse was appraised at $200,000, with a mortgage on it of $50,000. The townhouse contained antiques worth $50,000, and there was a balance owing of $5,000 on his father's credit cards.

Each province has different rules for calculating the value of an estate. Generally, an estate will include all real and personal property of the deceased in a particular province. Jointly owned assets are not included in the calculations. Certain categories of property such as life insurance and designated assets are also excluded unless benefits are payable to "the estate." No deduction is made for debts except for mortgages. Once you prepare an inventory of estate assets, you need to look at what is included or excluded for tax.

## Help Line

**Q:** Why is an affidavit of execution by a witness to the will required for probate?

**A:** This is a form of proof accepted by the courts. It confirms the legal formalities were complied with when the will was signed. (Two witnesses must be present and sign the will in everyone's presence.)

## How Do You Calculate Probate Tax?

For our example, we'll assume that Stephen Jenkins lived in Ontario. We'll calculate the probate taxes by looking at each asset.

**RRSPs are payable to the estate on death:** this asset creates an estate income tax liability that must be paid before proceeds are distributed. But the income tax bill is not deducted from the probate value of the estate. The entire value of the RRSPs, $300,000, is included.

**Life insurance proceeds:** they are payable to the estate and are included in valuing the estate for probate.

**Townhouse property:** it was a principal residence and is exempt for income tax purposes. Not so for probate. Since this asset passes through the estate by the will, its value as of the date of death must be included. David's current appraisal shows the townhouse's value. Only the mortgage of $50,000 is deducted in calculating the value.

**Personal contents:** they were given to a relative as specific gifts in the will. Just the same, their value must be included for probate.

**Credit cards or personal loans:** these liabilities are not deducted from the probate calculation. Only mortgages are considered appropriate deductions.

## Add, Subtract, and Multiply

Summarizing the above information, the probate taxes are calculated as follows:

| | |
|---|---|
| Total value of RRSPs | $300,000 |
| Life insurance proceeds | $100,000 |
| Personal contents | $50,000 |
| Townhouse property | $150,000 |
| **Estate value for probate** | **$600,000** |

The next step is to apply the provincial estate administration tax rate. In Ontario on the first $50,000, the rate is $250. On the remaining balance of $550,000, the rate is calculated at fifteen dollars per thousand. This is $550 x $15 = $8,250. Taxes for this estate would be $8,250 plus the base of $250 for $8,500.

David is upset because he believes he has no choice but to pay. He has to pay for appraisals, a bond, probate taxes, and legal costs just to get access to his father's money. He feels ripped off. The banks certainly didn't tell his father he'd need probate when he opened accounts with them. "Couldn't my father have avoided all of these taxes?" David asked the lawyer. Taking simple steps could have saved taxes. This is a key benefit of estate planning. So take a look at what could happen.

---

**Legal Lingo**

*Gifts* are voluntary transfers of property, without payment, between the living.

---

## Planning Can Reduce Your Probate Burdens

David's father could have reduced his estate probate costs if he owned assets jointly with right of survivorship. Another tax-saving method is to designate beneficiaries on his RRSPs. Life insurance policies can also be designated to a beneficiary other than his estate. Stephen could have saved some substantial costs. Here's the revised probate calculation when assets don't flow through the estate:

- RRSPs not designated to the estate – value for probate, nil;
- life insurance not designated to the estate – value for probate, nil;
- personal assets of $50,000 – included; and
- joint ownership of apartment with son – value for probate, nil.

The total value for probate would have been $50,000. In the Ontario example, $250 is the cost on the first $50,000 of probate value. Compare $250 with the $8,500 paid in the first example. On top of this reduction would be savings on executor and legal fees based on the value of the probated estate. So the smaller the estate, the lesser the fees. Avoiding probate also allows beneficiaries to get quicker access to and benefit from your assets.

## Ways to Save Probate Costs

Just by owning assets jointly or by designating them directly to beneficiaries, you can reduce probate costs. I'll take you through a number of these techniques:

- joint ownership with survivorship rights;
- life estate with remainders;
- living trusts;
- life insurance with named beneficiaries;
- annuities with designated successors;
- pensions with named beneficiaries;
- assets held through private corporations; and
- multiple wills.

## Some Specific Probate-Saving Tactics

**Jointly own assets:** joint ownership avoids probate only if one of the owners survives. This is perhaps one of the most common methods of property ownership between spouses. Joint bank accounts will also provide the survivor with easy access to money. Holding assets in joint ownership with children or anyone else is risky. I'll show you what I mean in a moment.

**Gift assets away:** gifting is a way of transferring assets during your lifetime, and it reduces the size of your probate estate. Remember to avoid the problems with the income attribution rules we discussed in Chapter 6. Capital gains consequences can arise with some gifts of capital property. This can be a probate reduction technique with a disadvantage — the cost of making a gift may be too high.

**Designate a beneficiary:** life insurance should be payable to a person other than your estate. This designation keeps insurance money out of the hands of estate creditors as well. Consider a secondary life insurance beneficiary designation if your first beneficiary dies before you do.

**Use a trust:** this method allows you to transfer assets to a living trust. You can be one of the trustees for purposes of control. Upon your death, the other trustees simply transfer title to your trust beneficiaries without probate. But remember — you can't get out of paying income taxes.

**Costs:** the costs of setting up a living trust are expensive in relation to a small estate — a couple of thousand dollars in legal fees for starters. You should consider a living trust only when you have substantial assets. If you need to keep your affairs private, a trust can help; it is not open for public inspection like a will.

**Create multiple wills:** this is a dangerous move without expert advice. Basically, two wills are prepared so that the second does not revoke the first. The first will is used to control the part of the estate that is privately controlled, such as shares in a family corporation. These are closely held corporate assets, for example, where no one requires probate. The second or secondary will is used to deal with probatable assets. Only the second will is probated. Taxes would be calculated on the lesser estate value of the public assets. You must have expert advice to guide you through this legal maze. It has drawbacks and uncertainties, including being eliminated by governments anxious to collect more taxes.

## Dangerous Surprises with Joint Ownership

Karl's wife had just died. Karl wanted me to register all his assets jointly with his only child, Andrea. The assets included a bank account and his home, which was not Andrea's principal residence. Karl figured that joint ownership with his daughter of all his assets was a good idea.

I advised him of the dangers of joint ownership with children. I call them the Five Terrible D's: death, divorce, debts, disasters, and disposition. Here's what I mean. Once Karl transfers assets to be jointly owned with his daughter, he has given up control. He won't be able to deal with that property without Andrea's consent. His daughter does not have to follow his wishes.

But that's not all. I warned him to watch out for the following problems.

**Death:** if Andrea and Karl die together, joint ownership doesn't avoid probate. Andrea's estate would also be responsible for any capital gains on her share of the home. They could be more than the probate costs.

**Divorce:** if Andrea marries or divorces, her spouse could make a claim to her share of the assets. Such a claim could force Karl to sell or mortgage the assets.

**Debts:** Andrea could go bankrupt, and her creditors could seize her portion of Karl's home. If she doesn't pay her income tax, her interest could be seized by the government for tax arrears.

**Disasters:** don't forget, people change. Karl could have a falling out with Andrea, which would be a disaster in many ways. What if she becomes abusive? If she becomes greedy, she could force Karl to sell and divide the proceeds with her. Joint ownership means that you lose control over the asset. There is no law that says Andrea must do as her father asks. If it's a joint bank account, either one of them could clean it out.

**Disposition:** what is it going to cost to reregister the deed into joint ownership? What about income tax issues that arise from assets that have capital gains? These costs may be higher than the probate taxes.

Once you make someone a joint owner, it's a gift you can't take back. The legal consequences are far reaching. Check with a lawyer and listen to advice you receive. Every lawyer can tell you his or her own probate avoidance horror story.

**It's Been Said**
..........................................................

"You can't escape the responsibility tomorrow by evading it today."
— Abraham Lincoln, 1809–65

## Gifts that Can Hurt You

Karl had a second income property. He wanted the deed to be registered so it would be joint with Andrea. Here's where making a gift can really hurt. If Karl transfers half of this second property to his daughter, he has income tax consequences. The property has appreciated, and he has capital gains to report and pay. Karl would also pay lawyers' fees and perhaps provincial tax on the land transfer. The transfer and income tax costs must be factored in to the risk and probate savings.

When you add it all up, Karl wasn't saving anything by conveying the property. His total costs were higher than the probate taxes he so desperately wanted to avoid, so he decided to retain the asset in his name.

Karl decided the loss of control and the Five Terrible D's were too much to worry about. If he had more than one child, his problems would be compounded. He realized that probate tax was a small premium to pay for continued control of his assets. Probate taxes were a price he'd pay for this protection until he died.

## Joint Accounts Can Lead to Lawsuits

Claudio took care of his mother's affairs after his father died. He even took care of his mother's banking. One day a bank employee suggested that Claudio and his mother open a joint account. It would make it easier to handle her bank investments, the employee said. For the next seven years, the mother's banking and tax information was mailed to Claudio's home address.

All traces of Mom's money disappeared as Claudio reported the interest income on his own tax return. He felt he deserved it for all his work caring for his mother. When she died, her other son, Tony, was surprised that his mother's bank account only had enough in it to pay for her funeral. Claudio did not tell Tony about the other account, and Tony had no idea what to do.

Tony hired an estate lawyer for advice. Together they reconstructed their father's estate. They discovered that when their father died Mom had inherited over $300,000 in bank assets. No one could understand how she could have spent $300,000 of her capital over the past seven years. Tony concluded that Claudio was hiding the money and threatened to sue him.

Claudio offered to give Tony $50,000 to settle out of court. Tony refused the offer. He figured the $300,000 had doubled over the seven years. He warned his lawyer, "If Claudio offers me $50,000, he must be sitting on half a million. He's going to pay big time."

When Claudio came clean about the $200,000 in bank term deposits, Tony still refused to believe him. Tony went to court so a judge would punish his brother and make him suffer for this dishonesty.

"Children, love one another, and if that is not possible
at least try to put up with one another."
— Goethe, 1749–1832

Do not fall into the trap of believing those who recommend joint accounts with children as the way to prevent all estate problems. Your beneficiaries can pay dearly for your carelessness. Besides, in most cases, income, not probate, tax is what most people should worry about.

## What if Things Change?

Your probate strategies must be kept up to date. One new development is the use of alter-ego and joint partner spousal trusts, and both are effective will substitutes. Traditionally, transfers to an *inter vivos* trust were deemed dispositions with taxable consequences. These two new trusts can specifically benefit those sixty-five years of age or over.

Deemed disposition rules don't apply for assets transferred to qualifying joint spousal or alter-ego trusts. These trusts must be created after 1999. Other requirements specify only the settlor or the spouse can receive or be entitled to all the income or capital from the trust. On the death of the last surviving spouse or the settlor of an alter-ego trust, the assets would be delivered to the contingent beneficiaries. These individuals would be specified in the trust documents. This process avoids the public disclosure necessitated by the probate procedure.

Only those in the highest tax brackets, however, will benefit from these trusts. Income earned in the trust during the settlor's life is taxed at the highest marginal rates. These trusts can help bulletproof estates and avoid probate taxes. Caution should be exercised, though. Ensure you obtain proper financial and tax advice before considering these new alternatives to bypass probate.

I've taken you through Step 2 of our plan and reviewed income and probate taxes. You've seen some strategies to help save and protect your estate and loved ones. As a bonus, you can be charitable and tax conscientious at the same time.

Now we'll learn about the cornerstone of your estate plan — how to make a will.

## The Least You Need to Know

- All provinces except Quebec charge a probate tax on assets passing through your estate.
- Use joint ownership and designated beneficiaries so you can reduce probate costs.
- Holding assets jointly with children can be dangerous and bad planning.
- Probate taxes are a premium you pay to retain control over your assets.

# Make Your Will

Welcome to Step 3, making your will. This is essential reading. You'll refer to this step over and over. It's the foundation of your estate plan. If you do nothing else, at least learn about wills. You may have made a will so long ago that you can't find it. Maybe you don't know what to do to make a will. And some of you don't know what one looks like. Be brave, read on, and your questions will be answered in the next four chapters.

I'll tell you some alarming stories that might motivate you. You'll learn some will terms and review a simple will. Most importantly, I'll help explain why a professional will is always your better bet. You can't afford to have an amateur make your will. Use my checklists to avoid the most common will mistakes. You'll also learn the inside scoop on what happens when a will is contested. Perhaps the best thing you'll learn is how to bulletproof your will.

# Chapter 9

# Have You Got a Parachute?

In this chapter:

- Prevent disasters.
- Avoid expensive dying.
- Enjoy twenty-four benefits from wills.
- It's your responsibility.

A fundamental goal of estate planning is to avoid dying without a will. When a person dies and a will can't be found, the problems begin to multiply. Do you know the advantages an up-to-date will can provide? I'll describe about twenty-four of them in a moment.

But let's start with what happens when you don't have a will. What the government does is write a will for you. What it does with your estate may surprise you. I think this can motivate you to keep your will current.

## Dying without a Will: Intestacy Is a Dirty Word

"I haven't made a will. I don't care what happens to my estate or my family. I want my death to be a real tragedy," Paul said.

Paul was a client who pretended to be serious when he made this statement. Unfortunately, his wife, Linda, was standing beside him, and she didn't laugh at her husband's sarcasm. She was upset. "Tell him, Ed, what's going to happen to me and the children if he has no will."

I told him he'd have no control over how his wealth would be handled. "I won't be here, so what does it matter?" he replied.

"You'd be surprised what will happen," I said. "They don't call intestacy a dirty word for nothing."

---

**Legal Lingo**

*Intestacy* means you've died without a will. Your estate is distributed by the intestate laws in your province. The government writes a will for you that may not be to your liking. Jointly owned or designated assets are not affected by an intestacy.

---

Intestacy laws dictate what is done to all your property except what's jointly owned or designated. Every penny is divided according to the government's rules. Your wish to provide for your family in a particular manner means nothing unless you have a will.

Provincial, intestate, or succession laws decide who inherits what if you don't have a will. Your own preferences don't count. A beneficiary's need or entitlement is disregarded. Your estate goes to your spouse and closest blood relatives by a strict code that varies from province to province. When you have no next of kin, your entire estate becomes the property of the Crown. No charity, cause, or religious organization can benefit from your assets.

---

**Time Machine**

In the 1970s, estate succession duties were abolished by most Canadian provinces. These duties were based on the value of your estate's assets passing on death and were similar to inheritance taxes.

---

## Who's Going to Get What?

Let's continue to use Paul and Linda as our example. What happens if Linda dies without a will? Paul would apply to be the administrator or estate trustee without a will of Linda's estate. He would have to pay all of her bills before he can get any benefit himself. His share is set by law according to the number of children that he and Linda have. Paul's children from a previous marriage don't share in Linda's estate unless she adopted them.

He would receive the entire estate if the couple had no children. He'd still have to go through the courts, though. A judge would confirm his appointment as administrator and that he's the sole beneficiary.

If Paul and Linda have children together, he receives any designated and joint assets plus the first share in the estate. It's called a "spouse's preferential share." Legally married spouses are usually the only ones entitled if one of them dies without a will. Depending on the province you live in, common-law spouses may also have inheritance rights. The size of this preferential spousal share varies from province to province. In Ontario, for example, as I write this, it is the first $200,000 of the estate after all the debts are paid. Alberta gives married spouses the first $40,000, while New Brunswick, Quebec, and Newfoundland have no preferential share.

What if Paul and Linda have one minor child? The balance or residue of the estate in most provinces is shared on a fifty-fifty basis. Sharing an estate with a child is not what many parents would want, especially if a minor's share of an estate must be paid into court. A judge would then have to approve all expenditures on behalf of minors. Most of the time you'd prefer that your spouse gets your entire estate because

- the children, even if not minors, may be too young to handle money wisely;
- the spousal tax rollover that provides a tax deferral doesn't apply to the children's share; and
- you want your spouse to control and benefit from the assets.

---

**Legal Lingo**

*Administrators* are persons appointed by the court to handle your estate if you die without a will. In Ontario, administrators are also called *estate trustees without a will*. Administrators must be appointed by a court. *Executors* or *estate trustees with a will* are confirmed by a court.

---

## Spouses Don't Automatically Get It All

Linda is an accountant in Ontario. She has a house worth $300,000 and a business valued at $500,000. If her estate is $800,000 after expenses, how would it be divided? Well, if she dies without a will, her married husband wouldn't get it all. Her assets may have to be sold to give her two children their share. There can be no trust for the children's share without a will. It would be paid into court and held there if they are minors.

### Intestate Distribution for a Married Spouse with Two Children

Step 1 Calculate total estate after debts – $800,000

Step 2 Deduct Paul's spousal preferential share – $200,000 (in Ontario only)

Step 3 Determine net estate for division – $600,000

Step 4 Divide the remainder – 1/3 to husband – $200,000   2/3 to children – $400,000

Step 5 Give each child – $200,000

Step 6 Give to husband his preferential share and a one-third share for a total of $400,000

How does Paul raise the cash to pay the children's share, which is $400,000? He has to mortgage or sell either the home or the business. If the children are minors, the $400,000 share is paid into court. It's held there until they reach the age of majority.

What if the children are twenty and twenty-three years of age? Can you imagine Paul handing them a cheque for that kind of cash? Are they ready for it? It could be gone in a few months or years. Even if you've always wanted to give the children an early start, they may have other plans than investing the inheritance. Finishing school may not be in their plans. They may want to spend a year backpacking in the Outback. Now that may be a valuable experience but not the legacy you'd like to leave.

## When Children Need a Lawyer

Once children reach the age of majority, they'll get their own lawyers. They almost have to. If they are underage or minors, each province has a children's lawyer or guardian to protect them. So back to our example of Paul and the two children. Yes, he will have to sell the house or business to pay them. Linda never left Paul much of a choice. She never gave him a chance and left a mess by not leaving a will.

So you may be saying to yourself, "Is that the most terrible thing that can happen if I don't make a will?" I'd like to say yes, but it's just the beginning of the problems. Paul must calculate the share for any minor children. He'll need professional valuations for the business — any land, building, inventory, and equipment. He'll have to satisfy a judge and the children's lawyer that the business is worth only $500,000.

What about Paul's salary? Since he took over Linda's job in the business, he's paid himself $2,000 a week, which is what Linda was earning. But the children's lawyer may object since Paul's salary is $100,000, and he has no experience. If that money were profit, the children would receive a share. Their lawyer is considering appointing an independent person to run the business until it's sold.

---

**Bulletin**

Provinces have different rules for what age you can drive, drink, and vote, known as the age of majority. Most jurisdictions consider eighteen a majority in wills and estates. If you've reached the age of majority, you're no longer a minor child.

---

## No Children — What Happens?

What if Paul dies first in an accident that also takes Linda's life? Every province has different rules if the last-surviving spouse has no children. Most intestate laws would distribute the estate equally to Linda's parents. Paul's family would get nothing. Linda's parents are divorced; she had lost touch with her mother, and her father has Alzheimer's and wouldn't know what to do with the money.

If her parents were predeceased, Linda's estate goes to her brother and sister. Her brother, Ted, hadn't spoken to her in years, but he would get fifty percent. Linda would have preferred leaving it all to her sister, a single parent, but she never made a will. With no surviving siblings, everything passes down to the next line in Linda's family tree — her aunts and uncles.

## Help Line

**Q:** How can I afford to make a will?

**A:** You can't afford to die without one. You may be surprised how reasonable these legal fees can be. You can find a lawyer by contacting provincial bar associations or law societies. Investing hundreds of dollars now can reap much larger rewards; you can save thousands of dollars later.

## Let's Review

Provincial intestacy rules vary, but assume all debts are paid in our example. We'll look at Ontario's laws, which divide things as follows.

- A married spouse gets everything if there are no children. And in the few provinces where a common-law spouse is treated as married, this rule is the same.
- If Linda had only one child, then her husband first gets a spousal preferential share. Then half of the net estate residue would go to the child and the other half to Paul.
- If Linda had more than one child, then the net estate residue would be divided into thirds. One-third would go to Paul. The other two-thirds would be divided between her two children who survive her.
- If Linda had more than two children, Paul would get one-third of the net estate residue, and two or more children would share the remaining two-thirds. Linda's parents and any brothers, sisters, and grandchildren would inherit nothing from her estate.
- If Paul died only moments after Linda in the same car accident, their children would get it all.
- If Linda had no spouse, children, or relatives, the Crown would step in to take everything.

The government intestacy rules tell you what must happen, which may be completely different from what you'd like to do with your estate.

## Not Legally Married — So What?

If you're not legally married or treated as married, you don't share in a partner's estate if he or she dies without a will. So in Ontario, for instance, common-law and same-sex partners must protect their partners by having an up-to-date will to avoid provincial intestate laws. Common-law and same-sex spouses do not have the same rights as married spouses. In some provinces, these partners are recognized as married only for tax or support purposes.

Without a will, your partner could receive absolutely no portion of your estate. The succession laws don't give a legally unmarried partner a share in an intestate estate. Your partner would have to commence legal proceedings to get anything, even support. Until recent legislative amendments, even this was hard to do.

If Linda were a common-law spouse, Paul's children from a previous partner would not inherit her estate. Paul would need to start legal action to claim a division of property or support. Doing so would pit him against Linda's family and even their own children. Imagine the emotional and financial costs.

### It's Been Said
......................................................

"When it comes to divide an estate, the politest men quarrel."
— Ralph Waldo Emerson, 1803–82

## Holding Assets Jointly Is No Will Substitute

Don't think a cohabitation or marriage contract is a substitute for a proper will. You can't eliminate the need for a will by holding all your assets jointly with a partner. What happens if both partners die in a common catastrophe? Your estate would be divided according to provincial laws as if you had predeceased the other joint owner.

### Bulletin

You can't avoid probate taxes by dying without a will. The government still charges the same taxes on your estate assets.

Take Louise and Moira, who have a joint bank account and jointly own their home. If they die simultaneously or in an event in which no one knows who died first, their estates would each receive one-half of the assets. Since they have no wills, their assets would be distributed on an intestacy. Dual deaths can be addressed only by a will that deals with this issue.

## You Must Protect Your Loved Ones

Wanda and Frank wish their adult children from their first marriages to inherit some of their assets. Their residence is jointly owned with the right of survivorship. They figure the survivor will sell the house whenever it's no longer needed. They promise each other that money will be paid to the deceased's children from the sale of the house. What could go wrong?

Let's look at just two scenarios. First, Wanda dies suddenly, and Frank remarries. He sells the home and uses the proceeds to buy a home with his new spouse. He dies of a heart attack and never makes a will. Frank's new wife inherits everything. Guess what Wanda's children receive? A broken promise.

Second, Wanda learns she is dying and wants to protect her kids. She worries that Frank may not keep his promises. She severs the joint tenancy by having a lawyer write up a deed to transfer her half to herself. She now owns fifty percent of the home as a "tenant-in-common." Her will gives her half of the home to her children. Frank gets notice after Wanda dies that the home must be sold to pay her children. What's he to do?

Since Wanda's will was made in the hospital, Frank could contest it. But he doesn't want the legal hassles. Then Wanda's children start fighting over the contents of the home. They believe they are entitled to everything since it was Wanda's before Frank moved in.

So just owning your assets jointly doesn't eliminate the need for a will. Small estates can be more easily and cheaply handled when there's a will. Protect yourself against the possibility of a common catastrophe in which both owners die.

Help Line

**Q:** What if the guardian named in a will turns out ten years later to be the wrong person to have custody of your children?

**A:** Always name an alternative guardian just in case. Remember that guardians must be confirmed by a judge who considers what's in the best interest of the child.

## Five Disadvantages of Intestacy

You're starting to understand the disasters that can be created inadvertently by dying intestate. Your precious possessions are divided among your relatives — even the undeserving ones. You cannot allow for any special treatment of your property or business. Everything must be sold and the proceeds distributed. The money from the sale of all your assets is passed down by provincial rules. Your children could end up inheriting your home and becoming co-owners with your surviving spouse.

Succession distribution doesn't skip a generation of beneficiaries; it just moves to the next in line. The law treats everyone within a category of statutory beneficiaries the same way. Those people share equally in your estate, and you don't have the chance to cut out an undeserving, undesirable, or underhanded relative. Charities, best friends, and nonrelatives can't benefit.

**Provincial succession laws dictate who benefits from your property:** if you don't make a will, you still end up paying for the one the government writes for you. Believe me, it will be a lot more expensive.

**Your estate can't be distributed until a court appoints an administrator:** the court places a person in charge of your estate in an intestacy as estate administrator, while a will lets you choose one. When you die intestate, the law dictates which relative can administer your property. Administrators are not authorized to act until appointed by a judge. Some relatives may have to waive their rights or let a judge decide. Delays, extra costs, and uncertainties arise, especially if an argument starts over who's in charge. A court-ordered bond may be required. This creates only more frazzle for your heirs.

**It's Been Said**
............................................

"Where there's a will, there's a way, and where there's no will there are always lawyers."
— Anonymous

**Your estate incurs extra court costs even if there are no disagreements:** your loved ones' unmet needs or sense of fairness can create problems. Broken promises and disagreements among your relatives can start court fights. Estate expenses increase with legal costs, especially if everyone involved hires a lawyer. Money payable to minors would have to be paid into court and held there unless the court directs otherwise.

When an administrator, guardian, or spouse is not provided for by a will, your estate will be reduced by the cost of court appearances. Disagreements are bound to arise when relatives are forced to agree on the process, timing, and distribution of the estate.

**You lose tax-saving opportunities, which leaves less for beneficiaries:** without a will, there can be no tax deferrals or savings achieved from planning. The tax department wins, and your loved ones lose. The proper transfer of your wealth should reduce the share the government takes through taxes. A will, as an estate planning tool, can help you achieve tax savings.

In an intestacy, all your taxes have to be paid. There is no option to defer or postpone, and the tax blow can't be cushioned. Look at Paul and Linda, for example. Any assets that Paul left to Linda would normally qualify for a spousal tax rollover. If Paul had no will, the portions inherited by the children would not qualify for a tax rollover. The estate would sell or liquidate assets to pay Paul's income tax bill.

**Your minor children can't have guardians designated:** guardians are the persons you appoint by your will to assume responsibility for minor children. If both parents die, there will be no one authorized to have custody of any minor children. A will can appoint a guardian to care for your children, their money, or both. Guardians must still have their appointments confirmed by a court.

## Everyone Benefits from Wills

Here are some reasons to make a will, some of which you probably haven't thought of.

- Rather than the government, you can specify who gets what and when.
- You can use trusts to postpone the immediate distribution of your estate.
- You can benefit lifelong friends who are not family under an intestacy.
- You can give special funds and directions for disadvantaged family members.
- You can specify burial arrangements, investment powers, and organ donor instructions.
- Charities, causes, and religious organizations can receive donations.
- You can select who will be your children's guardians and how their money is to be held.
- You can explain how to provide for your children, causes, or pets.
- Your spouse can receive your entire estate even if you have children.

## Help Line

**Q:** If your signed original will is lost, is your estate intestate?

**A:** Yes, intestacy can arise when no one can find your will. Store your original carefully. Treat it like gold. Tell your executors where they can find it. Dying with a will that nobody can find is like dying intestate.

Here are nine benefits relating to executors and guardians.

1. Executors must comply with your lawful instructions set out in your will.
2. Executors and guardians for minor children in your will can act immediately.
3. You can give your executors a reward, gift, or share of your estate.
4. Naming an executor prevents contests over who will be appointed.
5. An alternative executor can be named in your will for protection.
6. You can authorize your executor to borrow money or manage a property or business.
7. You can choose a person familiar with your affairs and family.
8. The executor can operate a business so these assets are not wasted.
9. You can authorize your executor to settle disputes without going to court.

Now here are some tax benefits from wills.

- Taxes can be deferred and not paid immediately at your death.
- Income-splitting devices can be used to minimize taxes.
- You can postpone when beneficiaries receive their inheritances.
- You can protect your assets from creditors and tax collectors.
- Trusts can shelter and protect infants, including grandchildren.
- Wills can be updated to capitalize on new tax-saving strategies.

There, you've got twenty-four more reasons to make a will!

## It's Your Responsibility to Make a Will

You have the right to choose your beneficiaries, guardians, and executors when you make a will. Only you can exercise this privilege, so choose to make a will. No one can do it for you. You have to personally assume this responsibility. In the next three chapters, I'll show you the steps involved in making the best will you can. You'll benefit if you are making your first will or reviewing or revising an existing one.

You spend a lifetime acquiring property. Yet, while you're alive, you seldom think of how it will be disposed of after you die. You probably spend more time planning a two-week vacation than preparing your estate plans. The biggest benefit of having a will is peace of mind. You make a will and estate plan so you can enjoy this benefit during your lifetime. Then you know you've provided for those you love.

Everyone needs a will, even people in their twenties or thirties. It's not just something you do when you get married or retire. So get going and make one, because there's no reward in waiting. Even if you have just a life insurance policy at work or a chequing account, having a will can make a difference. Your loved ones and friends will never understand why you didn't bother to make one.

## Wills Don't Cost Money — They Save It

Remember this saying. You've learned twenty-four advantages, but here's the best one yet. Some wills can cost you absolutely nothing to prepare. I'll explain this and what goes into a sample will in Chapter 10, "Easy Fundamentals."

### The Least You Need to Know

- Wills transfer your property at your death to your beneficiaries.
- Dying without a will means the government divides your property by law.
- Wills control who administers and benefits from your estate.
- Wills save money and protect what you leave behind for your heirs.

# Chapter 10
# Easy Fundamentals

In this chapter:

- Mysterious wills are explained.
- Do-it-yourself wills are a dime a dozen.
- Understand holograph, codicil, prenuptial, and joint wills.
- Look at a sample will.

Kyle decided to make his own will. He wanted his niece Jessica to inherit his car, so he used his computer to print a letter for Jessica to confirm this wish. She took the letter to a lawyer after learning of Kyle's death. "He told everyone in his family that's what I was to get," she said.

"Great, but the letter is not a valid will," the lawyer said.

Kyle died intestate. His estate can't honour this letter. Although it's in writing, it's not a legal will. In a moment, I'll explain what Kyle should have done for Jessica.

Wills are a mystery to many people. What kind of will should you have, and where do you get one? Can you order the forms by mail or pick one up at the store and fill it in? Should you just download one from a Web site? With all these options, it's no wonder so many people don't know where to start. I'll also show you a sample will and explain it in plain English.

## What Kind of Will Do You Need?

The law does not say you need a lawyer to make a will. That's correct, you heard me say it. But there's a big difference between needing a lawyer and investing in professional advice. No law says that you need a lawyer to witness, notarize, or prepare a will. There's also no law that says you have to see a doctor if you are sick. But in both cases, you may be sadly mistaken to believe professional help won't make a difference.

Kyle's letter didn't comply with the legal formalities. Kyle never signed it in front of two witnesses. Even an amateur such as Kyle must satisfy the legal tests for a valid will, and not knowing the law is no defence for or comfort to Jessica.

## Common Do-It-Yourself Disasters

So what can go wrong if you create a do-it-yourself will? Here's a common shortlist of mistakes I have found in homemade wills.

- You forget the "children" doesn't include your common-law spouse's.
- You don't identify or name your beneficiaries properly.
- You don't get the will witnessed, so it's invalid — and you're intestate.
- You forget to deal with all your property, causing partial intestacy.
- You give away assets that no longer exist when you die.
- You forget to consider what happens if a beneficiary dies before you.
- You don't consider the tax advantages of spousal rollovers.
- You have no backup beneficiaries, executors, or guardians.
- You give away property that's not yours to give.

If you are like most people starting out, you may find wills confusing.

Here's a list of the top ten wills you may have heard about (I'll take you through each in turn):

1. lawyer prepared;
2. do-it-yourself;
3. holograph;
4. codicils;
5. multiple;
6. foreign;
7. prenuptial;

8. joint;

9. living; and

10. invalid.

I'll explain the potential problems and advantages of each will in turn.

## 1. Lawyer-Prepared Wills Are Best

You work with a lawyer to prepare a will to satisfy the formal legal requirements. Your lawyer will be an expert witness in any legal challenge to the will. When you use a lawyer, you get greater certainty that your objectives will be carried out.

Lawyers are like doctors — some are general practitioners licensed to do many things. Find a lawyer who spends thirty percent of his or her time in wills and estate work. Individuals with complex trust or corporate tax needs require more specialized help. Your province's bar association or law society can refer and certify specialists in estate planning, wills, and trusts. Check out your lawyer on the Web. Conduct research and get referrals from friends or advisors.

Legal fees to prepare wills vary from a few hundred dollars to much more. The fee will depend on the time spent, the complexity of issues, and your lawyer's experience. Some lawyers provide free telephone or initial consultations to discuss your estate-planning needs. You'll want to ask lawyers about

- the cost of a will to cover your type of estate plan;
- what legal documents to take to the meeting;
- how long it will take to prepare the will;
- what other services or estate-planning recommendations you need; and
- whether you will meet with a lawyer or a law clerk.

## Help Line

**Q:** Can my financial advisor prepare my will?

**A:** Be careful — anyone can offer to review your will or even prepare it. Distinguish between legal work and financial advice involved in making a will. Don't get legal work done or opinions from individuals unauthorized to practise law.

Like most professionals, lawyers use language of their own. But don't be afraid to ask your lawyer to explain terms in any documents prepared for you. You'll get more for your money when you have your questions answered. As with all professionals, price is not always an indication of quality. You get what you pay for in most cases.

It doesn't hurt to educate yourself about your choices before you meet with a lawyer. Read this book to get your money's worth from your lawyer. It will help you save costs and give you more control to make the best decisions.

> **Legal Lingo**
>
> *Testator* means you're a male writing a will, and a *testatrix* is a female will maker.

## 2. Do-It-Yourself Wills Are a Dime a Dozen

So what is wrong with a preprinted will? How can they be sold if they're not legal? Well, that's not the point. You still have to do work, which, as an amateur, you can screw up. Generic forms can be purchased from stores or Web sites to fill in the blanks. Some computer-generated forms come with explanations on how you fill in the blanks.

The problem with preprinted wills is that they fail to offer you or your beneficiaries certainty. No one guarantees what you do with this kind of will is legally valid once you touch it. Most will forms contain disclaimers saying the company that supplied the forms won't be responsible if anything goes wrong. Does that give you any comfort sleeping at night?

I know what you're thinking — I am a lawyer, so I have a vested interest in this question. Yes, but it's also scary because I seldom see will kits filled out correctly. They are a dangerous, quick fix that may end up, like most

> **Bulletin**
>
> It's true you don't need a lawyer to prepare your will. But only a lawyer can give you a legal opinion about its validity. Lawyers are the only professionals trained in trust, tax, property, will, estate, and family law. They also carry professional malpractice insurance to cover their errors.

quick fixes, costing you a lot more money and time than if you'd done it right in the first place.

I hear you saying, "Ed, I do my own tax return. Why not my own will?"

Making your own will is not the same as doing your own tax return. The government will quickly tell you if you made a mistake in calculating your tax bill. You'll be charged interest or a penalty or even be prosecuted. If you do your own will, no one can tell you if you make a mistake. Whoever finds your will won't be able to talk to you. You won't be able to explain what you intended. Questions can arise requiring a court to clarify your will or, worse still, declare it invalid.

It doesn't matter how smart or rich you are — mistakes happen when you do it yourself. It's a poor investment. Contrast that with what it can cost in legal fees to fix a will. Sometimes it's not even possible if you've died without a valid will.

### 3. Holograph Wills Are Free

Holograph wills must be 100 percent in your own handwriting. Blanks cannot be filled in by another person or a typewriter. Witnesses are not required, but your handwritten document should be dated and must be signed. The holograph will is not valid in every country and province. It therefore can't deal with assets in some provinces or foreign jurisdictions. Documents that are typed or printed forms with fill-in-the-blanks spaces don't qualify. They are not 100 percent handwritten.

### Help Line

**Q:** How many pages is a will supposed to be?

**A:** Some lawyers will want to cover your tax, trust, and business investment decisions in twenty-five pages of details. Other lawyers will tell you a few pages are just the right length. There's no legal limit; just make sure your wish list is covered. Understand what you're signing.

Mistakes commonly occur when part of the will is handwritten and part is a printed form. Holograph wills, while the most inexpensive to prepare, are also usually more expensive to probate. This is especially true if your estate has to pay an expert to prove it's your handwriting. After you pay a few thousand for an expert, you still have to satisfy a judge.

Holograph wills seldom anticipate tax or interpretive problems from using imprecise or ambiguous words. Does "my money in the bank" include all banks, RRSPs, mutual funds, and term deposits? Use holograph wills only for an emergency, such as when you don't have time to prepare a formal will before a vacation. Even then I recommend you have a lawyer check it. Holograph wills carry all the disadvantages of preprinted wills but are even more complicated. Consider them an emergency measure until formal documents are ready.

### 4. Codicils Amend or Revise Wills

Codicils are used to make small changes when a new will is not required. You use them to deal with only minor amendments. Codicils can be used, for instance, if the name of a charity has changed or an executor has to be replaced. At a small cost, they do provide an opportunity to update your will temporarily. Because codicils alter an original will, you should consult a lawyer to ensure that the changes are not inconsistent with the will being modified. If you're just deleting paragraph 6(a) in your will, check to make sure it's the only clause that needs changing.

### 5. Multiple Wills Are Used for Complex Plans

You can have more than one will when your assets are located in different jurisdictions. Probate may be required in each jurisdiction where your assets are located. Having separate wills in each jurisdiction can make this process quicker and easier. Multiple wills in one province may also reduce probate taxes. This is usually done in the form of a primary and a secondary will, as I described in Chapter 8. Don't attempt this technique without professional advice.

**It's Been Said**
••••••••••••••••••••••••••••••••••••••••••••••••

"A good marriage is that in which each appoints the other guardian of his solitude."
— Rainer Maria Rilke, 1875–1926

### 6. Foreign Wills Cover You Abroad

Experts should be consulted in each state or country in which you own or keep significant assets. They can advise you on the best way to minimize probate, taxes, and legal fees. You must also comply, for example, with each place's local laws of probate. A foreign executor may be required to appear in court to obtain probate. Use separate foreign wills in each country, especially where you own real estate, to speed up your estate's administration.

### 7. Prenuptial Wills Are Made before Vows

Prenuptial wills are expressly stated to be made "in contemplation of marriage." You need to specify this in the will (e.g., "This will is made in anticipation of my marriage to Kim Wong on July 11, 2006"). The date and time of the ceremony are not required to be in the will, but it must refer to the anticipated event.

Remember that marriage revokes all prior wills. However, it does not revoke a will specifically made in contemplation of matrimony. These prenuptial wills can also be used to reflect the terms of a marriage contract or prenuptial agreement. Don't worry, gifts in the will can be conditional on the wedding taking place.

### 8. Don't Sign Joint Wills

Joint wills are made by couples and start like this: "We, Sarah and John Bridges, state that this is our last will. . . ." Joint wills are not the same as having two identical wills prepared that each spouse signs separately. Problems can arise when you change your mind and wish to amend a joint will. Must your spouse agree to the amendments? Can you change your will if your spouse dies first?

In joint wills, spouses ill advisedly sign one will document, usually with common beneficiaries. Instead, you need separate and signed wills.

Can you ensure your spouse won't vary or amend a mutual will with a marriage contract? If you want to make sure a partner won't change a major gift after you die, you draw up a contract saying that.

If you revise a joint will, your beneficiaries may object. Courts have to decide if the surviving spouse is bound by the terms of the will. If so, that spouse can't make changes even after the death of the other spouse. Avoid joint wills in which both spouses sign one document. They are not a good way to save money.

## 9. Living Wills Are Not Wills

The term "living will" is really a misnomer because the legal requirements for a valid will are not present. This term is usually used in some jurisdictions as a directive for medical or health issues only. It's not really a "will" because it's intended to be read before you die, not after. Since a living will deals with your medical directives and health, not property, it's not a will. But everybody calls it by this name. I'll consider living wills in more detail in Chapter 22, "Look down the Road," when you look at powers of attorney for personal care.

Now that you understand this, you won't make the mistake one couple made. Leaving for a vacation, they told me they had protected themselves with living wills. I asked them if they also had powers of attorney. They told me, "We have something better — a living will that protects us both while we are alive and when we die." Now you'll never make that mistake. Living wills are not wills.

## 10. Invalid Wills Are Avoidable Disasters

Incomplete wills are not valid wills. People may hope that they have some legality. Some documents are letters, lists, or final instructions. If not incorporated into a will, they can't bind your estate. Your incomplete will can cost your estate a trip to the courthouse to find out if a signature on a shopping list is a will.

Kyle thought he was typing up a valid will. But unless the document complies with the legal formalities, it's worthless. Compliance with these minimum requirements is essential.

So what does a proper will actually look like? Let's look at one now, and I'll explain each part.

# A Simple Will

So you're going to get a lawyer to help make your will. What kind of will do you need? Is there a list like a restaurant menu to choose from? If you have never seen one, take a look at the basic will that follows. Like any of the documents in this book, you can't use my sample as a legal document, especially in Quebec, where the laws for wills are completely different.

This will is for Roberta, who wants to leave everything to her spouse, Nick. If he doesn't survive, everything will go to her children. Roberta has taken extra precautions to protect the children if they are underage. Look at the provisions she's made for her children in paragraphs 6, 7, 8, and 9.

---

### SAMPLE — NOT TO BE USED

I, ROBERTA STEVENS, of the City of Sunnytown, in any Province, declare this to be my Last Will.

1.   REVOCATION
I revoke all former Wills and Codicils made by me.

2.   APPOINT EXECUTOR AND ALTERNATIVE
I appoint my husband, NICK STEVENS, as my Executor. If he does not survive me, or is unable or declines to act, or, having accepted the appointment, ceases to act as my Executor, I appoint my brother, ADAM SINCLAIR, to be the Executor of this, my Will, and refer to him as my Trustee to deal with my estate as follows:

3.   DEBTS, EXPENSES, TAXES
Pay out of my general estate my debts, my income taxes for the time up to my death, my funeral expenses, and estate inheritance and succession taxes and duties that are payable because of my death in any country. Pay the costs to administer my general estate out of my general estate; pay the costs to administer a trust under this Will out of the trust.

---

### 4. SPECIFIC GIFTS

Give all my jewellery and $5,000 to my sister, TARA SINCLAIR.

### 5. GIFT OF RESIDUE

Give the residue of my estate to my husband, NICK STEVENS, if he survives me by 30 days.

### 6. ALTERNATIVE BENEFICIARY

If my husband does not survive me by 30 days: Divide the remainder of my estate equally among my children, SARA STEVENS, CALLAN STEVENS, and BETHANY STEVENS, who survive me, and do this equally subject to the trust conditions set out below.

### 7. TRUST PROVISIONS

If anyone is to receive part of my estate and is under 18, set a part aside and hold it in a trust fund on these terms: Give what remains of the fund to them when they reach 18. Before then, you, my Trustee, may use the fund for them. You will decide how much of the fund to use, when to use it, and whether to pay amounts to them or to others on their behalf. You may use income of the fund or capital of the fund, as you choose. If any child dies before 18, divide what is left of the fund when he or she dies equally among my other children who are alive when this happens.

### 8. APPOINTMENT OF MINOR'S GUARDIAN

If my spouse predeceases me and if I die before any child of mine has attained the age of majority, I appoint my brother, MICHAEL SINCLAIR, to have custody of such child and act as the guardian of the property of such child. It is my wish that before the expiration of 90 days from the date of my death the said MICHAEL SINCLAIR apply in court to have custody of such child and to act as the guardian of the property of such child. If MICHAEL SINCLAIR declines or is unable to act, I appoint my sister NADINE SINCLAIR to be my children's guardian.

9.   FAMILY LAW EXCLUSION

I hereby direct that the income from any property acquired by a beneficiary pursuant to my Will shall be excluded from such beneficiary's net family property under the provisions of the Ontario Family Law Act, or any similar or successor legislation.

DATED the 22nd day of May 2005

**WITNESSES:**

This will is signed by the Testatrix and by us, all in the presence of each other.

_____

*Witness #1 (name)*


*Address*

                                   _____
                                        **ROBERTA STEVENS**


_____

*Witness #2 (name)*

*Address*

---

**Legal Lingo**

*Lapsed gifts* are lost and disappear because the beneficiary has died before you. *Ademption* is when the gift is gone and no longer exists by the time you die.

## An Explanation of Will Clauses

Roberta took steps to include clauses 6, 7, 8, and 9 in the above sample will. If you read on, you'll see why everyone with children needs these items. But let's start at the top of the will and look at what's called the preamble.

**Preamble:** you'll want to include your full legal name on the will. It's the one you use on any deeds, passports, and insurance policies. You may also want to describe yourself with your commonly known name if it's different. Nicknames such as "Fast Eddie" aren't appropriate, though. Your will must identify you so that everyone knows it's yours.

Historically, wills dealt with real property or real estate, and you needed a testament to deal with everything else. Now it doesn't matter, but the sentence "This is my last will and testament" is commonly used. The words "being of sound mind and body, I make this my last will" don't have to appear. The document must be testamentary, which means it is intended to be effective only once you've passed on.

**Revocation of previous wills:** this makes it clear that you want all your prior wills and codicils to be cancelled. If you have a foreign will that you don't want to revoke, then say so here. Wills are dated so that only the last one is valid. You can have more than one will, as when you deal with foreign assets, provided they don't conflict with or revoke each other.

**Appoint executor and alternative:** all the chapters in Step 4 will cover this subject in detail. Now all I want you to know are the basics. The gender-neutral term for executor is "estate trustee." For simplicity, the word "trustee" is used. Older wills use words that mean the same thing: "executor" (male) or "executrix" (female). All your property automatically vests in the executor at death when you have a will. An alternative executor should be named whenever a will is prepared, but don't name alternatives without their consent.

**Pay debts, taxes, and expenses:** executors are directed first to pay all bills, which only makes sense. They are personally responsible if they don't. You can't escape the payment of your taxes and bills even by dying. The will makes it clear these items are to be paid first and who is to pay them. If there's not enough to pay debts, there will be no gifts.

**Give specific gifts or legacies:** here's where you can give gifts of cash or items you want to go to friends or family. It's sort of a first-things-first listing. If you leave your car to someone but sell it before you die, the gift is gone. The law says the gift has failed or adeemed. If you leave a gift to a person who dies before you, the gift lapses and is cancelled unless certain exceptions apply. If you gave it to Sharon, but stated that if she does not survive you it would go to her children, you've made your intention clear. Some provinces have rules that prevent a lapsed gift for special categories of beneficiaries such as a child, grandchild, brother, or sister. Gifts to these beneficiaries will go to others and not automatically lapse or fail.

## Help Line

**Q:** Can I videotape my will?

**A:** No. Wills must be in writing and be witnessed. Videotaped or tape-recorded wishes are not valid wills.

**Residual clause, transfer what's left:** this is what's left of your estate after taxes and expenses are paid and specific gifts are made. It's known as the residue. In accounting terms, it's the net estate left over to distribute. The remainder or net figure must be given to someone. If there is no one entitled to this residue, the intestacy rules will apply to distribute it.

In our sample will, a gift is made to Roberta's spouse, Michael, if he survives her by thirty days. This condition avoids double probate costs. Executor's compensation, court filing, and legal costs do not have to be paid twice on the same assets, which would happen if both spouses die within, for example, fifteen days of each other.

**Name alternative beneficiaries:** if your spouse dies first, you'll need this clause to prevent an intestacy. In this case, the clause protects the children as alternative beneficiaries.

**Minors need trust clauses:** if your children are minors (under the age of majority), you need this clause. It says how money can be used during the period the children are underage. The children who benefit from the trust funds while they are alive have a life interest. They are also called life tenants

---

**Time Machine**

Beneficiary or heir, what's the difference? Not much nowadays. Beneficiaries can get benefits under a trust, life insurance policy, or pension. Heirs by law inherited the estates of people without wills.

---

of the trust. Their interest may cease when they die. What is left over from the trust, not used by the life tenants, is left for the trust's residual beneficiaries. Your grandchildren could be these beneficiaries.

**Appointment of guardian for minors:** this provision is reviewed at length in Chapter 19, "Children's Needs." You name an alternative guardian in case your first choice predeceases you or dies in an accident with you. A codicil can deal with a change in guardian without major legal expense.

**Family law exclusion:** if your beneficiary separates or divorces from a spouse, you'll want this clause. Otherwise, a beneficiary's spouse shares in the income, appreciation, or growth of inherited assets.

**Signature:** use your regular cheque-signing signature since your bank records are usually checked if there's any question about a forgery. Anything added after or below your signature is not a valid part of your will, so please don't add a P.S.

**Witnesses are present:** every will needs two witnesses who are not beneficiaries or spouses of beneficiaries. They must sign as witnesses in each other's presence and the person making the will.

OK, I have covered the basic will, but what if you already have one? In the next chapter, I'll show you ten will mistakes you'll want to avoid.

## The Least You Need to Know

- Wills must be in writing and are best prepared by lawyers.
- Avoid do-it-yourself wills — you can't guarantee you completed them properly.
- Holographic wills (100 percent in your handwriting) are not legal everywhere.
- You and your partner should never sign a joint will.

# Chapter 11

# Avoid Will Mistakes

In this chapter:

- Make will wish lists.
- Use building blocks.
- Take a quiz.
- Avoid the top ten mistakes.

Rachel died, leaving behind her fifteen-year-old son, Austin. She also had a new husband of six months. She didn't think she had enough assets to bother with a will. All Rachel had was her furniture and a life insurance policy from work. After she died suddenly, her husband walked away with her estate. Austin was abandoned when his stepfather moved away. Rachel was only thirty-seven and never thought she was old enough to need a will.

You're never too young to have a will. Even someone with an estate as small as Rachel's can benefit from a will. So don't sit back and wait until you're rich to make a will. I'll show you the first steps to take. Do you think your existing will is good enough? Read on and check it to see if you have avoided the top ten mistakes. Make sure your will is more helpful than harmful.

## When Should I Make a Will?

Any time is the right time. I've had clients in all age ranges finally get around to making their first will. Everyone tells me they're going to get a will some day, just not today. They have excuses: they are going to wait until after the baby is born, after they move into the new house, or after their vacation. Many come back years later, without a will, still unsure of where to start.

Begin with some professional advice. You don't book a foreign vacation without talking to a travel agent. Admit you need some help. Yes, this book is a good start. I can give you essential information for a six-step estate planning process. But it is no substitute for professional advice based on your personal situation.

## Do It for the Kids

Here's how it happens for some people. A couple are planning to leave on a holiday. Usually, a plane or car is involved. Someone suddenly thinks of the children.

"What if we never come back?" one spouse asks.

"Well, we can always have Ted and Priti take care of the kids," the other spouse responds.

"Anyone but your side of the family."

"What's the matter with my relatives?"

So Ted and Priti get a phone call. "We've decided to let you have the kids if something happens to us on our holiday."

"That's great, I guess," Ted replies. "But don't we need to have something in writing?"

"That's another great idea. We better go see our lawyer before we leave on vacation."

And that's how I get a lot of rush business.

Help Line

**Q:** How often should I change my will?

**A:** There's no set schedule for you to update your will. You should review it regularly to make sure it continues to meet your needs. Death, disability, or divorce of a beneficiary or an executor may force you to make changes. Remember, marriage revokes your will.

## Making Your Will Is Step 3

If you are making a will for the first time or need to update a will, you'll want to follow this next bit. Each time you make or update a will, you are answering three basic questions: who gets everything, who will be in charge, and who will be your backups? Sounds simple, so let's keep it that way.

In the first two steps of estate planning, you prepared an asset inventory and looked at the income and probate taxes you'd consider before you draft a will. Now I'll take you through what should go into your will. You'll consider key decisions such as your executors and beneficiaries in Steps 4 and 5.

---

**Bulletin**

Wills don't come with a "best before" date sticker on them. Update your will when it no longer reflects your circumstances. Just moving to a new province may require a new will to reflect different provincial laws. Check with your lawyer.

---

Before you sit down to fill in a will form or visit a lawyer, do some homework. Clarify your thinking and save some time and frustration later. First, prepare a wish list of your assets to be dealt with. In Step 1, you already identified each asset, what you own, and how you own it. Does anyone automatically inherit it? If no one has a prior claim or right to the asset, then you can deal with it in your will. You'll want to check off any tax issues that come up.

So here's a list to use to help you prepare your will wish list. It lists the property you may want to leave by your will.

| | |
|---|---|
| Property | home |
| Approximate property value | $75,000 |
| How I own it (alone, jointly, or designated) | alone |
| Does anyone automatically inherit? | no |
| Tax consequences to my estate | none |
| I wish to leave it to | children |

When your will wish list is completed, you've identified the major items to be covered by your will. It is handy when you make a will or visit a lawyer.

## Help Line

**Q:** How do I deal with the art, books, and glass I've collected?

**A:** Talk with your beneficiaries. Are you sure they'll appreciate you leaving these collectibles or valuables to them? If the answer is yes, then consider making a gift during your lifetime of some of the items. You can refer to the balance in your will by making a testamentary gift.

## How Detailed Must You Be?

People sometimes come into my office with very detailed personal inventories. They've taken the time to list their furniture, bank balances, and even the names of the stocks in their portfolios. They apologize that the information is not up to date. Some people think they can't make a will because they never finished completing their inventories.

Understand that wills don't deal only with what you have on the day the will is signed. They deal with all your property at death. That could be more or less than you have today. A detailed inventory is not essential to get you started on your will, because your will is not going to name specifically each asset you have. For example, you are not going to specify who gets your brown leather couch.

Wills are works-in-progress evolving with you and your beneficiaries' requirements. Your will may come into effect ten, twenty, or thirty years after you sign it. Accounts at a credit union, trust company, or bank may no longer exist in ten years. If you specify that the money in a bank account goes to your grandchildren, there could be problems. If the institution fails, amalgamates, or merges with another, your will needs to be revised to identify the gift.

Here's another example. You want to make a gift of your home at 707 Riverside Drive to your children. What if you are no longer residing there at the time of your death? It is preferable that you clearly specify your intention. Is it to give away any residence or only the one on Riverside Drive?

This is why it is important to establish your estate planning wish list and that you not skip Steps 1 and 2. If it's your intention to establish a trust fund for your grandchildren's university education, that should be incorporated into the will. Assets can be channelled into this trust fund on your death. However, if you have only $10,000 in your bank account for this trust now, there is no point in creating a $100,000 education fund.

## Help Line

**Q:** Is there a difference between a gift and a bequest?

**A:** Yes, technically. A gift is a voluntary transfer of personal property made when you are alive. Testamentary "gifts" are those made by a will after you have passed on. Bequests or devises are also testamentary gifts.

## Build Your Will with Building Blocks

Your will may be simple or complex. Use these typical five building blocks to make your gift plan in your will.

**1. Personal effects:** these are items such as jewellery, heirlooms, or the contents of your apartment. Specific wishes for each item of value can be incorporated either directly or indirectly in your will. A lawyer can help you decide which method is best for you.

**2. Specific gifts:** you may wish to make specific gifts of cash or property to charities or individuals. This can be a fixed sum or share of the estate. Don't forget that the net value of your estate can be substantially reduced. Your home is sold, your stock portfolio slides, and you've paid for a retirement home. Consider specific cash gifts so they don't exceed a portion, say ten percent, of the residue of your estate. Preview your estate's worth to ensure you have enough for specific gifts of cash.

Usually, it is preferable to have your executor sell real estate and divide the proceeds. This approach is easier and avoids any disputes. If minor children are given a house, you have to make sure separate funds are available to maintain it. Minor children will usually relocate to live with guardians, and the home will be sold, so don't expect guardians to move into your house.

What if you own a number of properties that you wish to transfer to individuals? Be aware of their legal descriptions, ownership rights, values, outstanding mortgages, and liabilities. If your desire is to make an equal distribution, specify the net values after tax on your will wish list. For example, if you want to leave each child a rental property, don't create a dispute if, at the time of your death, they have unequal values or include tax and mortgage liabilities. This is complex planning requiring help from an experienced estate lawyer.

**3. Business interests:** you need special provisions in your will if you have a business. The disposition depends on the type of interest and whether you liquidate or actually transfer it. A partnership or shareholder agreement may have a clause for a buyout of your interests. You can specify that the proceeds be a specific bequest under the will or part of the residue of your estate.

You may wish to authorize the executors to sell the business, corporation, or closely held family enterprise to achieve the highest yield. A buy/sell agreement should usually be in place to help you realize on your investment.

**4. Special trusts:** you may want to create a trust to benefit your surviving spouse, children, or any other dependants. I discuss trust benefits in greater detail in Chapter 15, "Hold Something Back." Always include a trust for minors if any beneficiary could be under the age of majority.

**5. Estate residue:** this is what's left over after all these specific items, including estate taxes and expenses, are dealt with. This residue can be allocated as an outright gift or a trust distribution.

Following are more options for the residue.

**Divide it into shares or parts:** you can place one share in trust, and the other can be an outright distribution. The trust could be for minor children, and the outright distribution could go to a surviving spouse.

**Place it entirely in trust:** you can provide an income for your disadvantaged children, grandchildren, or spouse as long as they live. Upon the death of the life interest, the remainder could go to charity.

**Authorize trustees to make staggered distributions of capital to children:** at certain ages or intervals, executors can pay out trust capital in stages. Typically, this is done at eighteen, twenty-one, and twenty-five. Children can thus cope with a substantial inheritance and still have their needs met.

Help Line

**Q:** I am separating from my married spouse. How soon can I change my will?

**A:** Anytime, since you probably don't want a separated spouse to be your executor or trustee. Changing a separated spouse's share is a lot trickier. You'll need legal advice, and you may have to wait until a separation agreement is signed.

## Top Ten Will Mistakes to Avoid

Here are the top ten common will mistakes that I see people making.

### Mistake 1: Forgetting to Mention Your Spouse in Your Will

First, let's make it clear what kind of spouse we are talking about. Married, common-law, and separated are but a few. You could leave a marriage and start a new family with a common-law partner. Having multiple spouses is not uncommon, but having more than one at the same time may not be desirable!

The treatment each spouse receives under the law is different. Married spouses have claims to share in your assets under each province's intestacy laws. Common-law spouses, depending on changes to their province's laws, may have no property rights. They can also be left empty-handed if they do not have assets of their own. I'll take you through a couple of options of both married and common-law spouses. For more on spouses as beneficiaries, see Chapter 20, "Spouses: Good, Bad, and Divorced."

---

**Bulletin**

Every kind of spouse needs to be provided for by your will. If you don't mention your spouse, married, common-law, or same-sex, you're gambling with your estate. Still don't want to leave anything? See a lawyer who is familiar with your provincial family property and support laws.

---

When you are married, you *have* to leave a spouse something in your will. If you don't, you run the almost certain risk that your spouse will take your estate to court. Legally married spouses are, after all, entitled under provincial family law to a share of your property. Unless you have a marriage contract, that's the law. However, if your spouse has millions more than you do at the time of death, you may be able to get away with it.

Don't try leaving a symbolic dollar to a spouse and all the rest of your estate to children. It will only backfire. Your estate plan would be upset and distribution of assets delayed until the court case (which your estate will lose) is resolved.

You may be tempted to give your children a larger share of your estate than your spouse, especially if your spouse is understanding or has sufficient funds or if this is a second marriage. You can differentiate their shares through a will, but you'll have to do so carefully with legal advice. In this way, you can avoid disputes between your spouse and children. You can provide for each person, taking into account separate needs, expectations, and entitlements.

What about common-law and same-sex spouses? Common-law spouses are a different matter altogether. If you don't mention them in the will, they could be out of luck. It depends whether your province gives them property rights by treating them as "married" on your death. In Ontario, for example, common-law spouses have no property rights unless they are named in a will. They would have to sue your estate if they have grounds.

Look at what happened to Patricia and Joseph, common-law spouses. Joseph went to the hospital for a routine procedure and never went home. He was a forty-eight-year-old businessman who left a baby for Patricia to care for. Joseph had just started his own business and couldn't make the mortgage payments on their home, which he owned. Patricia had loaned him money each month to get by. She never got anything in return or in writing. Joseph died without mentioning his common-law spouse in his will. Patricia had to sue his estate to recoup her money and get support for their daughter.

One of the biggest mistakes people in common-law relationships make is not having a will. If you have purchased real estate with a common-law spouse and it's not jointly owned, watch out. Your partner could be forced to sell the home he or she shared with you to pay your estate. Protect your partner with a will. Even if you are recognized as a spouse for income tax purposes and live common law for many years, you still don't inherit without a will unless your province treats you as "married." In many provinces, preferential spousal shares on an intestacy work only if you're married or treated as such.

Same-sex couples are in the same situation as common-law couples. A surviving partner may be forced to sell property not registered with a right of survivorship. This can happen when there's no money to pay the next of kin who share in an intestacy.

---

**Bulletin**

Your new marriage revokes your previous wills. You and your spouse would be considered intestate. Consider making a new will in contemplation of your marriage. Discuss your beneficiaries' needs before the marriage if you have support obligations to a dependant.

---

## Mistake 2: Forgetting to Name Guardians for Minor Children

Parents with children must name a guardian for them in a will. Guardians can take custody and administer minor children's money. If you're a single parent and die, what happens if the surviving biological parent doesn't take custody? Couples must consider the possibility that both spouses may die in a common catastrophe.

Wills can specify which friend or relative has consented to these responsibilities. In Chapter 19, "Children's Needs," I give you my checklist to guide you in selecting your guardians. If you don't, your relatives could fight for custody. Worse still, children could be orphans, leaving a judge to decide who should look after them.

The only way to specify your choice is by naming guardians in your will. Think of the consequences if you don't. Name a backup as well. Remember that your suggestion is not binding on the court. A judge must confirm that your choice is still appropriate five to ten years after you made your will.

## Mistake 3: Forgetting to Change a Will to Reflect New Marital Status

Your will must be revised if you marry, divorce, or separate. I'll examine all three to show you why. A divorce cancels all gifts and appointments as executor under a will to a former spouse. A divorced spouse can't be your executor, so name a replacement. Divorcing a spouse who is your executor and sole beneficiary means trouble. You'll have an estate with no executor and no beneficiary. It's like having no will. Your estate goes to your next of kin on an intestacy.

Separated spouses don't lose their share in your estate if there's an intestacy. You must have a separation agreement signed by a spouse to release your estate to other beneficiaries.

Separated spouses also inherit whatever you have given them in your will. What about the problems this can cause for your children and a new common-law spouse? You need a new will to appoint a trustee other than a separated spouse. If you remarry, your old will is automatically cancelled by law. Did you know that once you remarry you're intestate if you don't make a new will?

## Mistake 4: Forgetting to Protect Disadvantaged Children and Adults

You can't forget that intestacy laws don't differentiate between needs. Special needs, care, and directions can be incorporated only in your will. On an intestacy, a full lump-sum distribution of your estate must take place. Assets can be frozen for up to a year after your death. What will these people do for support? If you have a disadvantaged child with substance abuse problems, giving that child money directly may do more harm than good.

---

**Bulletin**

Beneficiaries with special needs who are on social assistance can receive limited benefits under your will. A discretionary trust called a Henson trust with set capital and income limits may be needed. You need to see a lawyer to include certain provisions not to jeopardize government benefits. Rules change constantly, so check with an expert.

---

Only a will lets you set up a trust so you can control or postpone the distribution of money to avoid financial disasters. Your will can create trusts to hold funds for years. You can give discretionary powers to trustees. Periodic payments of income or capital can be given for those with special needs at your executor's discretion. This way they don't lose benefits, social assistance, or the right to live in a community residence.

### Mistake 5: Forgetting to Prepare for the Transfer or Sale of a Business

When a small-business owner dies without a will, the business assets are frozen. An administrator must be appointed by the court. Your surviving beneficiaries cannot pay the bills or sell the business until they are authorized by a court to do so. What will happen to your employees? Competitors capitalize when a business is left without someone at the helm.

Unless instructions are left in a will, a sole proprietor can't specify who will run the business and when it is to be sold. The value of the business can fall dramatically if it is not run properly after your death.

Your will can allow your executors to operate the business without fear of being sued for loss. Make sure your will does reflect your business transfer plan, including any buy/sell agreement.

### Mistake 6: Forgetting Pets and Other Animals

If you are single, or if you and your partner die, who will take care of your pets? Your wishes are not legally binding unless you leave specific instructions in a will. A person to provide care for your animals should be specified after that person has agreed to take on the task. Friends, even with the best intentions, can't spend your money without the approval of beneficiaries. Set aside money in a will to care for your animals, and the beneficiaries' consent won't be required.

### Mistake 7: Forgetting to Support Charitable Causes

Your favourite charities and causes will all mourn your death for good reason. Financial and personal volunteer commitments you provided while you were alive will be gone. Intestate rules of succession do not allow for gift giving. Your religious organizations will be out of luck unless you have a will. Don't miss an opportunity to make yourself and others happy. After your own family needs are taken care of, you can be generous to charity. Check out Chapter 7 for more details.

### Mistake 8: Forgetting to Keep a Promise

Your family took care of your uncle after his wife died. How many times did he repeat his promise to leave you everything? If that promise is not in a will, what happens? Well, it has no legal effect. Unless, that is, a court is prepared to honour it. Get ready to hire a lawyer. A will can honour your promises after death and avoid court procedures. Don't think your previously expressed wishes carry any legal weight? Oral promises broken by your death may be enforced by the court system. Doesn't that sound like a mistake?

### Mistake 9: Forgetting to Make a Will for Grandchildren

If you want to leave anything to your grandchildren, you'll need to mention them in your will. Otherwise, the intestacy rules provide for only your spouse and children. But in a will, you can create an educational trust fund for the grandchildren. Don't leave the future to chance.

### Mistake 10: Waiting to Make a Will until You Need One

Yes, people make this mistake frequently. That's why wills are made in hospitals. It's also why it's harder to make a will for someone who is ill. When you have serious health problems, you need to deal with medical issues, denial, and new ideas of reality. How would you feel trying to learn intestacy laws while you're taking radiation therapy?

## Did You Do the Following?

|  | Yes | No |
|---|---|---|
| I did provide for my spouse in my will. | ❏ | ❏ |
| I did name guardians for my minor children. | ❏ | ❏ |
| I did change my will to reflect my new marital status. | ❏ | ❏ |
| I did protect disadvantaged children and adults. | ❏ | ❏ |
| I did prepare for the succession or sale of my business. | ❏ | ❏ |
| I did provide care for my pets and animals. | ❏ | ❏ |
| I did support my charitable causes. | ❏ | ❏ |
| I did keep a promise. | ❏ | ❏ |
| I did make a will for my grandchildren. | ❏ | ❏ |
| I did make my will in time. | ❏ | ❏ |

Yes is the correct answer to every question.

### It's Been Said

"Experience is the name everyone gives to their mistakes."
— Oscar Wilde, 1854–1900

## Who Suffers from Your Mistakes?

You may think making a will is not a big deal. You're not a lawyer, so you believe you don't have to get things perfect. But unfortunately the laws relating to wills are very strict. Judges have no right to rewrite your will to correct it. Some provinces do not allow a court to ignore even minor technical breaches.

Here is what happened to Christy. Her uncle Victor made his will from a computer program and asked Christy to read a draft copy. She was surprised to see that her uncle left her a bank account and his stock portfolio.

Uncle Victor was glad she approved of his will. He told her he would print out another revised copy and sign it before his surgery. Unfortunately, the surgery was not successful. When Victor's will was read, Christy had another surprise. Victor had signed the will, but two lines were missing — the ones that included her gift. Had he not noticed there was a printer malfunction?

Christy thought that she could use the draft will to prove Victor's intention for her gift. Unfortunately, the courts have strict rules about repairing wills. Christy saw it only as a minor problem that needed to be repaired. The other beneficiaries who stood to inherit those assets disagreed. They said Victor's omission was deliberate.

The result was an expensive court case in which everyone hired a lawyer and took sides. The results of the case would vary depending on which province Victor lived in. Christy may have been disappointed and could have faced the cost of losing the case to boot. What if Victor had seen the mistake before he signed the will? Let's say he did sign it — but in front of only one witness, not the two witnesses that the law requires? Victor's will would not be valid, and no court could rectify that error. Getting only fifty percent (one out of two witnesses) is still 100 percent wrong.

Not using a lawyer to make your will to satisfy all the legal formulations could be your biggest mistake. When you spread the cost of your will over the years, it can be pennies a day. A court fight over your estate can cost thousands of dollars a day in court. Invest in professionally prepared wills.

Don't wait too long before you make or review your will, because it can be contested. You'll find that out in the next chapter, in which I'll show you how to protect yourself.

## The Least You Need to Know

- Young or old, you need a will, especially if you have children.
- If you separate, marry, or divorce, you need a new will.
- You need a will to support religious organizations or charities.
- Common-law or same-sex partners need wills to inherit.

# Chapter 12

# Bulletproof Your Will

In this chapter:

- Let the battle begin.
- How are wills contested?
- Avoid bitterness and blame.
- Protect your will.

Sound mind. That's what they say in the movies: "Being of sound mind, I hereby declare this to be my last will." Were you in your right mind when you made your will? Courts are frequently asked to answer that question when someone challenges a will. If you were not capable of making a will at the time you signed it, then it's simply not valid. Your medical condition is only one of the factors that must be considered by a judge. Fraud, suspicious circumstances, and undue influence can also defeat your will, as I'll explain.

If a court sets aside a will, you can lose an inheritance that your family or friends intended you to have. This chapter will show you how wills are challenged and how to prevent yours from being taken to court. Your loved ones can become victims if you don't take these precautions. I'll wrap up with why, regardless of your bias, lawyer-prepared wills are a good investment. What you learn here can help bulletproof your will.

## Help Line

**Q:** How do I contest a will?

**A:** See a lawyer as soon as possible. Strict time limits exist on when and how you have to record your objection. It starts with a court document called an objection or caveat, which is filed with the court in the district where a deceased lived.

## What Happens if Fights Start?

Wills are challenged all the time. If you're a disappointed relative upset about losing a promised inheritance, what do you do? Usually, you contact a lawyer to investigate.

Johnny came into my office and said, "My uncle promised he'd leave me the vinyl record collection in his will. He thought he was Elvis Presley. Can I contest his will to get what he promised me?"

Hearing that someone can contest a will could make anyone turn in the grave. Why should someone object to how you want to divide your estate? Can a judge really overrule your will? Is this possible after you are dead and buried?

Think twice before you cut someone out who's expecting something. A battle over your will can start even before you're gone.

Even if your will is valid, a court challenge can result in the following problems.

**Legal costs:** everyone in a will dispute runs to a lawyer to find out his or her rights. Lawyers run to court to get a decision from a judge. Someone has to pay for all this running around. Usually, it's your estate and beneficiaries.

**Family feuds:** you never expected any problems, but now members of your family aren't talking to one another. Brothers, sisters, aunts, and uncles are taking sides. If they're not talking, they're arguing with each other, and the bitterness can last years.

**Estate holdups:** if your will is contested, your estate can't be distributed to your loved ones until the challenge is resolved. It can take years to finish a court case. The most needy may have to compromise or give up the battle. They call it a holdup for good reason — that's what it feels like.

**Court process:** this is a legal world that you don't want to enter dead or alive. Even lawyers get scared by the legal system. Justice is something the court procedures can't guarantee for any just cause. Get good professional advice from an experienced estate lawyer. Consider it a wise investment to keep your estate out of court.

## Old Wills Can Become Valid

Will disputes are all about money, greed, hurt feelings, and doing what's right. If your last will is thrown out by a court, a former revoked will can become valid. I'll explain that in a minute, but if there's no last will your estate could be distributed on an intestacy. Dramatically different results can occur.

### It's Been Said
........................................................

"The law does not say that a man is incapacitated from making a will if he proposes to make a disposition of his property moved by capricious, frivolous, mean or even bad motives. . . ."

– Sir James Hannen, *Boughton* v. *Knight*, 1873

Franco writes out his last will by himself while under heavy medication. No one witnesses the holographic will, which leaves everything to his sister. His previous will left everything to his wife, Gabriella. So she sees a lawyer because she believes his sister took advantage of Franco. The couple talked about a possible reconciliation and stopped their divorce. Gabriella wants an expert to examine the handwriting on the will.

In the opening round, Franco's sister and Gabriella each get a lawyer or two. Gabriella believes all her legal costs should come out of Franco's estate, especially if she wins. She thinks that if she wins she'd prove Franco's sister did something wrong. The sister would have to pay for everything because the previous will gave the estate all to Gabriella.

What is everyone looking for? Answers. Was Franco capable of making a valid will? What kind of test can a judge use to decide if Franco's will was valid? His holographic will had no witnesses and wasn't prepared by a lawyer. Someone would have to collect evidence about his health, medication, and mental condition. Who was present (if anyone) when he wrote his will? The case could settle before trial. Otherwise, a judge hears all the witnesses give evidence. The judge then decides if Franco had testamentary capacity, the ability to make a will.

## Help Line

**Q:** My brother won't show me my late father's will. He tells me that he is the executor and that nothing was left to me. What can I do to find out if this is true?

**A:** Have a lawyer request a copy or visit the court office to see if any will was probated. If necessary, get a court order to require your brother to produce it.

## Testing for Testamentary Capacity

Franco's will has to pass this legal test, which includes four factors. The judge will determine whether Franco had testamentary capacity: that is, whether he knew

- he was making a will;
- the nature and extent of his assets;
- the persons who would normally be his beneficiaries; and
- the actual dispositions being made under his will.

You may be able to make a will even if you suffer from a delusion. At one extreme, a delusion is insanity. At the other, it is only a mild interference in your day-to-day activities. It's all a question of degree for a judge to decide.

Go back a moment to Johnny's uncle, who thought he was Elvis. You'll want to find out if his uncle only thought he sounded like Elvis when he sang. Perhaps he signed his cheques as "Elvis Presley" or used his real name. This information can call into question the uncle's capacity to make a will.

## The Presumption Is that It's Valid

In the majority of cases, no questions about mental capacity arise. Your executors just file papers to probate your will. Assuming all the legal formalities are complied with, no court trial is necessary.

A judge can still throw out your will if it does not comply with the following legal formalities.

- You must be eighteen years of age to make a will.
- The will must be in writing and signed in front of two witnesses.
- The witnesses and their spouses cannot be beneficiaries under the will.
- Holograph wills (where permitted) are entirely handwritten and signed.
- No deletions, markings, or erasures are permitted on the document.

Yes, you can question a will's validity if both witnesses didn't sign it. But if a will meets the minimum formal requirements, it is presumed to be valid by law. Your executors should receive probate in due course.

Each will proven to be properly executed is presumed valid. However, it can be challenged by a person who has an interest in your estate. If Johnny alleges his uncle's will is invalid, he may have to prove it. The Elvis delusion may not have stopped his uncle from making a valid will — as long as it did not interfere with his testamentary capacity. The hard thing, however, may be to prove it after he's gone. The only expert evidence readily available may be from the lawyer who prepared the will.

What if you can't find a will or no executor comes forward? You'll ask a judge to name an executor during the lawsuit. He or she may be called an "estate trustee during litigation." You don't want to go through all these legal steps unless there's a fair bit of money involved. Make sure that the estate isn't financially insolvent and unable to pay creditors and beneficiaries, including yourself.

---

**Time Machine**

Alfred Nobel is immortalized because of his 1896 handwritten will creating Nobel prizes. He disliked lawyers, so he made his will himself. He couldn't avoid years of court proceedings to interpret it, though.

## Who Can Challenge Wills?

Here's why estate litigation is so costly: more than one person can challenge a will. Yes, that's right. People whom you have never met can spend your money in the legal battle. They'll expect your estate to cover their legal costs. Many wrongly believe they won't pay any legal costs, even if they lose.

Let's see how there can be multiple claims against your estate. Here's a list of the people who can make a claim:

- all persons named in your last will;
- all persons named in your prior wills;
- all persons who share in an intestacy; and
- all persons who have a financial interest in the estate (e.g., dependants or spouses of all descriptions).

So you can see how a lot of individuals can be involved in a will dispute. Your estate can be depleted by the costs, which probably scare some people from making a will. What's the point of bothering with a will if this is what happens? However, many nuisance cases get mediated or settled in the early stages, so do everything you can to avoid a will contest. I'll give you suggestions how to do this in a moment.

## How Is a Will Challenged?

A will can be challenged in several ways. The first consideration is whether the will complies with the formal requirements of law. If you sign a home-made will in your kitchen, it must still comply with all the legal requirements. It's no excuse to say you didn't know the law or didn't use a lawyer. All wills are held to the same legal tests.

Questions of interpretation can also arise. Your choice of words can create confusion or misunderstanding. "I'll leave my money in the bank to . . ." may be ambiguous. Does the money include bank certificates and term deposits? If your will is ambiguous, the executor will need a judge to resolve these issues.

> **Bulletin**
>
> Questions of testamentary capacity are practical ones. The court must find if the testator possessed a "sound and disposing mind" based on evidence of observation and experience.

Challenges are commonly based on fundamental flaws, which can make the will invalid even if it complies with all the legal formalities. The person challenging your will can claim that any of the following exists.

**Lack of testamentary capacity:** can you meet the fourfold test we discussed for a sound mind? Your capacity can be affected by drugs, major depression, illness, or plain incompetence. You may be eccentric and leave money for relatives to visit Elvis's birthplace — but it doesn't mean you lack testamentary capacity.

**Undue influence:** this occurs when you feel compelled to honour a direct or implied threat. Your will does not reflect your true intentions. Lack of free will invalidates the will. Alcohol abuse, a weakened mental state, or manipulation can create signs of possible undue influence. This is especially true if you give benefits to a person who helped you make your will. Evidence must show more than persuasion to win.

**Fraud:** fraud exists when you are told a lie, such as someone's sister is dead so that someone else can inherit. Once fraud is proven, your will can be set aside by a judge. Examples also include forging signatures, destroying a will, or changing pages in the will.

**Suspicious circumstances:** a court can declare that your will does not reflect your true intentions if any suspicious circumstances exist. They usually surround the preparation and signing of your will. The court can investigate suspicious circumstances. For example, a will prepared by your hospital nurse that leaves everything to the hospital may mean that the nurse has to remove the court's suspicion.

### Deciding to Contest a Will

First remember that this book is not a legal do-it-yourself manual. I can't give you legal advice because each province and jurisdiction has different rules of law. Since contesting a will is a legal procedure, I recommend you do nothing without expert legal advice because the consequences can be financially disastrous. The sooner you get advice from an experienced lawyer the better.

A lawyer can explain what evidence you will require to be successful with your challenge. You must understand who will have the burden of proof in a court of law.

If you go to court, you must understand the rules of the legal game. Not everybody who should win does, and not everybody who loses is wrong. Not every whim or personal slight can be rectified by a three-year legal battle.

If Johnny's uncle's last will is not valid, then it can't be probated. His prior will that left Johnny everything may not have been legally revoked. What if Johnny can't find it? If there are no other wills, the uncle would have died intestate. That's not the way he would have wanted to go. He had no children but did have a separated spouse. Yikes, his spouse hadn't signed a separation agreement releasing his estate. She could get it all if she's not prepared to honour Johnny's claim. Moral: make sure you're satisfied with any prior will before you challenge the last will.

What if you were promised money for work you did for Johnny's uncle? You may not need to set aside the will. It may be easier just to sue the uncle's estate by giving notice of your claim. Executors have a duty to defend the estate from legal action. Their duty includes defending the will in court. After hiring a lawyer, the executor could deny your claim, negotiate a settlement, or pay it in full.

---

**Legal Lingo**

*Litigation* is a contest in a law court to enforce rights. To litigate is to carry on a *lawsuit*.

---

**It's Been Said**

"[A man] may disinherit either wholly or partially his children, leave his property to strangers to gratify his spite or to charities to gratify his pride and we must give effect to his will, however much we may condemn the course he pursued."

– Sir James Hannen, *Boughton* v. *Knight*, 1873

## Temporary Court Trustees Are Estate Managers

You've decided to challenge your uncle's will. Who will handle and preserve the estate's assets until the case is finished? Judges may need to appoint an interim executor during any lawsuit. Your uncle's choice of executors usually can't be adopted by the courts unless it's a unanimous decision by all parties. "Estate trustees during litigation" must be appointed by court and are paid to manage but not distribute your uncle's estate. If an asset such as his empty home has to be sold, everyone must agree. Otherwise, a judge decides after everyone argues his or her case.

Temporary measures may be costly but necessary. An estate court case can feel like it's taking forever. Spouses and beneficiaries may need financial assistance while the case goes through a legal maze. Those dependent on your estate for support may need to apply in court for temporary relief. Children from a first marriage may argue about their share. They may argue about how much a surviving second spouse should get for living expenses. It's embarrassing and expensive.

Timing is everything in a will contest. You want to stop everything in its tracks. There is no point in fighting a will if the money has all been spent. Relatives could squander all the estate money at a casino. You will have to file an objection or caveat with the courthouse to stop the probate process.

## Resolve Estate Disputes through Mediation

Are you involved in an estate dispute? You know it can be an expensive wait for a judge's decision. There are shortcuts that can help through mediation. Mediation involves the persons in a dispute and their lawyers meeting to use a neutral mediator to try to reach an agreement. Mediation is different from litigation.

---

**Bulletin**

At mediation, the information exchanged between the parties cannot be used later on in the proceedings in any way. Therefore, the parties are free to exchange information that may encourage a settlement. The mediator, however, does not try to make judgments on the merits of either side but to help both reach an agreement. This is a unique role, and mediators can help the parties but not compel them to settle.

---

# Mediation: Five Things to Know

Many legal disputes are resolved without going to trial. This is typically called an alternative dispute resolution, which has been part of the legal landscape in Canada and the United States for several decades. Large corporations, governments, and individuals have always searched for faster ways to resolve disputes through out-of-court proceedings. Why? They are usually quicker, less formal, and less expensive.

## 1. What Is Mediation?

Mediation is a way for people in a dispute to meet with a neutral person (the mediator) to find a solution to their dispute. Unlike a trial, with its winner-take-all approach, mediation starts with the idea that persons in the dispute wish to reach some out-of-court settlement. Mediation allows everyone to make a deal without the complex process to get to trial.

## 2. How Does Mediation Work?

Mediation gets everyone together to start talking sooner. The courts are clogged with disputes, and mediation is an early way of making your point to the other side. You can make sure that the other side understands the risks of proceeding to trial.

### Help Line

**Q:** What are the costs of mediation?

**A:** Typically, a mediator can charge between $200 and $400 per hour. The costs are based on a half-day session and can be shared by the parties to the dispute. Each party will pay its own legal costs to attend mediation and for the time to prepare the mediation brief. Although mediation can be expensive in the short run, it can lead to considerable savings if the case can be resolved without going to trial.

## 3. Who Is the Mediator?

In most estate mediations, a lawyer or retired judge with estate experience is a preferred mediator. Mediators take different roles in the process and have different styles, just like judges. Unlike judges, mediators can help steer the parties to a satisfactory resolution that a trial judge would not be able to do. The all-or-nothing approach is what one is faced with in going to trial. In mediation, the parties must use the dispute as an opportunity to resolve any impasse or disagreement and to formulate a new agreement on how to proceed in the future.

## 4. Who Goes to Mediation?

Usually, mediation involves the parties and their lawyers in a neutral setting, such as the mediator's office. No court officials or representatives of the court are present at the mediation. No recording, transcript, evidence, or statement is taken. The process involves having the parties prepare mediation briefs, which are submitted to the mediator prior to the mediation. The brief sets out what the parties' versions of the facts are, their disagreement with the other side, and what they hope to accomplish by mediation. In some cases, everyone is encouraged to submit settlement proposals to consider options in advance of the meeting.

## 5. Why Is Mediation Successful?

Mediation allows the parties to discuss, in an off-the-record format, their concerns and to approach settlement without risk. After one or two mediation sessions, most cases do reach settlement. Why? The costs of proceeding to trial after mediation are usually made clear to both sides. These costs are an incentive that lawyers and mediators can use to reach a settlement.

## Help Line

**Q:** Should I insist on going to court and refuse to go to mediation?

**A:** Mediation is not something to be feared but encouraged in all legal disputes. It is an opportunity for the parties to reach an out-of-court settlement in a process that will be much more satisfactory than getting your day in court. You can settle through mediation.

---

**Legal Lingo**

*Citations* or *court orders* can compel the executor to comply with requests for information. Sometimes you don't need to contest a will but simply need to get information, which could be an inventory of estate assets if you have a financial interest in the estate. Ask the court to cite or summon the executor to file material that you're entitled to see.

---

## Court Costs — Who Pays, Winners or Losers?

Estate disputes can settle outside the court system by arbitration or mediation. Get sound legal advice, more than one opinion if you want, but understand what your chances are. You'll get nothing if you lose and maybe get hammered with legal costs to boot. Be sure that your case has merit.

What kinds of costs can be awarded by the courts in an estate case? The rule is that the judge hearing the case decides who pays for the proceedings. Here are some cost options the judge could order if you lose the case.

- Everyone's legal costs may be paid out of estate funds.
- Just a portion or all of your legal costs may be paid from estate funds.
- You may personally pay the other parties' legal costs and get nothing for yours.

If you win, don't expect your costs to be paid automatically out of the estate. The courts have discretion, meaning anything can happen. Weigh your options carefully. You don't want to rack up thousands of dollars of legal costs and exposure to pay anyone else's costs without proper advice.

> **Bulletin**
>
> Don't think that leaving a dollar to a beneficiary will stop him or her from challenging your will. Nor can you disinherit a beneficiary if he or she contests your will. Judges can declare such clauses to be unenforceable and against public policy.

## Eleven Ways to Bulletproof Your Will

Here are some topics to discuss with your lawyer to prevent trouble.

**Convene a family meeting:** discuss your estate plan with beneficiaries and, if tax and legal issues are involved, have professional advice available. Remember, you don't have to please everyone. You can even mediate disputes before you are gone.

**Give it away while you are alive:** consider how a financial counsellor can be used to prevent and mediate problems to reconcile family members.

**Get written agreement from your family:** individuals who receive a share of the estate while you're alive can agree not to contest your will's distribution. Independent legal advice will usually be required. In some cases with spouses, you'll need a marriage contract.

**Transfer assets into a trust or holding corporation:** leave little to fight about in the estate controlled by your will.

**Record your instructions with your lawyer in writing:** make sure beneficiaries are not present to avoid possible undue influence. This should be the rule from when you meet your lawyer until the will is signed.

**Get expert opinions on capacity:** if you're elderly and not well, confirm your testamentary capacity. More than one opinion will be better if a lot of money is at stake.

**Keep your will up to date:** update your wishes regularly to establish a pattern of giving using a competent estate lawyer.

**Carefully cut out beneficiaries:** be sure your reasons for disinheriting a relative are clear and reasonable. Leave a letter with your lawyer expressing convincing reasons. A penalty clause that says gifts are forfeited by those who contest the will may be ineffective. Your lawyer must draft such clauses carefully so they are not invalid. In some cases, public policy prevents you from denying others access to the court system.

**Avoid holographic or store-form wills:** these are risky and bad investments when you have so much to lose.

**Don't make a will in the hospital:** if you make a will at the last minute while suffering from a terminal illness, problems undoubtedly will arise. Even the most meticulous lawyers take shortcuts making hospital wills. This always looks suspicious to someone left out of a new will.

**Use an estate lawyer to make your will:** you'll want someone other than your cousin Ester, who just graduated from the bar. Find lawyers you feel comfortable working with who spend at least thirty percent of their time preparing wills.

## Are You Afraid?

People don't like talking about their money. Some of you will not discuss money with members of your own family, let alone a lawyer who is a stranger. We keep secrets from our own partners because we are afraid of divorce and death. Is it any wonder that we are reluctant to discuss details of an estate plan with a lawyer? Some people prepare their own wills, buy a computer program, or get a book with forms to fill out. They keep their secrets, and it doesn't cost them much until they are gone.

### It's Been Said

Regarding the expertise required to find a sound and disposing mind: "This is eminently a practical question, one in which the good sense of men of the world is called into action, and that it does not depend solely on scientific or legal definition."

— Sir James Hannen, *Boughton* v. *Knight*, 1873

Can a cheap, "fill-in-the-blanks" form work if you do not have a large estate? Well, a do-it-yourself will kit may save you money today, but what's it worth when you die? Have an estate lawyer prepare your will. Most people can't afford a costly legal challenge while they are alive. Why would you want your estate to fuel a family feud after you are gone? The costs of a lawyer-prepared will may be pennies a day spread over five to ten years.

## What Lawyers Can Do for You

People are afraid of lawyers for a lot of different reasons. Clients usually tell me this is one reason they did not make a will sooner. But once their wills are signed, they feel relieved that they have secured the future for their loved ones. A lawyer can help you avoid unnecessary expenses in your estate plan. Lawyers can also suggest methods to save probate and income taxes. Passing title to property by joint ownership, instead of through your estate, will lower estate costs. Tax planning advice alone may justify the cost of a consultation.

Costs for estate legal services will vary depending on where you live, the experience of the lawyer, and the complexity of your estate. The costs of preparing a will with a professional are a fraction of the costs of a future legal challenge. Educate yourself about your options to keep your legal costs in line.

If you decide to make a will by yourself, can you avoid a legal challenge?

A disgruntled relative may be suspicious about provisions in your will. Remember, your executor's duty is to uphold your will after you are gone. You can't tell him or her how much to spend to defend your will. Using a qualified lawyer avoids legal challenges, which alone justifies the fee.

## Lawyer's Duty When Preparing a Will

Most people do not realize a lawyer's duty to keep notes when a will is prepared. A lawyer must also confirm your instructions independently and privately. He or she is your chief witness to uphold your will. Only lawyers are qualified to give legal opinions in court on the validity of your will. Your financial advisor is not authorized to give legal advice. Your lawyer also confirms that no one influenced you when your will was prepared and signed.

Why is it important to make a will before you lose capacity? Let me tell you the story of Betty and her elderly father.

## Don't Wait Till It's Too Late

Betty was in town for a few days visiting her sick dad. She called his lawyer and said, "I want him to update his will so my sister Joan and I will divide his house." Betty took Dad to a lawyer.

Her father clearly told the lawyer, "I want to leave my house to Betty and Joan when I die."

"Let me write this down," said the lawyer. "You want the home where you live to be divided between your daughters when you are gone."

"No, that's not correct! Only Betty and Joan are to share the property!"

"Why is that?" asked the puzzled lawyer.

"Because Lucy is not getting a share."

"You mean you have more than two daughters?"

"Yes," said the father, somewhat annoyed, "but I have not seen much of Lucy."

"So why are you cutting Lucy out of your estate? In case she challenges the will, I need to know what she did," the lawyer asked.

"I just do not see her much," said the father. After a moment's reflection, he recanted, "Perhaps you better give Lucy a share of the house too."

"The house, then, is to be divided three ways among all your children, is that what you want?" the lawyer asked again.

"No!" said the father. "I just want the house divided between my daughters. Who said my boys were getting anything?"

"You did not tell me about your sons," the lawyer said.

"You didn't ask me," the father replied simply.

"Tell me why each boy is being cut out of your estate."

"Just have Betty come in; she can explain it," said the father in frustration.

"My duty to you and to your beneficiaries is to confirm all your instructions privately and independently," said the lawyer. "That's why Betty is waiting outside while we speak in private."

The lawyer never made a will for Dad that day because the father had trouble remembering all the boys' names. Lawyers have a duty to ask questions.

## Wills Keep Your Promises

Remember Johnny at the beginning of the chapter? His uncle promised him his Elvis albums, but the bad news is that such oral promises are worthless without a will.

Prepare your will before it's too late. Make sure you choose the right executors. In Step 4, I'll show you why and how to get the best executor.

## The Least You Need to Know

- Anyone of legal age with testamentary capacity can make or change a will.
- Your will can be contested or challenged if you are not of sound mind.
- Estate distribution is delayed and legal costs paid when wills are challenged.
- Your lawyer's fees for a will are small investments to bulletproof it.

# Choose Your Executors

Every estate needs to have someone in charge. Selecting the right legal representative, trustee, or executor is a key estate planning step. Executors are named in your will to manage your estate. You must choose wisely because the wrong executor can sabotage your plans and steal your legacy.

Here's how you can reduce the risks. First, understand the essentials of an executor's duties to your estate. Second, list your own particular requirements to narrow your choices. And third, analyze all your alternatives with my executor's worksheet.

As fiduciaries, your executors must act for the benefit of others. They must account for all their actions and keep proper financial records. That's why they are entitled to be paid. An executor's compensation can be a percentage of your estate. I'll show you tips, traps, and choices to save and protect money and how to invest it in a safe bet. That way you and your beneficiaries get your money's worth.

# Chapter 13

# Executor Essentials

In this chapter:

- Who's in charge?
- Review the job description.
- Take Managing Estates 101.
- Get answers to frequently asked questions.

You want honest and trustworthy executors to manage your estate. At least you hope they're reliable. You can do good or evil with what you leave in their hands. You're the one who chooses the people who distribute your estate under your will. In some provinces, the term "executor" or the feminine "executrix" has been replaced with "estate trustee." I'll use executor to mean the person who deals with your estate under your will.

The advantages of having an executor were covered in our discussion about wills. Now I'll review some essentials about executors so that you know what they do. I'll show you the steps they'll take to settle a typical estate. This discussion should help guide your selection of the right person for the job in case you are grieving a death in your family and are uncertain of what happens next. This section should help you understand what an executor does.

## Who's the Boss?

Go ahead and appoint an executor by naming one in your will. It's easy enough. Executors deal with your assets, children, and even pets under the terms of your will.

> **Bulletin**
>
> Make your executor's job easier and more rewarding. Prepare an asset inventory before you go. Let the executor know where to find your original will, property deeds, and insurance policies for your valuables. Don't cause executors extra work trying to locate these items once you're gone.

If you're married, then your surviving spouse is your logical choice to be your executor and beneficiary. But your spouse may not always be the best or only appropriate choice, especially in second marriages.

In this section, I'll share with you some alternatives that you may wish to consider, depending on your circumstances. I don't want to discourage you, however, from making a family member your first choice of executor. Bear in mind, though, that you always need a backup or an alternative executor named in your will. Without a will, you'll have no say over who'll be in charge. Your family will have to apply through the courts to become your court-appointed estate administrator.

Executors, since they carry out your will wishes, have no authority to depart from its terms. The closest you can come to ruling from the grave is to give them discretionary powers so they can do as they "see fit." It doesn't

> **Bulletin**
>
> Play it safe before you start handling a person's assets as an executor. Make sure you have the proper authority. A later will or codicil could revise or revoke the one you are holding. Make inquiries to see if a more recent will was prepared. You don't want to be liable to the real beneficiaries or third parties. Always check with an estate lawyer.

mean they can withhold a gift or bequest from a beneficiary. For example, if your child marries inappropriately, the executor can't take away his or her inheritance. If you do give discretionary powers, it's a good idea to specify in what cases they can and should be exercised.

Normally, a year is allowed to settle your estate. If you're an executor, a lawyer can confirm if more or less time is allowed in your province. Executors who are also trustees for any testamentary trusts created by a will can have extra duties. They also manage, invest, and distribute income and capital from a testamentary trust. This could go on for years — say until children or grandchildren reach the age of twenty-one or twenty-five.

### Do Executors Need a Licence?

Absolutely no licence, prior experience, or qualifications are required. Your executor's "licence to operate," so to speak, comes from your will. Provided they're not challenged, wills give executors the authority to act. The probate process has a judge confirm which is your last will and whether it complies with all legal formalities.

If you're an executor, you'll take the will to a lawyer to be sure. An executor's first act may be to arrange and authorize payment out of the estate for the funeral. The cost must be in keeping with your standard of living and social position. So don't overdo it. Keep in mind that funeral wishes expressed in wills are not legally binding on the executor. If you want certainty, pre-arrange and prepay your funeral while you can.

> **Bulletin**
>
> An executor is an executor even before the will is probated. That's why executors can legally arrange funerals before probate. That's why executors arrange and have the estate, not your family, pay for the funeral.

### Executors Get Confirmed

Executors can't walk into a bank, produce a will, and walk out with your money. If it was that simple, wouldn't we all do it? The bank manager, unless we're talking small amounts, will want the will probated. A court will usually process the paperwork in thirty to sixty days depending on its workload.

Provided the paperwork is in order and no one objects to the will, that is. If someone objects, you'll want to review Chapter 12.

Executors, especially those from out of province, may need to file a bond. A judge can require this bond before issuing the probate papers. Getting bonds can be time-consuming and an added expense paid for by the estate. The bond is usually purchased through a surety company. It's security if an executor skips town with the estate's cash. The bond can replace what was taken in the same way as an insurance policy.

What if you have named all your children as your executors? Before the court confirms their appointments, they can renounce or give up their right to be executors. Once their appointments are confirmed, they will need permission from the court to resign or retire from their duties.

Now let's describe an executor's duties as if you and your cousin Janet were executors for your Aunt Mary's estate.

## Job Descriptions, Please

So you've been asked to be a relative's executor. I'll explain some of the basic things you'll be expected to do, which may help you decide if you'll accept or decline the offer. I'll take you through each stage as if you were an executor.

An executor's work is carried out in stages, which usually overlap. These stages are obligations to do the following:

- secure assets;
- protect property;
- get probate; and
- distribute assets.

### 1. Your Initial Duty: Securing Assets

The telephone is ringing, and it's 4 a.m. You hear a doctor say your aunt Mary passed away in her sleep. You're asked to make burial arrangements. Aunt Mary gave you and your cousin Janet copies of her will in sealed envelopes. Reading the will, you find it contains no burial instructions. Janet is named the co-executor with you because she was involved in Mary's business.

> **Legal Lingo**
>
> *Co-executor* is anyone who is a joint executor with one or more other executors.

Wondering if Mary ever changed this will, you call Francine, your aunt's lawyer, at a respectful hour. She reports that there are no codicils or amendments to the last will. You can now go ahead with Janet to make arrangements. You confirm with Janet that no formal reading of the will is required (except in Hollywood). Beneficiaries and next of kin are notified of the funeral.

Janet and you agree to divide up some initial tasks. She'll get someone to run Aunt Mary's store, and you can take care of her house. You secure the estate property by changing the locks, which is the executor's first duty. Here's what else you have to do.

- Review the will and contact a lawyer.
- Confirm the funeral arrangements.
- Take steps to secure estate property.
- Notify the next of kin and beneficiaries.

## 2. Protect Property from Harm

Next you and Janet collect Mary's property. Janet arranges to run the business until it is sold. You've changed the locks and taken Aunt Mary's valuable papers with you. The fire insurance company is notified and asks you to pay the premiums for fire insurance. You're now on a first-name basis with the lawyer. You pay the funeral expenses and probate taxes out of Mary's account. Until the court confirms your appointment, other bills can't be paid from her bank account.

You prepare an estate inventory, collect bills, and appraise the business and home. Canada has no estate tax, but you still must pay your aunt's income taxes. You calculate the estate's value to pay provincial probate taxes. In this second stage, you do the following.

- Secure all property.
- Guarantee insurance coverage on valuables.

- Preserve any business or investments.
- Prepare an inventory of assets and liabilities.

## 3. Go Get Probate

You're now ready to sign probate papers prepared by the lawyer. Executors can hire lawyers to provide such legal services. You and Janet obtain letters probate. In Ontario, it's called a *certificate of appointment of estate trustee with a will*. Everyone still calls it probate, though. Unless there are problems, you will not have to appear in court.

### Help Line

**Q:** What if you think you can't complete all your duties as an executor?

**A:** Renounce or give up your appointment before you start. If you resign after starting, you'll need beneficiary and court approval. You could be responsible for the cost of this procedure. Make sure you can finish before you start.

A question comes up about a loan Mary gave to Charles. Charles told Janet their aunt never expected to get her money back. Mary cut him out of her will because of his substance abuse. Her will, however, doesn't mention the loan. It would be difficult to collect the money from Charles, who is unemployed. Janet wants to sue Charles. The will gives executors the power to settle estate claims. After discussions with the estate lawyer, you agree not to pursue the debt because of the poor chance of recovery.

All transactions are recorded through the new estate bank account that you've opened. As soon as possible, you pay all the estate's bills and income taxes. The business and home are sold, and the proceeds are put in the estate account. You advertise for estate creditors in the local paper. A tax clearance is received, and you've just completed the third stage.

- Obtain probate of the will.
- Settle all legal issues.
- Sell assets to pay bills.
- Pay all liabilities and income tax.

## 4. Distribute the Estate

Jewellery and personal gifts are delivered to relatives. Beneficiaries have the right to review your handling of the estate. As court appointees for the estate, your actions can also be reviewed by a judge. You've kept records of your time and transactions to support your claims for compensation.

Francine sends out a report to the beneficiaries with two attachments. The first is your estate report and compensation claim that the beneficiaries must approve. The second is a release form for the beneficiaries to sign to approve your work. Any problems are resolved. All signed releases are collected before anyone gets his or her share of the estate. If one or more beneficiaries won't sign, compensation and distribution are held up until the issues are resolved, negotiated, mediated, or decided by a judge.

Stage four is complete when you have done the following:

- Account to the beneficiaries.
- Have your compensation approved.
- Obtain signed releases from all beneficiaries.
- Distribute the estate assets.

---

**Bulletin**

You don't need your executors to sign anything to consent to serve in that capacity. They don't have to sign the will as witnesses just because they're executors. Remember, they can renounce the position. You can't force anyone to accept the job after you're gone. Always name a backup or alternative in your will.

---

## Frequently Asked Questions

Now you know what services an executor typically performs. I'm sure you have some questions. I'll try to answer them before we go on to your executor options.

### How Do You Find an Executor?

The Yellow Pages is not the first place to look. Perfectionists probably postpone making a will until they find the right person for the job. For most of us, it's different — the choice is obvious. Family usually, but not always, comes first. A spouse of thirty years could be an automatic first choice. If your spouse has health problems and requires daily assistance, you'll look elsewhere. Your children collectively or individually are the second most common alternatives.

Finding an executor is not as difficult as you may think; executors don't need the skills of an investment advisor, an accountant, and a brain surgeon.

Your primary concern is to have a person who is honest and trustworthy. After that, your decisions will be influenced by your marital status, assets, and beneficiaries. One important rule is "usually, family comes first." Yes, there are professionals for hire if you need them. Perhaps you can't trust a spouse or your children to act on your behalf. Certain situations require you to go beyond your immediate family. We'll look at those situations in the next few chapters.

## Help Line

**Q:** What happens if an executor refuses to do the job?

**A:** A person with an interest in the estate can get a court order or citation (summons). This requires the named executor to appear or to file a probate application. If this is ignored, the executor loses all rights. The court can then appoint an alternative.

> **Bulletin**
>
> Having all your children act as your executors may be a good idea. But what if they don't get along? Consider whether it's necessary to specify how decisions will be made. They have to be unanimous unless you specify that a decision of the majority is binding.

Must an executor consent? A person named in a will can refuse to act. Avoid leaving your estate without someone in charge. Confirm his or her willingness to accept the job in advance. You just need to ask for permission or consent, and nothing further is necessary. If you don't ask, you can end up like Sara. She wanted to make a will but couldn't find an executor.

Sara was too embarrassed to ask friends. She thought she'd have to tell them about her personal finances. Finally, she gave her lawyer a name and signed her will. When Sara died, the law firm notified Tracey that she was Sara's executor. No one was more surprised than Tracey — who was her hairdresser! She'd never been asked if she wanted the job. Tracey would have told Sara she was too busy to handle it.

What happens if Tracey just says no, or died before Sara, or takes on the job but can't complete it due to an illness or incapacity? Always name an alternative person so you don't have a problem. You won't have to pay to have changes made later to your will. The court can confirm your substitute quickly if you named one. Otherwise, there are rules to follow. Your next of kin or beneficiaries must apply in court to administer your estate. Most provinces allow only those residing within the province to apply. Sara's foreign relatives would have to find someone in the province to act. It's easier and cheaper to have a second choice in your will when it's prepared.

## Can Executors Get Professional Help?

It's not often you'll find an executor who can do it all alone. He or she will need help from lawyers, accountants, and real estate agents. A law firm's support staff can do some of the administrative work. But executors can't delegate their decision-making powers to others. This is improper. They'll be liable for the conduct of those whom they hire.

Executors need to consult financial experts to prepare a plan for estate investments. They must manage the estate as if they were prudent investors. If they fail to get expert help, they can be held liable for any financial losses. Your estate pays for the cost of professional advice.

Surviving spouses may not want to be swamped with estate work. Professional or corporate executors may be an option to consider. However, spouses and children who will inherit your estate are often good choices for trustees. Who else would be better motivated to carry out their duties efficiently?

What if your kids can't balance their own cheque books? Would you let them manage your money when you're gone? Does a lack of financial experience prevent your children from acting as your executors? Perhaps, but it may depend on the size and complexity of your estate. Estates with long-term investment decisions, a business, and trusts may need professional assistance — at least as a backup. In such cases, consider a professional or a trust company as a co-executor.

Many people do not have family or simply don't get along with family members. Frankly, they don't want them involved in their affairs. In these situations, it makes sense to name a friend or trust company as the sole executor.

## Help Line

**Q:** Does each executor get a percentage of my estate as compensation?

**A:** No, the total executors' fees must be shared between them. Usually, if the work is divided equally, the fee will be as well. This is best dealt with between executors before they start working together.

## How Much Do Executors Get Paid?

Are you still not sure your spouse can handle your estate? One other factor may help you decide. Usually, family does the job for free. Would you rather pay someone to administer your estate? Before you say no, consider this question: would you take a different approach to your responsibilities if you were getting paid? Compensation helps to ensure the proper performance of duties.

Executors are entitled to compensation for their time and trouble by law. As a rule, this compensation represents a percentage of the estate, which can be sizable. Payment of a percentage is not guaranteed — it's only a guideline. Beneficiaries have the right to have the court approve fees. Time records and involvement in the estate's affairs are factors in setting remuneration.

Fees can be roughly five percent of the value of the estate's assets depending on local guidelines. The actual fees will vary with the circumstances of each case. Factors such as complications and the size and complexity of assets can raise or lower the compensation. If a non-family member might take a sizable fee, you may reconsider selecting family. Family members may protect and preserve assets at the lowest cost. After all, they may also be the only beneficiaries.

Be aware that family members can also charge a fee. Obviously, if they are the main beneficiaries, it doesn't make sense to carve out part of their inheritance as compensation that is taxable. If the executor is one of four siblings and spends significant time and energy because of "harassment" by the other siblings, then family members may claim a well-deserved fee.

If you hire a trust company, you'll usually also sign a compensation agreement with your will. Fees are negotiated based on the size and type of your estate assets and agreed upon in advance. But don't worry about having to pay your executor in advance, because that's not required.

## When Do Executors Start?

Boris made his son, Rob, his executor, but later he became worried. "Dad," Rob said, "you can't sell your house without my consent, because I am your executor." Boris didn't believe it and checked with a lawyer, who said his son was powerless. Until Boris dies, Rob has no authority to sell anything. Boris is still 100 percent in charge. He can also change his executor without his son's consent.

So relax. Your executor doesn't start to control your property until your will becomes effective. You can continue to deal with your own property as long as you are capable. Just naming a person in your will does not put you in any danger. Your executors have no power to handle your property until after your death. You can replace executors any time you change your will. Permission to remove them is not required. All that is required is that you remain legally capable of making the change to your will.

### What's the Difference between Attorney and Executor?

You give your attorney powers set out in a power of attorney document to act as your agent. This document, until revoked, permits attorneys to act while you are alive. Attorneys have no power to handle your affairs once you are dead. That's when the executor's job begins. An attorney may be entitled to act in case of your incapacity. Normally, you want an attorney to be authorized in those situations.

Executors, however, are involved only after your death. No conflict exists between attorneys since they operate under different documents and circumstances. You may want the same person to act in both capacities. Remember, executors have no power over or access to your money until your death.

Now that you know the essentials, in the next chapter I'll take you through the specific choices you can make for your executor.

## The Least You Need to Know

- Executors are named in your will to be in charge of your estate.
- Ensure your executor and backups consent to being named in your will.
- Executors secure, protect, probate, and distribute your estate.
- Executors are compensated by law based on approved legal guidelines.

# Chapter 14

# Extra! Extra! Obligations

In this chapter:

- Choose executors wisely.
- Understand legal obligations.
- Follow rules and checklists.
- Power up for success.

You learned in the last chapter how important it is to choose the right executor. It's one of the most important estate planning decisions you have to make. Step 4 often causes my clients the most concern, especially if they have no suitable relative to handle the job. Clients want to know who will sort through their personal effects, manage their investments, operate their businesses. They want to know about executors' duties, responsibilities, and powers.

You and your relationships, beneficiaries, and asset portfolios are constantly changing. So your choice of executor must be revisited regularly or as circumstances require. But let's first explain some rules about choosing an executor.

John and Marian's children lived in the United States. The parents didn't want to burden any of them. They were afraid that they might die together in an accident. Someone would have to close down their business and liquidate everything. John and Marian came into my office to discuss their options.

"We couldn't decide who should be in charge, so we haven't started a will," they said.

"Let's learn more about how to make this decision," I said. "But first let me tell you what happened to Jessica. Her story is an example of what can go wrong with a bad choice of executors. Here is what happened."

## Don't Pick the Wrong Person

Jessica had a drinking problem when she started acting as executor for her estranged husband's estate. She spent three years dodging questions from Tom's children about what had happened to all the estate money. The beneficiaries went to see a lawyer because they couldn't get any financial accounting from Jessica. What she had invested was doing poorly in risky ventures. What she had liquidated had been spent speculating. Jessica started gambling. She hoped to win back the money she had taken before she got caught.

Tom's children lost their inheritance. The family spent another small fortune in legal costs. They tried to clear up Jessica's fuzzy explanations and poor accounting. They wondered why their father had never changed his will after he separated from her. Does Jessica now file for bankruptcy? Does she go to jail?

It's bad news if this happens to you or your estate. You can choose the person who will console beneficiaries, control costs, and avoid conflicts. If you make a mistake, you can alienate friends, destroy families, and create civil wars.

### It's Been Said
••••••••••••••••••••••••••••••••••••••••••••••••••

An executor is "the person or corporation empowered to discharge duties of a fiduciary, appointed as such by a testator in his will."
— In re *Walkins' Estate*, 113 Vt. 126

## Executors Help Write Your Legacy

Dishonest executors can cause irreparable harm if estate assets are stolen or wasted. Don't make a mistake and let a mean-spirited executor create a painful legacy of loss. This chapter will show you how to choose executors and how to help them do a better job.

## Review Your Selection Regularly

Choose executors wisely. Courts can refuse to appoint anyone with a criminal background or bankrupt past. But it's difficult to remove them once they're appointed. Such a legal process is costly to both beneficiaries and your estate. Even worse, it may be too late. Criminal or incompetent handling of your estate can cause irreparable damage.

After thinking about all these risks, you may pick a family member. Sometimes family members are the only ones you can trust. Yet they can be just as incompetent or dishonest as nonfamily. Relatives may not be able to act without emotional involvement. Conflicts can cloud their judgment, preventing them from being objective toward other family members. Do you feel confused at this point? In Chapter 16, "Analyze Your Alternatives," I set out a worksheet to help you choose an executor, and I'll review this worksheet in a moment. You can use it to identify the skills you need.

> **Legal Lingo**
>
> *Fiduciary* is a person in a relationship who is bound to exercise rights and powers for the benefit of another. Fiduciaries must act without personal gain or advantage and are accountable for their actions.

## Executors' Legal Obligations

In the previous chapter, we reviewed the executor's job description. Now let's look at an executor's legal obligations.

**Obligation as fiduciaries:** executors have a fiduciary duty that requires them to act for the benefit of others. (Fiduciary duties are created by law.) You can add fiduciary duties by the terms of your will, for example, by allowing executors to use their discretion. You can let them divide your personal property and knick-knacks among relatives. They must act reasonably and not arbitrarily when using their discretion.

**Obligation to treat beneficiaries equally:** executors can't prefer one beneficiary over another or show bias. They can't give a larger share of your mom's diamonds to a sister and a smaller share to a brother unless instructed to do so by the will. They must appraise the diamonds and then divide them equally.

**Obligation not to profit from the estate:** executors can't buy estate assets without court approval or the consent of all beneficiaries. However, you can give them this specific right by including it in your will. Partners who are also executors and potential buyers for the business need this clause; otherwise, they can't profit from their relationship with the estate. Payment for executor services is permitted as legal compensation and not considered profit.

**Obligation to account for their transactions:** the court that appoints executors can review all their dealings. They must keep financial records and explain their conduct to the court and beneficiaries. Funeral arrangements, for example, cannot be outlandish. Executors must be reasonable if the will provides no guidance.

**Obligation to pay your creditors:** filing tax returns and paying all creditors are part of this duty. No distribution can take place until all bills are paid. That's why advertising for creditors is necessary. Executors incur personal liability if taxes and the estate creditors are not paid. This exposure extends only to the extent that estate assets exist to cover the debts. If you die without much, don't worry — your executor doesn't have to pay your bills with his or her own money.

**Obligation to defend your will:** if your will is contested, your executors must defend it in court. This means hiring a lawyer to protect the beneficiaries' interests. This obligation extends to defending the estate from creditors' or beneficiaries' claims as well.

**Obligation to act as a prudent investor:** your executor must develop an investment plan for estate assets. This involves obtaining professional advice and making investments authorized by law or under the terms of the will.

## Help Line

**Q:** Are you sure I can't leave money to my monkey?

**A:** Pets can't inherit. You can, however, give money to an executor or others willing to carry out your intentions. However, be aware that these types of gifts are hard to enforce.

## Rules for Selecting an Executor

You need to look at five criteria to assess the qualifications for your executor. Consider your needs under these headings:

- Special Duties
- Estate Assets
- Distribution Plans
- Available Choices
- Interest Conflicts

Make your decision based on all these factors. Remember, the relative weight that you give to each factor is a personal decision.

### 1. Special Duties

You may have eccentric or mundane duties you wish your executor to fulfil. They can include

- finding a home for your pets;
- getting a museum to accept memorabilia or collections;
- locating lost relatives;
- delivering personal property to relatives abroad;
- operating a business until children can take over; and
- keeping children from each other's throat.

### 2. Estate Assets

You probably have no special requirements if you own only a car. But the location of your assets may make a difference to whom you select as executor. Can you expect your brother in Newfoundland to sell your dental practice in British Columbia? An executor in such circumstances should live close at hand. Your choice of local executors makes it more likely that they will accept and complete the job. A person from another province may also need to post a bond with the estate court.

Selling family heirlooms and art may require your executor to have special expertise. Running a business can be challenging for those without such skills. On the other hand, disposing of your investment portfolio may just be routine.

## Help Line

**Q:** Do I need three different people to be a guardian for my children, an executor for my estate, and a trustee for my children's trust?

**A:** No. You can have one person do everything or give each job to a separate individual.

## 3. Distribution Plans

This issue isn't serious if you simply need a bank account divided. But most of us will have more than that. Ask yourself if all your assets will be distributed immediately or held in a trust under the will. Outright gifts to surviving spouses may not require special skills. Managing trust accounts over several years, however, will require extra care. Impartial assistance may help to keep the peace over the long haul.

You may wish to consider a trust company for developmentally challenged children who require long-term trusts. Be cautious, though, about developing an overly complex estate plan. Is it really in your family's interests that long-term trusts are set up? Make sure that the advantages of the trusts are clearly identified. Get a second opinion from an estate lawyer if you have any doubts.

Often clients tell me that their advisors told them to include long-term trusts in their wills. They do not understand the advantages and disadvantages. Are you in that boat? This book will help you understand options to discuss with your lawyer.

> **Bulletin**
>
> Special-assignment executors can fill an estate role. You can assign a partner, a business's lawyer, or an accountant to operate a business until it's sold. Your spouse can then take over estate administration as the sole executor. Arrange this with your lawyer when you draw up your will.

## 4. Available Choices

If you have no spouse, relatives, or trustworthy children, whom can you consider? Consider friends, neighbours, a professional advisor without a conflict of interest, a charity, or a trust company. If you have foreign assets, you may want a foreign-resident trustee appointed in a separate will in that jurisdiction. He or she will be able to deal easily with any real estate interests.

## 5. Interest Conflicts

Conflicts of interest in a family will cause problems. Choosing your son, Mark, to administer his stepsister Darlene's trust fund can create tension. The potential for animosity can arise if you give Mark discretion over her spending. If he gets whatever is left over in that trust, he may try to reduce her spending. Darlene may be forced to have the courts intervene. They may censure or remove Mark as the trustee, and of course your estate could bear those costs.

Brokers, investment advisors, and business partners may be disqualified as executors because of their conflicts.

> **Legal Lingo**
>
> *Guardians* are not executors, but executors can be guardians. Executors have the larger responsibilities to handle your entire estate for all beneficiaries. Guardians handle the needs of those without full legal capacity, such as your minor children.

# A Worksheet to Help Choose

Assess the complexity of your estate plan before you select an executor. The tasks you require of this person will influence your decision. Here are some additional factors you may wish to review.

My executors will need to take care of the following:

|  | Required | Not Required |
|---|---|---|
| **1. Special Duties** | | |
| Sell a home | ❏ | ❏ |
| Deal with collections | ❏ | ❏ |
| Locate missing relatives | ❏ | ❏ |
| Operate or sell a business | ❏ | ❏ |
| **2. Estate Assets** | | |
| Investment portfolio – sell or manage | ❏ | ❏ |
| Contents of home – distribute | ❏ | ❏ |
| Second property – sell or rent | ❏ | ❏ |
| Foreign accounts, pets, collections | ❏ | ❏ |
| **3. Distribution Plans** | | |
| Immediate outright distribution | ❏ | ❏ |
| Special trust for children or spouse | ❏ | ❏ |
| Collect rent or mortgage payments | ❏ | ❏ |
| Deal with guardians | ❏ | ❏ |
| **4. Available Choices** | | |
| Spouse – second or common-law | ❏ | ❏ |
| Children – underage or adult | ❏ | ❏ |
| Relatives in province | ❏ | ❏ |
| Professional or trust company | ❏ | ❏ |
| **5. Interest Conflicts** | | |
| Backup beneficiary of trust | ❏ | ❏ |
| Your partner in the business | ❏ | ❏ |
| Children who don't get along | ❏ | ❏ |
| Second-marriage rivalries | ❏ | ❏ |

## Customize Your List

This list is not exhaustive, but you may find it helpful in highlighting some of your needs. Having an apartment, a house, or rental income properties can make a difference to you. Make your own custom requirements list. Based on your wish list, inventory of assets, investments, and beneficiaries' needs, set out the five most important things you require of your executor.

1. _____

2. _____

3. _____

4. _____

5. _____

You may wish to type up a letter detailing any special instructions for your executor. But be careful you don't inadvertently amend or contradict your will. Executors can read your notes when the time comes, so leave them with your will. Remember, though, your notes are not legally binding on your estate.

# Help Your Executor Succeed

So you've done a preliminary review. You've narrowed your choice of executor down to your brother or a trust company. Consider improving the odds your brother won't be scared away from the job. Tell him he won't be sued by your children for mismanaging their investment portfolio. Well, not exactly, but you can include comfort clauses in your will. This can reassure him that his exposure to liability is not open-ended if he acts prudently.

Here are some samples of protective clauses you can include in your will. Review your will with your lawyer to make sure you have included some or all of these powers.

**Power to settle claims:** what if your spouse is dissatisfied with your bequests and sues your estate? Will the lawsuit take years to finish? Empower your executors to settle claims without going to court or through mediation. Let executors fix values for assets by appraisal without fear that a beneficiary will question them.

**Power to invest:** your province may have an approved list in which estate funds can be invested. Expand the range of investments for your estate funds. Eliminate personal liability for any prudent investment decisions. This won't cover a breach of trust or dishonesty, only losses reasonably incurred. Make it clear that professional advice is an estate expense and not paid from the executor's compensation.

**Power to postpone a sale of assets:** your executor may need to delay the sale of assets, real estate, or a stock portfolio, so allow this option as part of his or her discretion to act reasonably.

**Power to take compensation:** executors can be shy about asking for payment. You may wish to give them more than what they're entitled to. Don't make them hesitant to ask for a fee from a belligerent family. Make it clear you want them to accept payment and when it can be paid.

**Power to use discretion:** you can't anticipate everything that will happen after you're gone. Rely on your executor to make the right choices and decisions for the estate. Let him or her decide whether to sell the stocks or hold them till the market turns around. If a children's trust is created, the executor needs discretion on when the children can encroach on capital. Can they lend trust money to family members? Let the executor decide how and when this happens. It helps to give them some guidance, for example, to permit tax elections or postmortem tax planning.

**Power to operate a business:** would you want to be responsible for any losses or drops in profit from a business? If you are the only person involved, or a key shareholder, your death will make a difference. You don't want a rush liquidation but a managed transfer to new buyers. Your executor should be authorized to run the business, to borrow money, or to use estate funds without fear of personal liability. If a corporation is involved, allow for corporate reorganizations and shareholders' agreements or buy/sell agreements to be honoured.

**Power for specific miscellaneous purposes:** your executors will thank you if they don't have to go to court, which may happen if you haven't empowered them.

### Let's Recap

You've learned that executors are fiduciaries with extra obligations imposed by law. Your particular estate needs may require specialized skills. You'll want to visualize the services you'll need performed. Give your executor powers in your will to handle your assets and beneficiaries.

I'll take you for a closer look at executors who handle testamentary trusts. These trusts require special services from executors, which you'll see in the next chapter.

### The Least You Need to Know

- Executors are fiduciaries with legal obligations.
- Executors can't be bankrupt or criminals or have a conflict of interest.
- Review your executor choices regularly to reflect your estate plan.
- Give executors special powers in your will to protect them.

# Chapter 15

# Hold Something Back

In this chapter:

- Use executors or trustees or both?
- Know these concepts for trust's sake.
- Protect loved ones with trusts.
- Understand long-term management options.

Are you interested in managing all or part of your estate from the grave? Do you want to control your money so that your beneficiaries don't blow it all? The answer may be to use a testamentary trust created by your will. Such trusts take effect on your death to control estate assets placed "in trust."

You can ask your executor to hold assets in trust under your will, or you can have a separate person act as a trustee. Whoever becomes the trustee keeps "the keys," so to speak, to control assets held in trust. Your beneficiaries get the benefit. These different roles are analyzed in this chapter to help you understand how you can use testamentary trusts.

## So What's the Difference?

Let's look at the difference between executors and trustees. Although most wills give the same people both titles, they have different jobs and legal descriptions. Executors administer your entire estate as your legal representatives. Trustees may manage only a portion of the estate assets, those placed in trust. Your estate includes all your assets: your home, stock portfolio, life insurance, and so on. Perhaps you want to use the life insurance proceeds for your children's education. These proceeds could be held separately in trust. The person who does this is your trustee, who may or may not be your executor.

When you need long-term trusts, the age of your executor may become a factor. You may want a younger trustee to act for you. When you select an executor, ask yourself, "Do I require any trusts in my will? And how long will a trustee be needed?" These are questions that influence your choice of executors and trustees.

---

**Legal Lingo**

*Testamentary* documents or appointments are effective only after the death of the person making them. Testamentary means it must be revocable. The maker of the testamentary document keeps control over the property until death.

---

You can refresh your memory of trusts as covered in Chapter 6. Property is given to someone you have confidence in as a trustee. You specify the purpose of the trust — for example, your children's care until the age of majority. Remember, living trusts are created while you are alive outside your will to control trust property. I'm going to focus now on testamentary trusts, which control inheritances for the benefit of beneficiaries named in your will.

## Concepts You Need to Know

A trust is really a relationship recognized by law. Through a testamentary trust, you can arrange for assets to be earmarked by a will and controlled by trustees. Trustees hold these assets as trust property. For example, the life insurance proceeds we spoke of earlier might be the trust property. The funds would be held for the benefit of minor children as trust beneficiaries.

Trustees administer assets for the beneficiaries' use. If your executors are not appointed trustees, you need separate individuals to handle the trust. They are referred to simply as trustees. This is short for trustees of the testamentary trusts. If you look at my sample will in Chapter 10, you'll notice a simple trust clause that deals with a minor's inheritance. I also appoint the executor as trustee.

Canadian law clearly draws a distinction between the roles of executor and trustee. Executors complete their duties once assets are delivered to beneficiaries. Testamentary trustees don't handle executors' duties such as selling assets and paying bills. They are responsible only for trust assets placed under their control by a will.

Executors have broad powers to liquidate your estate assets. When assets such as a family business are transferred to trustees, they become the managers of that trust. They act according to any discretionary or administrative powers established by the trust or by law. They often have discretion about how payments are made from the trust funds to beneficiaries.

### Help Line

**Q:** Do I need to select separate persons to be executor, trustee, and guardian under my will?

**A:** Everyone needs an executor or estate trustee. If your will creates a trust, you'll also need a trustee, who can be your executor or someone different. Guardians usually manage property for minors.

## For Trust's Sake

Paul has two brothers: Frank, who is alive, and David, who has died. Paul's will appoints brother Frank as executor and creates a trust for brother David's two children. When Paul dies, Frank as executor will divide the estate and transfer David's children's inheritance to Jennifer, their mother. She was named in the will as their trustee to manage the trust funds for their education until they are twenty-five. After that, she is to use the trust funds to help the children buy homes.

David's children's trust received $500,000 from Frank, the estate executor. Jennifer, the trustee, will invest the money according to the terms of the trust. Interest earned on the trust funds is considered trust income and must be distributed or held under the terms of the trust. The trust capital is the $500,000 held in trust.

Paul's testamentary trust consists of

- the trust property — $500,000;
- a trustee — Jennifer; and
- the trust beneficiaries — David's two children.

The beneficiaries of a trust are named in the trust — in this case David's children. Jennifer will distribute capital and income earned to meet the trust's purposes. The trust says the children have a life interest in it. When one of the children dies, his or her share goes to the other beneficiary. This person is called the remainderman, who receives the remainder of the deceased person's interest in the trust.

## Problems Taxing Will Trusts

A testamentary trust is taxed like an individual, meaning at an individual's graduated tax rate. This rate varies depending on the amount of income earned. If the trust beneficiaries will not rely solely on the trust for their support, then it can be an income-splitting device. In some cases, income can be taxed in the trust at lower rates than what the beneficiary pays.

Donald asked his lawyer, "Can I hold my children's inheritance in trust until they become financially responsible?"

"How long will that be?" the lawyer asked. "Don't think you can place your assets in trust for an eternity."

"Well," Donald replied. "The twins are both twenty-something now. How about another thirty years or so?"

"There are big tax problems, though," the lawyer explained. "Every twenty-one years a trust is deemed to dispose of all its property. The government can then collect income tax on all accumulated capital gains. Practically speaking, I don't recommend you hold assets beyond that twenty-one-year period."

## What Are Your Options?

Testamentary gifts can be outright, with conditions, or held in trust. What's the difference? Outright gifts are made in one lump sum. For example, I can give Joanne $1,000. She can use the money once she receives it. A gift in trust does not allow the gift beneficiaries to deal directly with the trust property; only the trustee controls the gift through the terms of the will trust. For example, my executor is directed to deliver $10,000 to Scott's mother, who will hold this amount in trust for Scott's education.

You may not want to make outright gifts if beneficiaries are incapacitated or financially irresponsible. In such cases, your immediate gift of a large sum of money could be disastrous. A trust gift allows the trustee to assist the beneficiary in spending the money wisely and gradually.

In many provinces, a Henson trust is recognized as a "discretionary trust." This is one way of gifting to those beneficiaries who receive some form of social assistance. You can create this trust as a way to legitimately supplement the needs of beneficiaries who are disabled or unemployed. Henson trusts must meet the capital and income ceilings imposed by provincially prescribed limits. For this reason, you need expert help in drafting these trusts, as these rules can and do change.

Decide, with the help of your financial advisors, if a trust can achieve your estate planning goals. These are some of the different gifts that can be made:

- I give Scott $100,000 (outright gift).
- I give Scott $100,000 if he survives me (conditional gift).
- I give my trustees $100,000 for Scott's benefit (gift in trust).

In the third example, your trustees hold the property. Scott doesn't get the gift outright but does benefit from the money as your will instructs. Trustees invest the money for him. These ongoing trust responsibilities must be considered when you look for an executor as trustee.

## Does Everyone Need a Trust?

As you've learned, trusts are created for different purposes. Principally, they are used to separate the beneficiaries from the property they inherit. In this way, your trustees can protect the beneficiaries and manage the trust property. You must use testamentary trusts when you have infant children. If anyone inheriting under your will is a minor, you'll need a trust clause.

Minors can't hold property given to them by a will if they are underage. The hardship begins when their inheritance must be paid into court and held until they reach majority. Make sure you have trustees in place to manage their property "in trust" until the children can receive it. It's not enough just to create a trust; you must specify details for the trust. You need to give some directions to operate it. If you don't, it may fail. A court would be required to make a decision on this issue.

## Trusts Save Taxes by Splitting Income

Income-splitting is another benefit of a testamentary trust because of the graduated income tax rates. Here's an example. Your spouse earns $60,000 a year from her employment. You have a $1 million insurance policy. Consider to whom do you make the proceeds payable on your death? You can hold the policy benefits under a spousal trust created by your will. You can also leave the proceeds to a spouse as an outright gift. What's the difference?

Let's say the life insurance proceeds held in trust earn $60,000 annually in income. The trust's tax rate is much lower on the $60,000 than your spouse's tax rate on her employment and investment income of $120,000. The insurance trust income can be taxed in the trust even though these amounts are paid to the spouse. When this tax saving is spread over ten years, it can be substantial.

## How Trusts Protect

Since trustees control the trust property, trusts are a good idea if the assets are complex; you can avoid the risk of having inexperienced persons handling them. Select a person in whom you have confidence. Assuming you operate a business, ask your executors to operate the business until it is sold. Profits from the sale of the business can then be placed in trust so that benefits can continue to flow to your family without allowing them to run the business.

## Help Line

**Q:** What's the difference between a life interest and a remainder interest in a trust?

**A:** A life interest is given to a person who benefits from the trust during his or her lifetime. After the death of this person, the balance of the trust capital goes to the remaindermen.

Here's another example for you if you need a spendthrift trust. We all know a spendthrift is one who spends money carelessly. Gabor, a widower, has a son, Ivan, whom he wants to help financially. Ivan, however, gambles and has no steady employment. Gabor is not prepared to give Ivan his inheritance as an outright gift. The father can't decide how to provide for his son. Gabor wants to help Ivan buy a home but only if he settles down. Ivan has children, and Gabor does want to leave his grandchildren something as well. Gabor can't figure out the details. He selects Sophia, his daughter, to handle a trust fund for Ivan.

If Ivan can't control money, perhaps his sister can do it for him. Sophia will be in a better position to assess Ivan's needs when Gabor is no longer around. Gabor has selected the person he has confidence in to be his trustee. Sophia can help Ivan purchase a home with the trust. If he already has a home by that time, then the money will be used for the grandchildren's education.

Here is a simple outline of Gabor's wishes summarized for his lawyer to be incorporated into a spendthrift trust in his will. The drafting of these terms is complex. Don't expect to use this as a clause in a will. It's simply a summary, not an example.

> I want my executors to transfer one-half of all my estate to my daughter Sophia in trust. She shall be my trustee to hold this trust property for Ivan on these terms: the purpose of this trust is to help my son Ivan purchase a home. My trustee can, in her absolute discretion, pay out trust income and capital for my son Ivan's benefit.
>
> Should Ivan not require a home, these funds shall be used to educate Ivan's children. If Ivan has no children when he dies, I wish Sophia to pay the remainder of the trust funds to a charity that I have specified in my will. If Sophia dies before Ivan, the ABC trust company shall replace her as trustee.

## Discretionary Powers, Encroachments, and Payouts

Ivan can get money from the trust when he needs it as long as Sophia agrees. You can give trustees discretion but also clear directions.

Here's a different example of what Chantal did with her net estate of $350,000, which she left in trust. The trustees invested it, and annually $14,000 is left after expenses to distribute as income for her brother as a trust beneficiary.

However, Chantal's brother cannot manage on this amount and his own earnings. He asks the trustees for more money. They can't give him more unless the trust allows them to touch its capital. This is called an encroachment. Trust capital can be used if specifically allowed by the trust terms. Trustees can then use trust capital for the beneficiary's benefit.

This is referred to as a discretion to encroach on capital. You can state under what circumstances this is to be permitted. Capital or unspent income can also be paid out by your trustees. This payout can be done at predetermined intervals, annually, or at their discretion. Trustees may want to be able to wind up the trust by distributing whatever capital is left.

You can place recreational or vacation property into a testamentary trust as well. Your will can specify that property is held in trust for the enjoyment of your children or spouse. When a summer home is no longer used, the trustees can sell it. Then, after taxes and expenses are paid, the proceeds are divided among beneficiaries named in your trust. This is a method I look more closely at as a gifting strategy in Chapter 17, "Guidelines for Gifting."

## Help Line

**Q:** Can I hold money indefinitely under a trust?

**A:** Each province has rules that prevent property from being held forever. These laws control income and vesting of property. You must also remember the income tax rules that declare a deemed disposition of trust assets every twenty-one years.

## Help Line

**Q:** How can I take care of my beneficiaries' needs and give to charity?

**A:** You can create a trust to protect your beneficiaries while they are alive. If they die or no longer need the money, the trust remainder can be given to charity.

Do you have minor children and want to control their inheritance? Place their share of your estate in a trust. Authorize capital distribution at a predetermined age. The trust could pay out twenty-five percent of its capital at the age of eighteen. Another share, say fifty percent, can be paid out at twenty-one, with the balance at twenty-five. These payouts are appropriate where the amount of the trust assets warrants the expense of maintaining a trust. Remember, filing annual income tax returns, trustee fees, and accounting and legal costs can add up.

## Benefits to Consider

Trusts can also be used for a variety of purposes:

- to protect your infirm or incapacitated spouse or child;
- to handle investments for inexperienced investors;
- to channel benefits to the developmentally challenged;
- to provide professional and experienced management of assets;
- to sprinkle funds among a group such as grandchildren;
- to protect assets from spendthrifts, creditors, or other spouses;
- to maintain government services or benefits; and
- to benefit a charity as a beneficiary of the remainder.

In the above cases, a trust can be considered as an alternative to an outright gift of property. The beneficiary can obtain the benefit but not actual title to the property. What if your spouse will be pressured to give money to a financially irresponsible child? You can control access to the trust capital or principal with independent trustees who work with your spouse.

Trusts can secure your property from possible creditors or a former spouse. You can also protect property from a beneficiary unable to handle money. We'll learn more about how trusts can be used to bless your beneficiaries in Chapters 19, "Children's Needs," and 20, "Spouses: Good, Bad, and Divorced."

> **Bulletin**
>
> Decisions to create a trust can't be based on costs alone. Your first concern should be the protection of the beneficiary on a long-term basis.

## Second Marriages and Life Estates

Spouses in second marriages with substantial assets have different worries. You may not want to make an outright gift to a surviving partner. Can you cut out a spouse in this way? Remember that your obligations under marital property and support laws must first be honoured. You may even need to obtain a marriage contract to satisfy these spousal rights. You can then freely create a trust to benefit a secondary list of beneficiaries.

Marilyn has two children from her first marriage and a second husband, Luke. She is the sole owner of their home. Marilyn wants her children to be provided for, and Luke says he will do this if she is no longer alive. Marilyn, however, wants to set up a trust, just in case. Her home is a tax-free asset, which she wants to keep for the children.

Marilyn doesn't want Luke to suffer, so she'll give him a life interest in the home. Luke can use the residence as long as he's alive. After he dies, the home will be sold, and the proceeds will be divided between Marilyn's two children.

Marilyn's will must deal with contingencies that can arise before Luke's death. What will her trustee do about repairs, rental income, and renovations? If Marilyn doesn't want the trustees to be forced to sell the home, she may have to set aside money to cover these costs. If the property is sold at Luke's request, can her trustees purchase a replacement home for him with the proceeds? The trust must also specify what happens to the surplus funds if Luke wants to move to a smaller home.

Trust drafting must consider any unexpected events that can occur. A lawyer experienced in trusts can identify problems and suggest ways of dealing with them. Estate plans can be upset by an unanticipated event such as Luke's remarriage, incapacity, or filing an election to claim his spousal share in Marilyn's family property. The idea is to allow the trust asset to be used and then sold when certain events occur. The selling could be triggered by the death of a partner or the coming of age of the youngest child.

## Drawbacks to Consider

One problem with trusts is the cost to administer them. These costs include trustees' fees, setup charges, and annual fees to maintain the trust.

Trustees can generally charge a fee when capital is distributed or received. In practical terms, the trustees need to prepare annual financial statements and income tax returns. They'll consult with tax advisors and estate lawyers and vice versa. Corporate trustees charge an annual fee for their services. The income of the trust or estate may not be sufficient to cover all expenses, meaning that trust capital may need to be used.

In this way, trust capital can be depleted in a few short years, which defeats your original intention. That's not to say that a trust fund for adult children will not work. You simply must have sufficient money held as trust capital to warrant considering it. The beneficiaries should not need the capital held in trust, or they will collapse the trust fund.

> **Bulletin**
>
> Income earned by a testamentary trust must be reported in an income tax return. The trustee must file a T3 return and pay any tax. Even if tax is not payable, a T3 return must be filed to avoid penalties.

Another drawback with trusts is that they require specialized tax or legal advice. Trusts must cover many contingencies. If the wording fails to deal with changes in circumstances, problems arise, and trustees may be compelled to visit a judge to get answers. They may need help to interpret their trust authority because they are limited by the trust terms. Trust structures will also incur higher professional fees and add costly degrees of complexity to your estate administration.

If the trust requires interpretation, each party may get a lawyer. A court will be asked for an opinion to tell the parties who is right and who is to pay the legal costs. These costs may be paid from the trust fund even if a beneficiary was wrong.

## Your Long-Term Management Options

When trustees will be involved on a long-term basis, you have to consider their motivation. Will they be able to continue performing their tasks? This is why family members are usually the first choice for being trustees. However, without relatives, you'll have to consider alternatives, which usually place you in the hands of a corporate trustee.

A trust company as a sole, alternative, or co-trustee provides added benefits. Corporate trustees are experienced and routinely manage trust portfolios. They can serve as both executors and trustees to meet all your needs.

Trust companies must, like all trustees, consent to their appointment. Before consenting, they'll discuss your particular needs and enter into a fee agreement. Paying a fee to an independent trustee may be a small price for the protection of your beneficiaries. These fees, based on the nature and size of your estate assets, will be agreed upon in advance with a trust company. They are payable only after your death.

Your spouse may wish to avoid constant pressure or bickering from spendthrift beneficiaries. Do everyone a favour by placing control of the assets in the hands of a third party. Objectivity and experience in trust law obligations are a trust company's long suit.

## Conflicts of Interest

Do you prefer to have a relative's personal touch to deal with a difficult beneficiary? Make sure there's no conflict created between trustees and beneficiaries by the terms of your trust. Conflicts can arise if a trustee is also a beneficiary of the trust. You can't expect neutrality in such situations. Beneficiaries can apply in court to have the trustee removed for prejudice. The mere opportunity for a conflict to exist should motivate you to look elsewhere.

Executors and trustees must be objective to avoid family conflicts. Use a corporate trustee to avoid such conflicts.

Special problems come up for spouses who are the sole executor and trustee under a spousal trust. Their discretion to encroach can be abused.

They can remove all of the capital from the trust for their own use, which may not have been your intention. Your intention to benefit secondary residual beneficiaries under the trust would be defeated. In such a case, more than one trustee must handle the trust with your spouse. This can cause friction. A spouse may file an election to claim an outright share to avoid the trust restrictions.

## Let's Review

Testamentary trusts can be used to achieve the specific estate planning goals. But problems can arise if you don't have the right trustees. Trustees, unlike your executors, may have long-term obligations. These are factors to keep in mind when choosing your executors.

In the next chapter, I'll tell you a story that describes the terrible things that can go wrong with your executor. And, most importantly, I'll give you a checklist to compare all your executor options.

### The Least You Need to Know

- Trustees who manage trusts need not be the same persons as executors.
- You create testamentary trusts by your will to hold assets for trust beneficiaries.
- Trust beneficiaries can be entitled to benefit from trust income and/or capital.
- Trusts can funnel benefits to infirm, challenged, or spendthrift beneficiaries.

# Chapter 16

# Analyze Your
# Alternatives

In this chapter:

- Avoid common horrors.
- Use worksheets for review.
- Follow tips and avoid traps.
- Understand trust company benefits.

You may be wondering why I'm spending so much time on executors and trustees. The selection of these people is critical. Sometimes your choice of an executor is so obvious it's a no-brainer. It's so clear that you forget to consider contingencies. But ask yourself, "What if my executor dies before me in the same accident?" Your first choice could be gone. This chapter will review solutions to this and other problems.

I'll explain the advantages of the typical executor choices. Remember that you must review your choice of executor regularly; otherwise, you could end up like Emily's father, who left his daughter with a nightmare.

### How Family Feuds Start

Emily's father had trouble coping after his wife, Sharon, died. He hadn't reviewed his choice of executors in his twenty-year-old will. He'd appointed his two children, George and Emily, as co-executors, but they didn't get along. He thought they would work things out. But George had emotional problems, which had cost him his job and his marriage. These losses should have been a warning, but Dad didn't remove him as a co-executor.

> **Bulletin**
>
> Executors can't assign their decision-making responsibilities by giving a person a power of attorney. As fiduciaries, they can't transfer their legal obligations. Administrative matters may be delegated, but that's it. If an executor becomes incapacitated, he or she must be replaced.

Heartbroken, Dad refused to talk about his wife's estate. No one filed her tax return. The stockbroker couldn't get anyone to convert her stock options. No one claimed her life insurance benefits. Dad became senile. He should have signed a power of attorney for property; his attorney could have handled some of the paperwork.

Dad became more depressed, and he didn't heed his daughter's warning. Emily told him to remove her brother as a co-executor. She hardly spoke to George and wouldn't be able to work with him.

When Dad died, Emily's nightmare started. George wouldn't go to the funeral home when his sister was there. They had to schedule visits so they wouldn't see each other. It took them three months to agree to use the same estate lawyer. Finally, they compromised so they could apply for probate.

George wrote to the law firm with his instructions. The law firm told him it had to take instructions from both executors. George's letters were passed on to his sister by the lawyer for approval. Emily just cringed whenever she got an envelope in the mail from her brother. She started returning the letters unopened. She was too upset to read them.

## Help Line

**Q:** What records should an executor keep?

**A:** Executors have their accounts (financial records) approved by the estate beneficiaries. If there's a dispute, executors "pass their accounts" to get court approval. Records are kept of revenue and capital receipts, which are recorded separately from expenses and disbursements.

## Could It Get Worse?

Almost eight months after Dad's death, his home was finally listed for sale. Emily had made three appointments to meet her brother at the house. He never showed up to divide the contents. He complained about her attempt to paint the house. She wanted to prepare it for sale to get a better price. George just refused to cooperate.

Emily drove by her father's empty house almost every day to check on it. She was afraid it would be vandalized. She threatened to sell it, contents and all. She gave George an ultimatum to take out his share of the contents. He never replied to her.

Emily wanted a few of her mother's things, such as the piano. She had been the only one in the family to play it. She cherished the sewing machine her mom had taught her to sew on. But the lawyer told her that she could not purchase items from the estate. The will didn't give her that authority; George would have to agree, but he didn't.

Emily had the contents appraised before she sold them all to a dealer. She didn't bother getting her brother's permission. Her children bought the piano and sewing machine for her from the dealer.

Emily hated to think of how much money was being wasted on an empty house. She had cleared the house, and it was ready for sale.

## The Horrors Continued

Emily's problems weren't over, though. George now started asking the lawyer for the china and antique pieces he wanted. He also asked Emily's son to pay the estate six months of back rent for living in Dad's home. Emily's son, a college student, had moved into the house to help his grandfather. The youth had taken him to doctors' appointments and done chores. But he'd never paid rent, and George refused to budge. He wanted his share of the rent, which he figured was $1,200.

George refused to sign papers to list the house until the rent was paid. Emily took money out of her pocket rather than keep fighting with her brother.

It took more than three years to finalize Dad's estate. Before it was over, Emily had to borrow money from the bank. She had promised to help her children get married and buy homes. She didn't want to take out the loan, but her brother refused to cooperate. He didn't want to agree to an interim payout from the estate. Emily lost the chance to invest her share of the estate for over two years. She would have done well had she just had her money.

## Getting Rid of a Bad Apple

Emily was under terrible stress, losing sleep and weight dealing with George. Her brother, she thought, was being totally unreasonable. If only she could get him removed as a co-executor. She consulted a lawyer. The procedure would be complicated, she was told. George would hire a lawyer to oppose her in court. Likely, he'd want an independent trustee to replace Emily because of his concerns. He was complaining about the china he never got. Emily was upset because she did all the estate work and wanted compensation.

George claimed Emily's refusal to reply to his letters showed a bias against him. The estate lawyer warned Emily she would have to hire her own lawyer. The lawyer suggested a neutral party such as a trust company to take over the job. George and Emily would still have problems. They would have to get permission from the court to resign. This would mean their accounts would have to be approved by a judge.

George would agree to resign if Emily would give him the piano. That's as far as she got. The thought of so many lawyers involved in a court fight was too much for Emily to bear. On top of it all, a new executor would charge compensation and hire a new independent law firm. It drove her wild with rage. "My parents worked all their lives. They never intended their money would be spent on legal battles," she sobbed.

Emily dropped her compensation claim. She capitulated. Her brother got everything he'd asked for. And Emily never spoke to him again.

> **Legal Lingo**
> _____
>
> *Even-hand rules* require your estate's legal representative to manage the assets in a manner fair to all beneficiaries. An encroachment of all the capital for a life tenant may not be justifiable — especially to the remainderman, who would receive nothing. That's why beneficiaries are treated evenly.

## Are There Grounds to Do It?

It's not that it's impossible to remove a bad executor; it's just plain difficult and expensive. You may need a court hearing and even a trial. A judge must have good reasons to remove an executor for cause. Being convicted of a crime, failing to produce records, or causing damage to assets are obvious cases for a court to intervene in some way.

I can't give you definite rules to remove an estate trustee. A lot will depend on the details and proof of allegations in a court case. But assuming it's going to be a battle, you'll have to show things such as

- incapacity to perform duties because of illness, old age, or another reason;
- breach of trust, placing assets in jeopardy, or failing to act;
- personal misconduct that impairs the performance of duties; and
- unfair treatment of beneficiaries with competing interests.

## It's Going to Cost

What you may consider as unsuitable qualities or misconduct may not pass the court's test for removal. If you're successful, you'll want your legal fees to be paid by the estate. If you are unsuccessful, you may have to pay everyone's legal bill personally. Courts can pay the removed executors' legal costs unless their conduct was reprehensible. In many cases, your loved ones will be stuck, like Emily, with whatever you leave them. That's why it's so important to review your decisions regularly.

### It's Been Said
••••••••••••••••••••••••••••••••••••••••••••••••

To remove an executor, "one must show the acts or omissions [to] be such as to endanger the trust property or to show a want of honesty, or want of proper capacity to execute the duties, or a want of reasonable fidelity."
– Lord Blackburn, quoting *Story's Equity Jurisprudence* in *Letterstedt* v. *Broers*, 1884

How much of Emily's grief could have been avoided? Perhaps, just by updating his choices of executors, Emily's father's legacy would have been much different. It's your responsibility. Keep your choice of executors up to date.

Here's where you can use my worksheet to compare executor qualifications.

**It's Been Said**

......................................................

"In case of positive misconduct, courts of equity have no difficulty in interposing to remove trustees who have abused their trust; it is not indeed every mistake or neglect of duty, or inaccuracy of conduct of trustees, which will induce courts of equity to adopt such a course."

— Lord Blackburn, quoting *Story's Equity Jurisprudence* in *Letterstedt* v. *Broers*, 1884

## Executor Selection: A Worksheet

Let's look at the factors you should consider when choosing your executors. Here's how you assess all the different items and make your final decision.

You named your cousin Charlie as your executor, but he has just moved to the United States. He left behind his failed business and marriage. He keeps borrowing money from you and shows little desire to start repaying it. Charlie may not be your best choice. And your parents are too old to handle the job.

Let's look at a specific list you can use to finalize, review, and revise the alternatives for your executor.

| Possible Executors: | Spouse | Child | Relative | Professional | Trust Company | Combinations |
|---|---|---|---|---|---|---|
| capable | ☐ | ☐ | ☐ | ☐ | ☐ | ☐ |
| organized | ☐ | ☐ | ☐ | ☐ | ☐ | ☐ |
| responsible | ☐ | ☐ | ☐ | ☐ | ☐ | ☐ |
| honest, sympathetic, trustworthy | ☐ | ☐ | ☐ | ☐ | ☐ | ☐ |
| experience with assets | ☐ | ☐ | ☐ | ☐ | ☐ | ☐ |
| will want or need a fee | ☐ | ☐ | ☐ | ☐ | ☐ | ☐ |
| close by and available | ☐ | ☐ | ☐ | ☐ | ☐ | ☐ |
| no conflicts of interest, impartial | ☐ | ☐ | ☐ | ☐ | ☐ | ☐ |
| long-term trust issues | ☐ | ☐ | ☐ | ☐ | ☐ | ☐ |
| experience in estate work | ☐ | ☐ | ☐ | ☐ | ☐ | ☐ |
| relationships with family | ☐ | ☐ | ☐ | ☐ | ☐ | ☐ |

Now let's look at each of your possible executors in turn. I'll provide some additional comments as well.

### Family First

Should you always choose a family member first? Your family may be back home in another province or country. Or you may not have family that can handle the job. Frankly, some of your family should never handle your money, or your beneficiaries may never get to see it. Let's look at family members more closely.

### Pick Spouses First

Traditional long marriages make this choice simple. A spouse who is your only beneficiary will usually be your first choice. Your spouse will do the work without compensation, and that can be quite a saving. Other factors can override this choice, though. Will the executor's role impose a burden on an elderly partner? He or she may appreciate having some assistance. Giving up a small portion of the estate for co-executor compensation could be money well spent. There are other factors to consider.

If you create a spousal trust fund, an independent co-trustee can help avoid conflicts. If you only want to give your spouse an outright gift, you may not have the same needs. Long-term asset management is not an issue in an outright distribution. With testamentary trusts, your executor's age is a factor to consider.

What if you are married and have adult children from a prior marriage? Here's where a second spouse may or may not want to handle the estate alone. Don't assume arguments will not develop if you are no longer around. It's safer to assume that there will be dissension. Of course, if you're leaving everything to your spouse, it's a no-brainer. Your spouse will probably be your executor, but who's the backup?

A married spouse not satisfied with his or her share under your will has legal remedies to claim more. If your spouse wants a larger share or more support, he or she may have to sue your estate. Your spouse will then be in conflict with the estate and can't be your executor. Name an alternative as a precaution to save considerable expense and delay. Your second choice can step in immediately if an unresolvable dispute arises.

Help Line

**Q:** I've given one daughter a power of attorney. Should all my children be named as co-executors?

**A:** These are separate jobs, although they are financially related. This is a decision worth saying yes to in many cases. Your other children will want to review the attorney's financial dealings. As co-executors, they will find this review easier.

Your business affairs can be complex, with sophisticated corporate investments and partners. Estate trustees may have to negotiate with landlords, creditors, and bankers. You may not wish to place a spouse in the middle of this turmoil. In such situations, you can appoint a co-trustee with business expertise to help your spouse.

## Children Must Be Eighteen

Parents usually share their estate equally among their children if they both die. This dispersal keeps peace in the family. Consider the following factors before you select your children as executors.

Children under the age of eighteen can be named as executors in your will. They cannot act, however, until they reach the age of majority.

Should you appoint all of your children as estate executors? Perhaps they may not always agree or be readily available. However, I believe you should appoint all of them unless there is good reason not to. Forget about it being easier to administer your estate with just one person. They want to be involved or at least supervise each other. Years later children may second-guess your decision not to name them as executors. They may feel left out.

A child who is a sole executor may not get the cooperation of siblings for major decisions. An alternative is to include a clause that all children need to be consulted on all major decisions and define what is "major." If they don't all participate, they may not understand the executor's actions. This can lead to mistrust, which most parents want to avoid. Parents don't want to see their children retain lawyers to argue over their inheritance.

Children who live out of province can still participate in the estate's administration. Let them decline or renounce their positions as executors if they wish. Couriers, fax machines, and e-mail make no place too far away. Allow each of your children to participate, at least initially, in your estate's affairs. You'll help them feel involved in the grieving process.

If all of your children participate, there may be an added benefit. They will see the need to complete the estate expeditiously to receive their share. If they choose not to serve, they can simply renounce their appointments. You or your estate lawyer can explain that there is no legal or moral obligation to serve as executor.

There is a further benefit to appointing all of your children. Hopefully, your will won't be probated until years after it was made. Some of your children may have moved out of the country or become unavailable. Naming all of them reduces the risk that no child is in the jurisdiction.

Five years after you make your will, your son John is alienated from his sister, Jeanette. This is a case where having both children act could be inappropriate. If this situation is likely, consider independent executors as a buffer between family members.

If you make a relative your executor, you do not have to make him or her a beneficiary as well.

## Business Partners May Have Conflicts

Your business associates may be trustworthy and well known to your family. Does this mean they are appropriate executors to run a business in your estate? If they are the only buyers of your business under an agreement, they have a conflict of interest. Resolve these issues and review the following.

Will the business interests be sold or continue to be operated and for how long? Your estate may be interested in an immediate sale of a business to maximize the price. Business associates may wish to spend money and reinvest profits in new projects. Ask yourself if the business is to be operated or sold and who the potential buyers are.

Doctors, dentists, and other professionals can appoint fellow practitioners. Professionally licensed help can facilitate a sale or interim management of the practice.

Court approval or beneficiaries' permission is required if executors wish to purchase estate assets. Don't forget this, or you'll eliminate the best buyer for your investment. Specifically in your will, permit a purchase by an executor without a judge's approval. Alternative safeguards to protect your estate can still be set up. Make your business partner one of two or three executors. This group can make unanimous decisions about the final sale price.

## Help Line

**Q:** My brother told me there was nothing left in my parents' estate. What proof am I entitled to?

**A:** Informally, you should get disclosure of all the material to support that position. Ask for an estate inventory and list of assets. If you're not satisfied, get a court to compel a formal production or accounting.

---

**Bulletin**

Don't assume your children will automatically get along as your executors. If you're gone, you can no longer act as peacekeeper in the family. Personal rivalries and jealousies can be brought to the surface. Don't forget to ask for your children's consent to act as your executors. You may be surprised by their answers.

---

## Getting Paid Twice?

Lawyers always get asked to be executors. Why not? If anything, an estate lawyer should know the ropes. Divorce lawyers may not know any estate law. You won't gain any advantage by choosing a criminal lawyer. Lawyers, if they practise in the field, may have a client relationship worth maintaining. Consider the following factors.

Have an independent law firm prepare or review your will if a lawyer is your co-executor. Professionals should make it clear that there is no obligation to select them as executors. They also must advise you of potential conflicts.

Accountants may be familiar with your tax and business affairs. Selecting accountants won't always lead to a saving of fees. Any professional can charge separately for professional work and estate services. You may not be getting two for the price of one.

Remember, your estate can always retain your personal lawyer and accountant for assistance. Their expertise can be used to administer the estate. It isn't necessary to make them executors.

An executor's compensation usually doesn't compare to the professional's hourly rate. Low fees may encourage carelessness or a lack of attention. Professional trustees may delegate all their duties to support staff.

Remember, friendly professionals will always be available on a fee-for-service basis to assist your family. You can avoid paying larger executor fees if you can keep it in the family.

Consider a professional as an alternative or backup. This is a logical choice if there are no family members in the jurisdiction. Travel expenses and extra costs may prohibit a distant relative from being named.

---

**Bulletin**
_____

Most major banks have trust divisions. Only a trust company is authorized by law to accept your appointment as an executor or trustee.

---

## Trust Company Considerations

Trust companies can act as professional trustees, but there are pros and cons. Let's consider six advantages first.

- They have experience in managing complex estates and court battles.
- Loss due to dishonesty is not an issue, and no bond is necessary.
- Long-term trust administration with continuity is possible.
- Professional management of investments is assumed.
- Regulation of your executor already exists by law.
- They have expertise and track records in estate and trust work.

But there are some disadvantages. A trust company will require compensation even for simple estates. Paying the minimum fees is not always a benefit if the estate calls for an immediate distribution. Simple transfers to a single beneficiary may make a trust company unnecessary.

For smaller estates, a trust company may not be prepared to act. For larger estates, fees may be negotiable, especially if other trust company services are used. In every instance, the decision depends on the nature of the trust company's duties and your assets.

Trust companies can be cautious in making investments. So it is important for you to provide clear powers and directions. Small business or minor equity positions may be difficult for them to handle. If these assets are in your estate, ensure that the trust company has this capability. It may not wish to be involved in modest estates. The nature of your assets will help you determine your choices.

Another disadvantage is that trust companies' decision-making processes can be cumbersome. Typically, a committee is set up with senior officers of the trust company who will meet regularly to make discretionary decisions. As a result, their decisions may not be immediate but will be well considered, balancing the interests of the beneficiary with the intentions set out in the will. Frequent personnel changes make it difficult to develop close and personal relations.

But trust companies can help in an obvious conflict-of-interest case. They can also be valuable alternative executors when family members may not survive you or become incapacitated.

The person you hire should be given the option to hire a trust company as an agent. This may be an alternative to appointing it as an executor. Your executor can hire the trust company for consultation and to perform professional services. It can explain its fee schedules for such services.

### Help Line

**Q:** I am confused by trusts, estate trustees, and trust companies.

**A:** Trusts are relationships in which someone holds property for someone else's benefit. Trustees manage all kinds of trust assets for the benefit of the beneficiaries. Estate trustee is another name for executors who are responsible for administering estates. Trust companies can act as both the executor and the trustee.

## The Best of Both Worlds

Trust companies are good choices especially as alternatives or if there are long-term trust obligations. But remember, as with all executors, you want to get their consent in advance. This will be the time to discuss the trust company's compensation package as well. Most trust company executors will want to review your draft will. They will usually make helpful suggestions for changes. Fee agreements will also be put in writing.

If your executor dies, resigns, or becomes incapacitated, a trust company can be a backup. Remember, unless you specify otherwise, all executors must act together. If you want one to have final say, specify that power or discretion.

A key factor to consider in your selection is whether you have a trust created by your will. It could be a testamentary trust for your spouse or minor children. If the trust must operate for several years, a trust company is a welcome choice.

Step 4 is now concluded. You should be able to navigate your way through all the available choices for your executors. Keep these choices up to date to avoid horror stories and preserve your legacy.

Now I'll show you how to take care of your beneficiaries in Step 5.

## The Least You Need to Know

- Review and revise your choice of executor regularly to avoid problems.
- Your first choice is family if they are trustworthy and competent.
- Removing an executor is costly, so choose wisely.
- Use a trust company if you require long-term and special expertise.

# Benefit Your Beneficiaries

Now it's time to think of your beneficiaries as you make your will. Here it is, your chance to leave a legacy. You can become immortal by leaving an inheritance so your beneficiaries never forget you.

Your gift to a beneficiary can cause problems, though. If someone can't handle it, the gift can do harm. Inherited money can destroy your family, create bitterness, and lead to costly legal proceedings. You must learn to give wisely, so I'll give you some rules.

You have a better chance of success if you follow my suggestions. Remember, life is a bowl of cherries, but you don't want to end up giving your beneficiaries the pits!

# Chapter 17

# Guidelines for Gifting

In this chapter:

- Follow simple rules.
- Gifts can have conditions.
- Spell out details.
- Use strategies for second homes.

Everyone knows what to do at this step — you just give it all away. It's not rocket science, right? My twenty-six years of experience as a lawyer has taught me just the opposite; people don't know how to give away their estates, and that's one reason they put off making their wills.

One of the joys of estate planning comes from knowing you'll leave a legacy. You want your last wishes respected. Even if your choice of beneficiaries is obvious, you'll benefit from reviewing this chapter. The people who inherit your valuables or just your collectibles will appreciate your thoughtfulness.

## Simple Ways to Give

What's the best way to make a gift? Isaac asked himself this question. He has investments and a mortgage-free home. He is sixty-seven and going to a nursing home, so his home has to be sold. He doesn't know how much he can get for it. Will the cost of his nursing care deplete his assets? How much money can he leave to his two nieces or his favourite charity? He worries about what will be left for his beneficiaries. Solutions to Isaac's problems are simple. Learn them and your worries will be over.

---

**Legal Lingo**

*Beneficiary* is one who receives or enjoys benefits, advantages, profits, or fruits under a trust, insurance policy, or will.

---

## Help Line

**Q:** If I want to leave someone a legacy, do I have to use the word *legacy* in my will?

**A:** No. There is no such formal requirement for legacies, which are gifts of personal property. You can specify from where the legacy is paid. For example, "Pay $2,000 from the sale of my car to my sister or from my estate residue."

## Give Shares, Slices, or Percentages

It's difficult to know what property you will leave behind. Estimates are the best you can do, unless you have enough cash to maintain your lifestyle regardless of illness or any other contingency. If that's the case, you can make gifts of some of your excess capital or income. If you're elderly, you may be able to make a gift from such excess while you're alive. And isn't that one of the pleasures of having wealth? You can help a relative buy a home. Remember, you don't have to restrict your gift giving to your will.

So what if you're twenty-five? You probably live on every cent you can borrow. You can't decide how much to leave each beneficiary in a will because you don't know what will be left after taxes and expenses. Start by previewing your estate as we did in Chapter 4.

Your solution may be to give each beneficiary a percentage or share of your estate. You can divide your estate residue so it is distributed as follows:

- to my niece Rani — twenty-five percent;
- to my nephew Mohammed — twenty-five percent; and
- to my favourite charity — fifty percent.

Dividing your estate by percentages makes the task easy. Just decide the exact percentage or share each beneficiary gets of the net residue and ensure the total is 100 percent. You'll find it even easier to give the charity two shares and everyone else one share each.

## How Gifts Can Be Made

As you know, a beneficiary named in your will can be a person or an organization. Gifts can be a share of your estate or specific items such as a car. Gifts can be conditional — for example, when someone reaches the age of twenty-one. Or they can be shared among beneficiaries, who can be primary or secondary. "For Rani, if she survives me," makes her your primary beneficiary. "If not, to Abdul, if he survives Rani," makes Abdul your secondary or backup beneficiary.

Sometimes you want to give only a small share of the estate to someone, with the bulk of your property or residue going to someone else. Gifts can be a specific item of property such as a piano or a cash legacy of $5,000 in a will. A bequest is a gift other than real estate. An inheritance can also be a share or percentage of a larger single asset.

---

**Bulletin**

Canada has no gift taxes. If you plan to make a gift while you're alive, you must consider the income tax consequences. Each time capital property is transferred, you have a disposition. You'll have to calculate and pay any income taxes.

---

Residues or remainders are what is left after debts are paid and all specific gifts are made. Those remaining assets would be converted into cash and are treated as estate residue. If you acquire property after your will is signed, you'll need a codicil or a new will to make it a specific gift. If you don't do this, the new property will be distributed as part of your estate residue.

## Plan to Give It Away Now

Estate planning doesn't mean you have to die before you can help your beneficiaries. Lifetime transfers, or *inter vivos* gifts, make sense. They can help you achieve your estate planning goals and give you a warm, generous feeling, especially if you can afford to continue your lifestyle without the money. Why not give to charity or your loved ones?

You should also consider ways to reduce taxes, including income and probate taxes. But don't forget to consider the taxes that can be due when you transfer property to beneficiaries. You'll remember these as the deemed disposition and income attribution rules that also apply.

## Don't Get Caught

Canada's tax system doesn't tax gifts in the hands of your beneficiaries. Nor is there a gift tax similar to the one in the United States. But Canadians need to be careful whenever property is loaned or gifted to non–arm's-length persons such as a child or grandchild. Usually, that includes those related by marriage, blood relationship, or adoption.

Attribution rules apply to loans, transfers, or gifts to a spouse or minors (under the age of eighteen). Income from such gifts, loans, or transfers is taxed in the hands of the person making the gift (the donor). The person who receives the gift (the donee) doesn't pay. These rules are designed to avoid income-splitting. Whenever you plan major lifetime gifts, you'll want to make sure you get tax advice.

But don't try to be cute. Finding creative loopholes won't make you look like a genius if you get caught with transactions considered abuse of the income tax rules.

Some income-splitting techniques with minor children even attract a special "kiddie tax." This tax on split income neutralizes certain tax arrangements to share dividend, partnership, or trust income used for the benefit of minor children. Instead of the lower tax rates applying, the government taxes the minor child's income at the top marginal rate.

## Consider Nontaxable Gifts

You can give away or assign non–income-producing assets to a beneficiary. Assets such as a life insurance policy, when given to a charity, can provide a tax credit as well. Giving away non–income-producing assets will also reduce your probate taxes but won't give you any income tax relief. Other lifetime gifts can include antiques, jewellery, or artwork. Although you pay any capital gains on the gift, you'll see your beneficiary use and enjoy the property or items during your lifetime.

## Gifting Strategies to Avoid

Occasionally, hard-nosed clients come into my office and only want to make gifts with conditions or terms. They fiercely insist that the gift must come with strings attached. It may be okay in the movies that someone inherits Uncle Fester's millions only if he or she marries. But generally, you can't control behaviour.

For instance, making a gift conditional on whether or not a person quits smoking is hard to police. Generally, if you want to control the gift, you can place it in a trust. Try to avoid illegal or invalid restrictions on gifts, which I mentioned in Chapter 2 are against public policy.

Here is an example of a gift that is not delivered until something happens. When your niece enters dentistry college, you want her to receive $15,000 to help establish her practice. Your lawyer must carefully word such conditional gifts because problems can arise while your niece is still in college. What happens if she fails or drops out? When is the money to be paid? Is it paid only if she opens an office? If she dies before graduating, do you want her spouse or children to receive the gift?

## Spell out the Details

Don't leave questions unanswered in your will. Don't believe that everyone will cooperate to work things out. Residual beneficiaries in your estate may have no moral obligation to help your niece. If your niece's gift fails, they may profit by the $15,000. Imprecise wording can force a judge to interpret your words to search for your true intentions. This procedure only costs your estate more in legal fees, leaving less for everyone. Make up your wish list before you see a lawyer. Consider all the contingencies so that you can cover them in your will.

### Help Line

**Q:** I am using a store kit to make my will. Can I just give everything to "my children in trust" so they'll divide it?

**A:** Most will kits are not designed to deal with trust complexities. The children and their spouses may all have different ideas about what's fair or what they deserve. Just using the word *trust* may not satisfy the legal requirements to create a trust. Consult an estate lawyer to draw up wills that involve trusts.

## Another Bad Gift Example

Here's another example of poor will drafting for a gift clause: "Each of my grandchildren shall receive from my estate enough money to cover university tuition costs." When this tuition clause was drafted, you may have had just two grandchildren and enough money set aside. Do you want to provide for any grandchildren born in the future? What if your children remarry and have more grandchildren? What about step-grandchildren or those born from donated sperm or frozen embryos? Did you leave sufficient reserves to fully fund the tuition costs, allowing for inflation? Do you intend to pay for their first degree only or for medical school as well?

Be careful not to attach conditions that violate public policy. You can't say there'll be no gift if a person marries out of a religion. A judge would likely decide that the gift could be delivered without any conditions.

## Alternative Beneficiaries for Gifts

So you want to leave your home to a partner who has lived with you for years. What happens if the partner dies before or with you? Avoid having to revise your will by naming an alternative beneficiary to inherit any major assets. Doing so will keep you from seeing a lawyer each time a beneficiary dies or becomes incapacitated. More importantly, it avoids an intestacy when assets have no beneficiaries. Another option is to specify that the gift goes to your partner only if he or she survives you.

Most provinces have anti-lapse rules that cover gifts to certain categories of beneficiaries, such as a brother, sister, child, or grandchild. Gifts to these individuals do not automatically fail. The anti-lapse law sets out a formula that distributes the property unless you specify otherwise in your will.

Do you want your second spouse's children to inherit your assets? If so, perhaps you could give them rights as alternative beneficiaries in your will. Also consider naming a charity or a worthy religious cause as an alternative beneficiary.

---

**Bulletin**

You can't wait to tell people that you left them something in your will. But are you afraid they'll be anxious to see your early departure to get their inheritance? Don't worry, the law is clear; a person guilty of murder can get no benefit under the will of his or her victim.

---

## Avoid Double Probate

You can attach survivorship conditions to gifts of a major portion of your estate. Doing so ensures that the person receiving the gift must survive you for at least thirty days to inherit. Is there any magic in the thirty-day period? No, the number is arbitrary. A period of fifteen, twenty, or forty-five days can be used as well. The intention of the survivorship provision is to avoid duplication of probate costs.

You'll want to consider this if you and you beneficiary could die together. For example, you and your beneficiary could suffer fatal injuries in the same car accident. If a beneficiary survives you by only ten days, your estate would go to him or her. Then when your beneficiary dies, that estate would incur a second set of costs for executors, probate, and legal fees.

## Double Disasters

Survivorship clauses for a common disaster can also avoid different tragic results. Donald wants his estate to go to Michelle, his second wife. If she dies, he wants it to go to his children. Michelle's will gives everything to Donald, but if he dies Michelle wants everything to go to her mother.

After a catastrophic car accident, Michelle survives Donald by twenty-four hours. Her mother is in a nursing home. She's not competent to realize that she has just inherited Donald's estate as well as Michelle's. Donald's children are still shaking their heads. Their father had promised to take care of them, but they received nothing.

What happens when children are cut out of wills? Can you disinherit your children and not expect a lawsuit? You'll learn that in Chapter 18, "Don't Ignore Your Beneficiaries' Rights."

## Gifts to Witnesses

If a witness to a will is a beneficiary, there is the possibility of fraud in the preparation of the will. The law usually cancels gifts to beneficiaries who are witnesses or spouses of witnesses. However, laws may exist in your province to salvage the gift, but it requires winning your case in court. You can best avoid this problem by having wills witnessed in a law office. It will be the lawyer's responsibility to ensure that no beneficiary or beneficiary's spouse is a witness.

### Help Line

**Q:** What about gifts to our feathered or furry friends?

**A:** You can't leave a gift to a pet. It doesn't matter how much the pet is part of the family. You can set up a trust to care for your animals. You can leave money for the animal's care. But specify what happens to the trust money after the pet dies.

## Strategies for Gifting Vacation Properties

You love your recreational property and recall all the good times the family shared there. But dreamy vacations at this second home can turn into nightmares after your death. You need to know how to handle the property in your estate plan.

Sheila and Bob, for example, had a nice place by the lake. They just couldn't get to it anymore since Bob stopped driving. The couple enjoyed the place only on holidays. Their daughter, Deirdre, seemed to live there most summers with her kids. The couple's other adult children never had time to visit it.

When Bob passed away, Sheila wanted to update her estate plan. She wanted to leave the property to all three kids equally but wondered if there was a better way to divide it. The cottage obviously meant the most to Deirdre. Her mother didn't want to deny, however, the other two children their share of the property. Sheila didn't have other assets to divide besides this property, so what else could she do?

Here are some options that Sheila could consider for the property:

- transfer it to a trust;
- sell it and divide the proceeds now;
- gift it now; or
- leave it through her will.

Let's look at each of these choices in more detail to find a recommended strategy.

### 1. Transfer It to a Trust

Under this option, a living trust agreement would be created while Sheila is alive. She would pay to have the property registered to the new owner, "Sheila's family trust." Unfortunately, she would also have to deal with any potential taxable capital gains on the transfer. Writing a cheque to the government for income taxes is not a comforting idea; she may want to consider her other options.

Sheila also has to pay the costs to create a trust and the transfer fees for the new real estate deed. These expenses, along with any capital gains, can add up. She may not have the money for these expenses. After the property is owned by the trust, Sheila and her brother (who is also her executor) could be trustees. She would put enough money into the trust to pay for the property's expenses.

**It's Been Said**
.........................................................

"Death twitches my ear. Live, he says; I am coming."
– Virgil, *Minor Poems*

All future capital gains, however, would be taxed in the trust and not her estate since Sheila no longer owns the property. The trust could sell the property and distribute the proceeds when she dies or later. The cottage would be available for the entire family's enjoyment, and there would be no need to dispose of it at the time of her death just to pay any capital gains or probate costs.

Trust terms could specify how the property's costs would be shared. After Sheila's death, the cottage could be sold if two of her three children agree.

Living trusts have the setup and annual maintenance costs I have explained. They are usually too costly and complex to consider for most families.

Are there better options?

## 2. Sell It and Divide the Proceeds Now

This is the least charming of the proposals but has its advantages. If Sheila no longer wants the burden of paying the property's costs, she can sell the cottage. After expenses, each of her adult children would get a share. They may wish to retire their own mortgages or invest the money in other ways.

Another variation would be to sell the property to Deirdre. Perhaps Mom would take a mortgage or help arrange bank financing. Perhaps you are like me and don't like to see mortgages between family members. Nonpayment problems can give you a major migraine. However, a mortgage may help protect Sheila's claims for payment if, for instance, Deirdre and her spouse separate and the cottage is sold.

If Sheila sells the property now, she'll include any capital gain in her income and pay taxes on it. This approach will keep the asset out of her estate for probate. Selling now doesn't sound like much of a strategy, does it? Well, in some families, it may be the best idea. If the children don't get along, making them partners on a second property will be more of a curse than a gift. Don't expect that dealing with the details of ownership will draw them closer.

## 3. Gift It Now

Here's how this works: all three children take title to the property. The deed can contain a reservation of a life interest for Sheila. She can continue to use the property while she's alive. The capital gain is dealt with at the time of the transfer, hopefully with cash Sheila can part with.

If she makes all three children co-owners, they are forced into a sibling partnership. Any partnership, as they say, is a tough ship to sail. Will Sheila need marriage contracts with the children's spouses so they can't make any claims on divorce? What about the dangerous surprises with joint ownership I listed under probate-gifting strategies in Chapter 8? What would happen if one of the children goes bankrupt? Is there a surprise behind door number four?

## 4. Leave It through Her Will

This option involves the least amount of planning and expense. By dealing with the property in her will, Sheila can defer making any payments or decisions. She can then specifically leave one child the first option to purchase the property. Then she can try to give the other children an equal share of other assets if she expects to have any at the time of death.

If Sheila is young enough, her children could purchase life insurance to cover payment of any income taxes. Life insurance could be used to create an "instant" estate for the other children who don't wish to share the summer home.

What if Sheila decides to leave the property to her daughter in her will? She'll tell Deirdre to buy out the siblings' shares. Uncertainty can lead to bitterness between children when they all must consent. You can't anticipate all of these issues when drafting your will. How is the sale price calculated? What are the deductions to be made? What about paying for improvements made by the daughter? There aren't any simple answers to these questions.

It may be easier to sell the cottage and divide the proceeds as part of the residue. In the final analysis, that is what I recommend. Deirdre, if she can afford to and still wants the property, can then buy out her siblings' two-thirds interest. If Sheila thinks the other children won't cooperate, she can have independent executors set the terms for the sale.

You can spend a small fortune in legal time and fees trying to deal with all the variables of future events. Besides, it all becomes academic if Sheila must sell the property to pay for her nursing home bills.

## Postpone Solving the Problem

After Sheila dies, the debates can degenerate until everyone goes to his or her respective corner. When round two starts, the siblings come out fighting each other with their lawyers. In my opinion, unless you can reach a consensus, sell the property as part of the residue of the estate. You'll pay probate and other estate expenses if you still own it. But then no one will be able to have first claims or rights to it.

If one person really wants to buy the property, he or she can always negotiate with the family but shouldn't expect a deal. There really is no good way to divide up real estate between multiple owners. Each has priorities and expectations. Don't force co-ownership on reluctant family members who may just wish to go their separate ways. Remember, estate planning is about people, not property.

In the next chapter, we'll look at what happens if you forget that principle.

## The Least You Need to Know

- Give shares of your estate whenever you aren't sure what to leave everyone.
- Don't force people into a partnership.
- Income attribution and capital gains rules affect any lifetime gifts.
- You can't make a gift in your will to witnesses or their spouses.

# Chapter 18

# Don't Ignore Your Beneficiaries' Rights

In this chapter:

- Spouses have a right to share.
- Understand a simple marriage contract.
- Dependants can sue your estate.
- Broken promises can cause problems.

Absolute power. You may believe you have it when you dispose of your property through a will. After all, you've spent a lifetime acquiring wealth. That should count for something. Why can't you be kind, cruel, or eccentric with your estate? You may be surprised to know that your power to give or to deny is not unlimited.

Your beneficiaries have rights. They can sabotage any estate plan by enforcing it through the courts. Beneficiaries, even those not mentioned in a will, can ask a court to intervene. Spouses, dependants, and those with broken promises can upset your distribution plans. This chapter is where I get into specifics about marriage contracts and cutting someone out of your estate.

## Spouses Treated as Married Have Rights

It's not true that you can get away with leaving your spouse a dollar in your will. No matter how much you may want to do so, it's not appropriate. You can't ignore a married spouse's entitlement to share in the property acquired by the other spouse during the marriage.

In most provinces, common-law spouses aren't treated as married. When it comes to your estate, they may only be entitled to claim support against a common-law partner's estate. In some jurisdictions, they wouldn't automatically share an estate unless they are named in a will.

Quick recap. Married spouses have property and support obligations to their spouses. Common-law and same-sex spouses, unless you are in a province that treats you as married, usually only have support rights. Spousal definitions change regularly because of court cases. You'll need to get the latest update from a lawyer in your province when you seek advice. That's why no book is a substitute for professional advice.

---

**Legal Lingo**

*Spouse*: the definition for this term varies from province to province and in each piece of provincial legislation. Terms such as "spouse," "child," or "dependant" are often defined differently in specific laws.

---

Provincial law grants a surviving married spouse certain elective rights. In this first section, I'll talk about property rights, which are restricted to married spouses. Common-law and same-sex spouses have traditionally only had rights to claim support and limited benefits under provincial property laws. If you are in this category, you've probably heard of recent legislative changes for same-sex partners. Consult a lawyer to clarify your rights.

Surviving married spouses don't have to take what's left to them in a will or under an intestacy. They can "elect" to take a forced share of a deceased spouse's estate. How much a spouse is entitled to is calculated under provincial family law.

## Married Spouses Share in Divorce and Death

Your married spouse can share in certain matrimonial property in the event of divorce or death. Provincial formulas for calculating what a spouse is entitled to on death or divorce vary. You'll need a lawyer in your province to guide you in this area. You'll find a maze of rules for what property is shared or excluded. It depends on things such as who brings the property into the marriage, who inherited what, and whether it's a business.

This is what's important to understand. Your married spouse may share in your property in a divorce, and your death won't necessarily reduce the claims. Spouses can get, asset-wise, what's coming to them. Even when you're in your grave.

## Spouses Can Elect the Bigger Share

So you want to leave your married spouse the house and everything else to the children? Don't think you'll get away with it. If you don't leave your spouse what he or she is entitled to, here's what can happen.

Sandra's estate in Ontario is valued at $500,000. Sandra wants Howard, her husband, to share in it. She also has four children from her first marriage. Her will gives Howard $100,000, and the $400,000 is to be divided among her four children.

Sandra wants to treat everyone equally. She thinks her gift of $100,000 to her husband is fair. The problem is that Howard may not agree, and this disagreement can lead to a legal challenge, pitting him against her children. Howard can accept her gift, or he can go to court to take his entitlement as a married spouse. In Ontario, he must contact a lawyer and start proceedings within six months of Sandra's death. Her executors would normally wait the six months before distributing her estate assets.

> **Legal Lingo**
>
> *Matrimonial home*: this definition varies from province to province. The home can be called family or marital property. Usually, it's the dwelling place ordinarily used by a married couple as their residence. Ontario law allows couples to designate which property this is for purposes of the Family Law Act, which gives spouses special rights to the matrimonial home. You can have a number of such homes.

## Married Spouses Are Guaranteed a Share

Howard's lawyer explains how the law guarantees Howard a share of Sandra's estate. Sandra can't cut him out unless he has more wealth than she does. Howard has to do a financial comparison with her estate.

It is the net value of all spousal property acquired during marriage that is compared. Howard has to deduct his debts and the value of property he brought into the marriage. Property has a broad definition. Under Ontario law, it includes almost everything from pensions, to income from a trust, to professional practices.

## Let's Try the Calculations

Here, for example, are four steps that Howard would follow in Ontario.

Step 1: calculate Sandra's "net family property" (wife's NFP).

- At the time of marriage, Sandra had no assets or debts.
- At her death, she owned property worth $500,000.
- Her NFP is the value of property at death less property owned by her on marriage. In this case, it's $500,000 NFP, with no deductions.

Step 2: calculate Howard's, the surviving spouse's, net family property, as above (husband's NFP).

- Howard had $200,000 of his own assets, and he brought $50,000 into the marriage.
- Howard's NFP is calculated as $200,000 - $50,000 = $150,000.

Step 3: calculate the difference between Sandra's NFP and Howard's NFP (Sandra's NFP = $500,000; Howard's NFP = $150,000).

- Difference between spousal NFPs is $500,000 - $150,000 = $350,000.
- Howard is entitled to $175,000 (half of $350,000) if he elects to take his married spouse's share under the law.
- Howard should be better off by $75,000 over what Sandra's will gives him. But he's not finished. After he makes the mathematical calculation, he must take one more step.

Step 4: calculate the advantages of making the family election against Sandra's estate.

- The dollar difference of $75,000 between the gift in the will and Howard's entitlement may not be sufficient reason to make the election. Going to court would put Howard in a conflict of interest against his wife's estate. He wouldn't be able to keep his position as executor and would certainly generate ill will from Sandra's children.
- If Howard and Sandra had young children with a trust set up in the will, he would have to give up the trustee's role and not handle the trust funds. He needs to review what

assets he receives from Sandra outside the will as well. What if he receives a life insurance policy of $200,000 outside the will? This is an asset that some provinces require him to include in his calculations.

---

**Bulletin**

What counts as family property? In some provinces, nonfamily assets are business assets, and spouses must show some contribution to the business in order to share after a family breakup. However, beneficiaries may be entitled to an automatic right to share family assets. Ontario, for instance, makes no distinction between family and nonfamily assets.

---

## More Variations of "You Can't Escape"

Dan was terminally ill. He decided to gift his property to his grown children from his first spouse. After Dan died, Veronica, his second wife, discovered he'd left her next to nothing in his will. She hired a lawyer to make an election to her spousal share instead of accepting benefits under his will.

"Veronica," the lawyer said, "Dan died broke. He has no assets in his name that you can claim."

She decided to sue Dan's children. She claimed they had cooperated with their father to defraud her by depleting his estate of all assets. Who won in court? Yes, you guessed it: Veronica. The point of the story is you can't intentionally get rid of property or incur debts to deny a spouse his or her share of your estate.

What if, after making the election and equalizing their family property, Veronica still couldn't support herself? A court could order Dan's estate to pay support to her. She'd be classified as a dependant for support purposes. A judge could order Dan's estate to maintain a home for Veronica and pay her monthly support or a lump sum. The court has wide discretion on how to support dependants. Better you take care of them yourself than have the court costs and your will overruled by a judge.

Look at this story in another variation. What if Veronica was a common-law spouse of twenty-four years? She can't make an equalization claim since she's not married. Following are some claims that she could raise as a common-law spouse.

**Unjust enrichment claims:** common-law or same-sex partners often contribute toward the purchase or renovation of real estate. If such a property is registered in only one person's name and that person dies, look out. Surviving partners can make claims to the property.

**It's Been Said**
..................................................

"Where there's marriage without love, there will be love without marriage."
— Benjamin Franklin, 1706–90

**Constructive trust claims:** what if Dan owned a farm and Veronica helped him operate it for over twenty years? When he dies, she has no titled interest in the property. Constructive trust claims could compensate her for her labour and spousal services. A judge could declare that Dan's estate holds a portion, say fifty percent, of the farm in trust for Veronica.

**Breach of contract claims:** Veronica and Dan entered into an oral contract when they started living together. Let's say Dan wasn't healthy. He promised Veronica that, if she took care of him until he died, he'd share his estate equally with her and his two children. But Dan broke his promise. Veronica could sue his estate for a breach of his contract. She may have a hard time proving it without good evidence. In the alternative, the court may pay for her services on a *quantum meruit* basis. That's where the amount of compensation for service has not been agreed upon but is set afterward by a court.

## Summary

The courts will provide relief to disappointed individuals who may not have status to legally challenge a will. These claims can disrupt your estate plan. You can be responsible for all the court costs if you are responsible for wrongdoing.

**Legal Lingo**

*No contest clause* in a will is designed to disinherit and punish any beneficiary who contests a will. In many jurisdictions, these clauses are not enforced by the courts. If you leave only a token amount to the beneficiary, he or she may have no financial incentive not to challenge your will.

## No Contest Clauses

What if Dan is dying and his children get him to leave nothing to Veronica in a new will? The children insist that their father put a clause in his will to punish her if she challenges his will. With this form of penalty clause, Veronica will forfeit her inheritance if she challenges the will. Can Dan protect his estate from her claims in this way?

Well, in some cases and jurisdictions, the wording of the clause may make it unenforceable as a matter of public policy. The public has an interest in making sure only valid wills are probated. Dan may not have had testamentary capacity or was unduly influenced to cut Veronica out of his estate. These are issues that a court would always want to open for judicial review. It must investigate the merit of these allegations. Dan's children wouldn't usually be able to hide their wrongdoing behind a no contest clause.

---

**Legal Lingo**

*Cohabitation agreements* have been used traditionally by common-law or same-sex couples not treated as "married." These contracts can specify your rights during cohabitation and after separation. Legal changes have been introduced for same-sex couples and common-law couples, so your existing cohabitation agreements may need to be revised to deal with support and other property claims.

---

## Spousal Elections Are Costly

If you still choose to ignore your married spouse's rights, the costs will be high. Probably as a minimum, your spouse's legal fees will be paid out of your estate.

---

**Legal Lingo**

*Marriage contracts* are also called *domestic agreements* and can be entered into if spouses are already married. If you are going into business, your spouse may be required to sign a marriage contract as part of a partnership or shareholders' agreement. It may list what rights a spouse may have to the business in a divorce.

---

The spouse and the estate will require separate legal assistance. In Ontario, special financial statements, sworn under oath, are provided by both sides. If the parties dispute property valuations, costly professional appraisals will be necessary for court or mediation. Until the calculations are made, no assets can be distributed. Ontario law prohibits distribution of a married spouse's estate until six months after that person's death.

If you are determined to get around the family property laws to plan your estate, consider prenuptial or marriage contracts, which are recognized by provincial laws.

### The Famous Prenup

You've heard of prenuptial agreements, especially between celebrities. Their agreements make the headlines. But regular people who are about to marry, or those already married, can make contracts. These agreements are also referred to as marriage or domestic contracts.

Marriage contracts are signed by both parties. You'll want one to cover ownership of property and estate planning needs, especially if you have children from a prior marriage. Details in the contracts can also deal with support, pension plans, and children from previous marriages. To a degree, these contracts can take precedence over a province's family property laws.

As a general rule, if you have substantial assets or are entering into a second marriage, you need to consider a contract. Why? Because the law discriminates in many ways against individuals who own certain types of property, such as a matrimonial home, that they bring into the marriage. For example, if you live in Ontario and have a $500,000 home, it gets shared immediately with your spouse. If, however, you hold the same value in a GIC or stock portfolio, you have to share only the increase in the investment value.

Protect yourself and both families with a contract. The more you have to lose, the more steps you should take to avoid loss. At a minimum, consult with your own lawyer privately.

### A Specimen Contract

To answer your questions about marriage contracts, I have included a specimen. You'll notice my sample covers a second marriage. Its purpose is to protect the value of the family residence brought into the marriage. These contracts can also deal with potential claims to the parties' estates, although this example does not.

If you have an existing business, you'll want to consider a contract as well. Without one, your province may not protect or exclude business assets from division in a divorce. In Ontario, for instance, a deduction is given for a business brought into the marriage. This deduction won't cover, though, any increase in the value of the business during the marriage unless you have a contract. You *can* deduct assets brought into the marriage, except for the matrimonial home.

Remember, do not use the forms in this book for your own purpose. Every province has different laws and requirements, particularly Quebec.

**SAMPLE — NOT TO BE USED**

THIS IS A PRENUPTIAL OR MARRIAGE CONTRACT
made this __14__ day of __February__ 2006.

B E T W E E N:
Tania
("Wife")
— and —
Simon
("Husband")

1. INTERPRETATION

    (1) In this contract:

        (a) "Wife" means Tania, who is a party to this contract;

        (b) "Husband" means Simon, who is a party to this contract;

        (c) "family residence" means the buildings and lot located at

_____ ,

and includes any other buildings or lot acquired in substitution for them;

        (d) "breakdown of the marriage" means:

            (i) the separation of the parties;

            (ii) the dissolution of their marriage; or

            (iii) the annulment of their marriage.

2. BACKGROUND

    (1) Tania is a widow, who is retired.

    (2) Simon is a retired professor.

    (3) They plan to marry each other on December 18, 2006.

    (4) They intend to live in the family residence.

    (5) The family residence is owned by Tania and is free of all mortgages.

## 3. PURPOSE OF CONTRACT

Each party agrees with the other to be bound by the provisions of this contract.

Each party intends by this contract to avoid any rights and obligations relating to the family residence and contents that arise or that may in the future arise at law or in equity from their marriage.

This marriage contract is to prevail over the same matters dealt with under provincial family law.

## 4. FINANCIAL PROVISION

The responsibility for making financial provision for the family during cohabitation under the marriage will be assumed jointly by the parties in proportion to their respective financial abilities as may be agreed upon from time to time.

## 5. SUPPORT AFTER BREAKDOWN OF MARRIAGE

If there is a breakdown of the marriage, each party will have such rights to receive financial support from the other and will be under such obligations to provide financial support to the other as are given or imposed upon each party by the province's family law or the Divorce Act.

## 6. FAMILY RESIDENCE

(1) Each party acknowledges that the family residence is owned by Tania, and each agrees with the other that it will remain her separate property and will not be included in any sharing of property.

(2) The family residence is acknowledged by the parties to have a current fair market value of $350,000.

(3) In the event the family residence is sold, Tania will be solely entitled to the sale proceeds.

(4) Simon will have no right to share in the increase in the value of the family residence.

(5) If any property is purchased by the parties in substitution for the family residence and if it is purchased with Tania's funds it shall also remain her separate property and not be subject to division or inclusion in the property of either party.

## 7. CONTENTS OF FAMILY RESIDENCE

If a breakdown of the marriage of the parties should occur, the contents of the family residence or any successor residence will be distributed between the parties according to ownership whether that ownership arises by way of purchase or gift, including gifts from the other party.

## 8. TRANSFER OR BEQUEST OF PROPERTY TO OTHER PARTY

Either party may, by appropriate written instrument:

(a) convey or transfer during his or her lifetime, and

(b) devise or bequeath for distribution after his or her death

any property to the other, or appoint the other as executor of his or her estate. Nothing in this contract will limit or restrict in any way the right to receive any such conveyance, transfer, devise, or bequest from the other, or, if so appointed, the right to act as executor or administrator of the estate of the other.

## 9. FINANCIAL DISCLOSURE

Each party:

(a) has fully and completely disclosed to the other the nature, extent, and probable value of all his or her significant assets and debts or other liabilities existing at the date of this contract, and in addition to this disclosure,

(b) has given all information and particulars about his or her assets and liabilities that have been requested by the other, and

(c) is satisfied with the information and particulars received from the other.

## 10. AMENDMENT OF CONTRACT

Any amendment of this contract will be unenforceable unless made in writing and signed by each party before a witness.

## 11. GOVERNING LAW

This contract will be governed by the law of the Province of Ontario.

## 12. CONTRACT TO SURVIVE DIVORCE

If a divorce is granted, or if the marriage is declared a nullity, the terms of this contract will survive the event and continue in force.

## 13. CONTRACT TO SURVIVE DEATH

This contract is intended to survive the death of a party or the parties and will be binding on their estates.

## 14. INDEPENDENT LEGAL ADVICE

Each party acknowledges that he or she:

(a) has had independent legal advice, or the opportunity to obtain independent legal advice;

(b) understands his or her respective rights and obligations under this agreement; and

(c) is signing this agreement voluntarily.

IN WITNESS WHEREOF the parties hereto have hereunto set their hands and seals.

SIGNED, SEALED, AND DELIVERED
in the presence of:

| | **Sample Only** |
|---|---|
| As to the signature of Tania | Tania |

| | **Sample Only** |
|---|---|
| As to the signature of Simon | Simon |

## What Does a Marriage Contract Cost?

It's hard to say. A lot will depend on the complexity of your assets and needs. As a minimum, expect two or three visits to your lawyer. Your partner or spouse will do the same with his or her own lawyer. This is key to having your agreements upheld as valid. Agreement terms must be negotiated before a consensus is built, so this process will also add to the cost.

Don't try to save money by using the same lawyer. Each party needs a separate lawyer throughout negotiation of the agreement. This approach ensures that no undue influence or unfair bargaining takes place. Full financial disclosure of existing assets and debts is mandatory. It's not sufficient to say, "What's yours is yours, and what's mine is mine." What happens if you're unaware that your partner is a multimillionaire? Your agreement will be flawed.

### Help Line

**Q:** To save money, I was told to sign my marriage contract in front of my partner's lawyer. Is that okay?

**A:** It depends. If no one complains or challenges the agreement, you're okay. The contract may be complied with until a problem arises or someone objects. At that point, validity must be decided by a court. Without separate legal advice, the contract can be declared worthless by a judge.

> **Legal Lingo**
>
> *Domicile* (from the Latin *domus*) means a home or dwelling house. Domicile can be fixed by birth or designated by choice or law. You can have numerous residences but always return to one fixed place of domicile.

## Are Contracts Unbreakable?

*Intolerable Cruelty* is a movie in which George Clooney portrays a divorce lawyer claiming to have invented an unbreakable prenup. The movie pokes fun at divorce and divorce lawyers. Clooney's character learns that inevitably someone can always find a loophole.

Let me illustrate with Marisa's story about her marriage contract. Marisa was young, and her husband took her to a lawyer who didn't speak her native language. She signed a contract she never read. Her husband's children had worked in the family landscape business for twenty years. They all thought the contract signed by Marisa was valid. When their father updated his will, he left his children the business.

Marisa realized that with her own limited investments she couldn't support herself. She had, however, signed a contract that stated she'd always be self-sufficient.

After her husband retired, they travelled together. Marisa never worked after her husband became sick. She visited a lawyer to learn about her rights. She was told that, since the contract hadn't been updated when she quit working, she could claim that it was invalid. There had been a material change in her circumstances. Plus, she hadn't been able to read English when she signed it.

The children asked the business lawyer who had prepared their father's will if he had reviewed the marriage agreement. He said that their father had refused to provide him with a copy of the contract, not wanting to pay for it to be updated. Now his wife was going to court to challenge the validity of the contract. She claimed she'd given away property and support rights without getting anything in return.

Marriage contracts can be reviewed by a court to confirm their validity. Courts regularly set aside contracts that

- are ambiguous;
- are coercive or one-sided;
- fail to exchange benefits;
- do not disclose assets and debts; or
- lack independent legal advice.

## Domicile Makes a Difference

Remember that marriage contracts need to be reviewed as you move from province to province. You'll need advice to decide your domicile. Take Athina and Robert, who have recently lost their spouses.

In the course of selling his business in Alberta, Robert seeks advice from his lawyer. He plans to marry Athina in the next year but isn't sure where he's going to live. Athina has a condominium in Arizona where they can both retire and live. After Robert sells the business, he will have very few assets left in Canada. He's not sure if he needs a marriage contract and in which province, state, or country.

His lawyer advises him that the marriage contract can designate a domicile for spouses. It can control family property in the event of separation, death, or divorce. Robert is advised to make a contract and to restrict any joint ownership assets with Athina. Such ownership would otherwise take assets away from his children from his first union.

You need to know other things if you don't want a marriage contract. We'll review a checklist for those getting married in Chapter 20, "Spouses: Good, Bad, and Divorced."

## Dependants Have Support Rights

Alfred supported his stepson Marco by paying the first year of his college tuition. But after Alfred died, his estate trustee told Marco he was on his own; he wasn't mentioned in the will.

Marco's lawyer saw things differently when he was consulted. Alfred had congratulated Marco on his grades and promised to help him financially. Alfred was supporting Marco at the time of his death with tuition payments. Marco could make a claim against Alfred's estate.

Claims for dependants' relief can again override the provisions in your will. Each province has different statutory requirements under which dependants can make a claim for support.

## Help Line

**Q:** How does a separation agreement affect my estate plan?

**A:** Separation agreements (or marriage contracts) usually contain clauses whereby a spouse waives his or her rights to your estate. Such agreements can also impose obligations (support) on your estate.

The judge in Marco's case must determine if Marco qualifies as a dependant. To qualify as a dependant means that Marco passes legal tests before a court can interfere. Judges can award him temporary support until trial. Lump-sum payments to Marco to cover the next few years at college are also possible. All the other beneficiaries under the will would be affected and have rights to attend court.

What if Marco tells his lawyer about Alfred's other promise? Alfred had asked Marco to live out of town and off campus to take care of Alfred's rental property. Alfred had told Marco that he'd give him part of the property in return for his services when he graduated. Marco was considering suing Alfred's estate for the services he hadn't been paid for or a share of the rental property.

Alfred had breached his promise and never paid Marco, who could claim a share of the estate for breach of contract or unjust enrichment. Marco settled out of court. He wasn't even mentioned in the will, but he received a share of Alfred's estate — because he enforced his rights.

### Same-Sex and Common-Law Partners

Obligations for support or benefits for these partners are recognized in law. Same-sex partners who aren't married are now entitled to go to court to claim support as dependants.

## What's Strange about This?

Strange cases happen all the time. Brad hadn't seen his father for twenty-five years and was left out of his father's will. Yet Brad got one-half of his father's estate. That was the result of a court decision in a 1997 case in British Columbia. It is significant because of the judge's comments and the result. The judge stated that there was no evidence why the father disinherited his adopted son. Even though they hadn't seen each other in the past twenty-five years, the son was entitled to a share.

Here is some of the background that you may find interesting. The father married Brad's mother when Brad was three years old. The father adopted him. When Brad was seven, however, the couple separated. Brad moved with his mother to Alberta. The father and son had no contact after that. Brad legally changed his name, no longer wishing to carry his father's.

### It's Been Said

...............................................

"As long as some evidence is provided of the testator's reason for disinheriting a child the court can then determine if those reasons are valid and rational."

– Re *Pattie* v. *Standal* (Estate)

When the father died, he left his entire estate to his common-law partner of two years. His will made no reference to Brad. Under the particular provincial law, the court concluded that Brad was entitled to relief. The father hadn't provided any financial support to Brad during his lifetime, and the court said that this lack of support created a moral obligation under the province's laws. Brad should have been provided for in his father's estate plans.

The judge exercised the broad discretion given to the court in that particular province. It was just and equitable for Brad to receive one-half of his father's estate. The court stated that there was no evidence why the father had decided to disinherit his child. The judge couldn't explain the father's reasons. She couldn't assess whether the father had acted as a judicious parent to discharge his duty.

Is there a moral? Yes. A recent court decision said that similar moral claims can be enforced by judges in Ontario. Planning your estate means you have to consider legal and moral claims, because a court can rewrite your will based on law or equity. Equity is that spirit of fairness that judges use to prevent wrongdoing when the law doesn't protect a victim from harm.

Disinheriting a child means cutting the child out of your estate. Can you do that? If the child is a dependant, the law says that you can't. If you have an adult child, it's another story.

**It's Been Said**
·············································

"As a general rule, nobody has money who ought to have it."
– Benjamin Disraeli, 1804–81

If you leave a dollar to your son, the courts will ask why. Is it because he married against your wishes? Did he break into your house and rob you to feed his addiction? Or is he estranged for reasons unknown? This information could make a difference.

I always ask clients if they are providing support to children. Is that support direct or indirect? You could be paying for vacations or helping with a student loan or a mortgage. I ask them if any person may feel dependent on them. If the answer is no, I continue. Will any child qualify as a dependant? If not, are there any moral or legal claims the child could make to share in your estate? What about any broken promises, unjust enrichment, or contractual trust claims?

At this point, if nothing unusual has come up, I ask for the reasons so I can record them in my file. If they're not inflammatory, the client may wish to specify them in the will.

You and your lawyer should prepare defensively for a possible challenge. I do that whenever a client wishes to cut out a child. Consider such preparation to protect your estate. Leave your executor, lawyer, and relatives a letter explaining your decision. You may mention an adult child's name in the will. For example, "I intentionally leave Robin nothing because he refused all my previous attempts to help him financially."

The reference to leaving a child a dollar is a common misconception. In some American jurisdictions, state laws require you to leave an adult child a dollar to specifically exclude him or her from a will.

The next chapter looks in more detail at children as beneficiaries.

## The Least You Need to Know

- Your estate can be sued by dependants who enforce their rights.
- A broken promise may give a person grounds to make a claim against your estate.
- Married spouses have rights to a share of your property, even after your death.
- Common-law or same-sex spouses can get support if you don't provide for them.

# Chapter 19

# Children's Needs

In this chapter:

- Treat children equally.
- Know exceptions to the rule.
- Trust your children.
- Protect your minor children.

Most of you will leave something to children, either your own or somebody else's. This chapter looks at children as beneficiaries. I'll share my experiences as a lawyer and a parent when it comes to how to give children their inheritance.

Some children dare to be different, and some are different because of their challenges. How can you treat them all the same if one has special physical or developmental needs? We'll discuss how a trust can help. If minor children are concerned, a trust is essential, as is appointing a children's guardian by your will.

## Father/Mother Knows Best

After a lifetime spent parenting, you probably know just what to leave your adult children in your will. No one knows them better than you do. They get along just great, and you never have to worry about them. You could be partially correct — after you're gone, their problems aren't something you can worry about.

But what happens if you're not there to act as the family peacekeeper? You can't count on things being the same after you're gone. Your skills as a mediator will no longer be available. Small rivalries between siblings can explode after years of being pent up. Children with no previous interest in china or crystal can squabble over every piece. Spouses may get involved, and an all-out war can start. Once Mom is gone, it's payback time. Who can stop them? Their sense of injustice, real or otherwise, can't be soothed away with reason.

## How to Treat Your Children

I hear your words of protest — "Not in my family!" Perhaps, but have you ever been involved in settling an estate? Clients frequently tell me that they don't want their estates to end up like a relative's did. But whenever there is money on the table to be divided, there will be disagreements. If someone isn't satisfied with his or her portion, lawyers may be hired. They can always find new ways to share the wealth in a family.

Dividing property in a divorce case is a piece of cake compared with that of an estate. Divorcing couples can ultimately be reasonable when they run out of money for legal fees. In estate cases, legal fees are often paid out of the estate. A child's sense of gratitude can quickly turn to greed. Whatever the cost, all or nothing can be the rule in some family estate disputes.

## Avoid Trouble: Treat Children Equally

Treat adult children equally. That is the standard advice I give all parents. If you want an unequal sharing of your estate, be prepared to justify it in my office. Years later, when your will is read, angry children will demand answers. Your reasons for creating an unequal division of your estate may be valid when you sign your will. But circumstances may change or not exist at the date of your passing. Reasons to discriminate against certain family members in 2005 may no longer be appropriate in 2012.

What if you forget to revise your will and don't treat everyone equally? Expect trouble. Equal must mean of equal value on a net basis. Leaving Miriam a $200,000 antique collection and Ben a $200,000 rental property is not equal treatment. You must factor taxes, future appreciation, and risks in each gift. If they are not equal, yours could be a different legacy. You'll likely create envy between brother and sister, which is probably the last thing you want to do.

---

**Bulletin**

Remember that minors can't receive an outright inheritance under your will. That's why you need an infant's gifts held in trust for minor children. Don't mistakenly leave property to a minor. The gift may be liquidated if you do not have an infant trust in your will.

---

## Forgive Family Loans

Theodore loaned his son Steve $50,000 for renovations to his home. Steve's wife, Marylou, stopped working after she had a second baby. Theodore was a new grandfather and no longer insisted on the monthly mortgage payments. Marylou assumed the loan was forgiven as a gift.

Theodore's will gave Steve's sister, Nancy, an extra $100,000 but didn't refer to the loan. When his will was read, no one could understand this extra gift to the sister. Theodore didn't have a lawyer make the will, which was unfortunate because a lawyer would have kept notes possibly explaining the unequal gifts. Theodore made it himself using a will kit.

Here's a further complication. Theodore never forgave the loan to Steve in his will. Nancy wants her brother to pay the balance of his loan and interest. No one can find the IOU with a list of all the cash payments Steve made to his father.

Until the lawyers advise them of their options, Steve wants credit to forgive the balance of the loan. But Nancy isn't ready to give up the fight. The executor must have the consent of all the beneficiaries to consider such a proposal. Legal expenses will be paid out of Theodore's estate to resolve the confusion.

## Equalize While You Are Alive

If you need to treat the children differently, then try to do it while you are alive. Don't leave them wondering why you waited until your death to play favourites. Even adult children will have trouble reconciling this with their grief. Avoid anything that could create friction or slight, however small. Pick all your children to be your executors. Give everyone a say in the estate. Don't let anyone feel left out of the process of sharing your bounty.

Whenever possible, equalize your children's share of your wealth while you are alive. Sometimes parents pay a small fortune to send one child to school and want to spend a similar amount on the child who didn't make it to university. If you have a legitimate reason why someone should receive more, make it known to your family.

**Legal Lingo**

*Child:* each law may have a specific definition of this word. For example, "child" has a different meaning for divorce, support, or a dependant's claims.

Tell the family that Alison is getting the house because she deserves it; she has promised to take care of her parents until they die. Everyone should know the score while you are alive. That way you can deal with any objections personally. What happens if Alison inherits and dies immediately after both of her parents? Your estate planning objectives can be easily thwarted. Alison's will may leave everything to a charity and not to her brother. If you have alternative beneficiaries for the gift, include them to avoid negative results.

## Let's Get Specific

Equal shares may not be fair if you have a developmentally or physically challenged child. In such cases, need outweighs fear of conflict within the family. Your obligations take precedence. This is a perfect example, however, of how you can make a special exception during your lifetime. Set aside funds and create a special trust for the support of your disadvantaged children. You can also do this while you're alive.

What if your son Mark's gambling problem is only getting worse? Your personal, religious, and philosophical background can affect your approach to money and children. If children must earn their inheritance, then Mark may be cut out of your estate. However, a special trust created by your will may be appropriate for him. It may help him make a fresh start. An inheritance from a parent to a problem child can also be a source of healing. Giving one last chance, so to speak.

Of course, giving everyone an equal share of the farm or the family business may be impossible. Tony runs the family restaurant without his sister Rose's involvement. It's not practical to give Rose a piece of the business. But what if there is nothing else in Dad's estate to divide? Life insurance or succession planning experts can develop ways to fund an equivalent share for her.

## Categories of Adult Children

Children can be put into different categories. The principal distinctions are single, married, born out of wedlock, stepchildren, and adopted children. Grandchildren also come under this heading because they can be dealt with under the will and require special instructions or precautions.

It's not sufficient to identify your beneficiaries simply as your children. You could be treating the children of a second spouse as your own, but legally they aren't your children. You could also be caring for a deceased brother's surviving children as your own. Children born out of a brief relationship can be dependants entitled to support from your estate.

It's a mistake to use the word *children* in your will. It can lead to costly court interpretations in front of a judge to determine who is entitled to share in the estate. Your will should identify each child individually by name. The same goes for nieces and nephews or brothers and sisters.

### Help Line

**Q:** What does the phrase "issue *per stirpes"* mean?

**A:** It's literally "by the root." It's seen in wills to describe how your issue share in an estate. It means, if a child dies but leaves issue (grandchildren), all issue will share what their parents would have inherited.

## What If a Child Dies?

You must decide what happens to a child's share of your estate if that child dies before you do. Normally, if a child dies first, you redo your will. If a child is born after your will is signed, you also make changes. A simple codicil or amendment can add the newborn's name. But what happens if the child dies, leaving your grandchildren alive? How can you address this in your will?

You can divide a testamentary gift between children on a per capita or issue *per stirpes* basis. Let me explain some terms first.

**Children per capita:** "by heads," meaning among your children individually if they are alive.

**Issue *per stirpes*:** "by branches," meaning issue, which can be a multigenerational group including more than children. If a child dies, his or her share would be divided equally among his or her issue. This means that your grandchildren would inherit only if their parents died.

Here's an example to help. Thomas and his sister, Theresa, share their father's estate equally. The will states that this is on a per capita basis. If his sister dies, Thomas would receive 100 percent of the father's estate.

If the will says *issue per stirpes*, a different result can occur. If Theresa dies but has children, her issue, the grandchildren, would inherit her share. Thomas would still get fifty percent of the estate. His sister's five children would each inherit ten percent according to the *per stirpes* condition in their grandfather's gift.

## Excluding a Child's Spouse

Every province has different family laws that deal with inherited property. Most provinces treat inheritances received during marriage as excluded property. Your children don't have to share their inheritance in the event of a marriage breakdown.

Ontario's Family Law Act can exclude increases in the value of an inheritance received during marriage from spousal property calculations. Increases are not shared with a child's spouse if there's an expressed declaration made in a will or at the time a gift is made. This is a significant provision that gives great comfort to parents.

For example, if the gift of $100,000 in stocks is worth $500,000 ten years later, then the increase in value is not shared. In Chapter 10, in my sample will, there was a provision to exclude any income from the gift.

**Q:** Is it okay to just leave everything to "my children" in my will?

**A:** No. Every province has rules to decide the meaning of "child" for different purposes. Stepchildren aren't automatically included.

## Setting up a Children's Trust

Here's one of the most common requests clients make. They want me to show them how they can control their kids' money. Parents want to make their children's inheritance last. The answers to this request may vary, but the result is the same. After you're gone, it's too late, too hard, and too expensive to keep teaching your kids. These are lessons they should have learned on their own.

You may not be able to control what children do with an inheritance. You can, however, control their access to estate funds. The most common way is to place the inheritance in a trust. For minor children, this is an essential clause in your will.

As we saw in Chapter 15, testamentary trusts allow your trustee to control the capital for the benefit of beneficiaries. Setting up a trust in your will is the most inexpensive route to go. Typically, your will creates a testamentary trust.

- Trust income earned on the capital can be distributed to children.
- Trust capital is encroached or used under certain circumstances.

## Staggering Payouts from a Trust

Capital and trust income can be paid out by your trustees at predetermined dates or events. Remember, you have the right to select trustees whom you trust. They'll exercise their discretion in these situations and can determine when the children's interests will take precedence over your stated desires.

A predetermined distribution can take place on a specified date so that

- twenty-five percent of the trust capital is distributed to my son at the age of eighteen;
- fifty percent of the trust capital is distributed to my son at the age of twenty-one; and
- the balance of the trust capital is distributed to my son at the age of twenty-five.

These types of payouts are more appropriate where there are sizable estate assets. A larger portfolio warrants the ongoing expense of maintaining a trust with corporate trustees and costs. You'll want to do a cost-benefit analysis to determine if your estate will be used up simply supporting the children to the age of eighteen.

## Drawbacks of Trusts for Children

The problem with trusts is the expense to administer them. The costs are twofold. One set is for annual tax filing and professional and trustee fees. The other is for court applications to vary or interpret the trust, costs that could be paid out of the trust's assets. The maintenance costs are annual until the trust ends, and there are costs to collapse and distribute trust assets. A trust can be collapsed for various reasons, including if there are no trust funds left to administer. This can happen when there has been mismanagement of the trust funds.

Trustees who are not spouses or close relatives will likely want an annual fee for their work. The income of the trust or estate may not be sufficient to cover all the trust expenses, and trust capital will have to be used, leading to a depletion of capital after a few short years.

This isn't to say that creating a trust fund for adult children won't work, just that you'll need sufficient wealth to fund the trust. Also, your children should not have immediate financial need of the trust money.

## Word Things Carefully

Trusts must be carefully planned. Living trusts must cover many contingencies. If they are incompletely drawn, problems will result. The trustees may need to visit a judge for an interpretation of the terms of the trust. The wording may restrict the trustee's ability to deal with both a beneficiary and the assets of the trust.

Educational trusts, for example, may cover room and board. What about foreign travel costs? If your son's school is in Japan, will Bob, the trustee, refuse to pay for travel to the school? If your son and Bob can't agree, each may get a lawyer and ask the court to intervene. The court must decide who is right. And what about the legal costs if your son is successful? Even if he isn't successful, the court can specify that this interpretation or a variation of the trust is necessary. In such cases, the legal costs may be paid from the trust fund even if the child isn't right.

## Infant Children Need Trusts and Guardians

Infant children have special needs. They must be provided for in your will with support and proper guardianship. You need to consider different scenarios, even the unthinkable. Most people don't plan for a common disaster (that's when both parents die in a common mishap). Wills must name a guardian for your minor children and their property.

### Help Line

**Q:** Who is a minor?

**A:** The age varies from province to province. For estate purposes, we'll consider a minor to be a person under the age of eighteen.

You should decide who will look after the children if both you and your spouse should die. A surviving parent would normally be expected to be the guardian. In most cases, that is the norm unless there's abuse or proven unfitness. In second marriages or common-law arrangements, there is real danger of a dispute, especially if along with guardianship come the keys to the family vault.

You may naturally think that your parents, the kids' grandparents, will automatically take over. Wrong! What if they are too old to be able to handle the needs of two or three active children? There are no automatic rules to decide who should have custody of the children after the biological parents die. By not specifying a preference, you are inviting an argument because the court considers that you have not properly taken care of the children. Don't leave it to a court to decide among competing interests and relatives.

If you die without a will, and children are minors, their money is paid into a court trust fund and held there. The court supervises release of the funds. Provincial law will dictate how the minors get use of the money held in trust. Access to your estate funds will be postponed until a guardian is appointed by the courts. In some cases, this may lead to difficult, time-consuming, and expensive court procedures.

## Courts Approve Guardians

If you specify your choice of guardian in your will, the courts must still approve your selection. The courts are the final decision makers when it comes to minors and their care. You can stop arguing with your spouse because you can't agree whose relatives will get the children. It may be academic. A change in circumstances can occur after your death, several years after your will was prepared. Perhaps your first choice of guardian is no longer alive.

Your suggestion for a guardian is not binding on the court after your death. It is only a statement of preference that the court may disregard. Higher tests, such as what's in the best interests of the child, apply.

This does not mean that your preference has no merit. It's not futile to express your wishes. The last thing you want is to have relatives fighting over custody of the kids at the funeral home. This can also happen because you left a sizable estate.

Consider that both parents could die in a common catastrophe. What would happen? Your choice of guardian must be confirmed by a court order. In Ontario, that has to be done within ninety days of your death. The court will confirm that the appointment is in the children's best interest.

---

**Time Machine**

Children born out of wedlock were normally excluded from a share of your estate. Now laws have been passed that automatically include them, along with adopted children, in the definition of children.

---

If you make a will, the designated guardian will care for the children immediately after your death. Your selection may not cause others to challenge it.

## Custodians/Guardians of Property

Sometimes parents wish to designate a person who is not the child's guardian to control the child's money. What if your designated guardian is overzealous and spendthrift? Use a different person as the guardian of the child's money. You can do so by specifying who takes custody and who guards the child's trust. Again, you can have your executor or a special trustee do this.

## Guidelines for Choosing Guardians

Jacques was sitting in my office and telling me why he and his wife, Lisa, had postponed making their wills. "We are arguing over the choice of guardian for our two children." If you are in that position, here are some helpful hints.

- Both parents need not name the same guardian. It's the will of the parent who dies last that settles the matter.
- If both parents die together, a court will ask the children, if they are twelve or older, for their opinions, which carry weight.
- Guardians do not get paid to raise your children. You can give them a gift in your will that is conditional on the children staying in their care.
- Always name alternative guardians in case your first choices have a change of heart.

Consider these additional factors.

- **Age:** elderly parents may not have the energy to go ten years with the twins.
- **Religion:** you may want guardians who share your values.
- **Marital status:** can your sister cope with your children and her own if she is divorced?

You've looked at children and how you can benefit them and control their inheritance. In the next chapter, I'll talk about all sorts of spouses.

· · · · · · · · · · · · · · · · · · · · · · · · · · · · · · · · · · · · · · · · · · · · · · · · · · · · · · ·

## The Least You Need to Know

- Treat children equally in your will to avoid problems.
- Have a family meeting to explain why you propose an unequal division.
- Specifically name your children if they are beneficiaries in your will.
- You need to name guardians in your will for minor children.

# Chapter 20

# Spouses: Good, Bad, and Divorced

In this chapter:

- Know traditional definitions of spouses.
- Follow checklists for brides and grooms.
- Learn tax-saving strategies.
- Understand spousal variations.

Do you remember your estate planning "wish list"? In Chapter 1, some of you, I'm sure, wrote down that taking care of your spouse is a key reason to plan. This chapter is dedicated to spouses, including every variation you can think of — traditional, separated, common-law, same-sex, divorced, and dying.

Spouses are in a special category of beneficiaries. For most of you, your partner will be the person who inherits your entire estate. Tax laws encourage most people to take care of their spouses, and traditional marriages make the choice of beneficiaries straightforward. Different questions arise in modern relationships with multiple marriages or less formal arrangements. There are always competing interests. I'll show you a variety of spousal situations. You'll get suggestions to consider as you change your spousal status as well.

## Marriage as a Partnership

As you well know, marriage is a partnership. And family law in every province reinforces that message. Laws protect the property and support rights of legally married spouses, meaning that you can't do whatever you want with your own property. So when you prepare a will or estate plan, you must satisfy your legal obligations to provide for your married spouse.

Marital property laws provide that some assets, such as the matrimonial home, are automatically shared. Assets such as a business or an inheritance may be excluded from family division. In most cases, property acquired during a marriage (including your pensions) is shared equally in the event of a divorce.

I know you're saying, "I'm not even married yet. Why are you telling me what happens if I divorce or separate?" It's important to understand the family property laws. You need to be aware of your rights and obligations before you marry to plan. Laws distinguish and create special property rules for married couples in case of death or divorce. In most provinces, common-law and same-sex relationships don't have the same property or support rights. This is an important reason for individuals in these relationships to plan and to write wills.

## Contracting Out

You and your spouse can agree in a contract that some provincial family law will not apply to your marriage. Most provinces allow you to set these new terms out in a prenuptial, domestic, or marriage contract. Agreements with a spouse can vary the property-sharing rules that would automatically apply. For instance, family businesses or particular assets can be excluded.

Prenuptial, domestic, or marriage contracts can deal with a variety of issues, not just who washes dishes and changes diapers. More important matters should be covered, such as support of spouses and children, under any federal support guidelines if they can be agreed upon. Cohabitation agreements can provide similar benefits for common-law or same-sex partners.

**It's Been Said**
......................................................

"He never say never before today,
What was able to take his breath away,
A face to lose youth for, to occupy age,
With the dream of, meet death with."
— Robert Browning, *A Likeness* (1864)

What if you're getting married for the second time? You'll definitely want to consider a marriage contract, especially if you have children from your prior marriage or a business to protect. You can modify, if you don't want to entirely negate, provincial family law to protect your beneficiaries. This modification can allow you to plan your estate in the event of divorce or a spouse's death.

## An Illustration Makes It Clear

Rachel and Joshua marry in Saskatchewan. Rachel is hired by a computer software company for a job in western Canada, and the couple relocate. During the marriage, she continues to do well financially. She earns stock options and purchases a home and a vacation property in her name. After a few years, Rachel inherits her father's estate. She uses the proceeds to pay off the mortgages on both properties.

The marriage is suffering, so Rachel decides to find out what her rights are just in case. She is told by a lawyer about her province's property laws, which require her to share assets. Her husband will get a share even though he didn't contribute financially to the purchase of either property.

Rachel, however, wants to assist financially her sister Ruth, who is unable, through illness, to work. Rachel asks the lawyer to clarify what she can or cannot do with her estate for Ruth.

## Jointly or as Tenants-in-Common

The lawyer tells Rachel it depends on how she currently owns her properties. If she owns them jointly with Joshua, then he would automatically inherit them, and Rachel couldn't control them by her will as part of her estate. Even though she is sole owner of the properties, she can't deal with them by her will. Her husband has rights to share in property acquired during the marriage.

Rachel asks her lawyer, "What can I leave my sister?" The lawyer explains that her husband's entitlement can't be taken away. Rachel is surprised. It was always her money or inheritance that was used, yet she has no freedom to deal with the properties as she wishes.

Rachel could enter into a marriage contract with her husband. They could agree to exclude the operation of some provincial family law, which would enable Rachel to provide for her sister. The lawyer also suggests that Rachel designate her sister as a beneficiary of a life insurance policy. This is a temporary measure until the marriage contract is signed. In the contract, Rachel and Joshua can agree through negotiations what their entitlements to each other's estates are.

So what if you are planning to get married?

## A Checklist for Those Getting Married

Congratulations are in order. But before you walk down the aisle, you and your spouse-to-be need to review your financial affairs to make sure you're cleared for takeoff on your honeymoon. Here are a few of the legal matters you'll have to consider (other than getting your marriage licence).

**Your wills:** marriage revokes all existing wills except those made specifically in contemplation of marriage. Both you and your spouse must make new wills. If you have children from a prior marriage or relationship, it is vital to prepare new wills to appoint new executors and guardians. Remember to stay away from signing one joint will.

---

**Time Machine**

Before 1890, a married woman couldn't make a testament to give away her personal property unless, among other conditions, her husband gave his consent. These laws weren't changed until the 1890s. Today either spouse can make a will without the other's consent or permission.

---

**Employee benefits:** you'll probably want to change the beneficiary of any benefits through your employer, such as life insurance policies, retirement plans, and medical coverage.

**Designated beneficiaries:** apart from benefits through work, you may have RRSPs, RRIFs, or life insurance policies. To save probate costs, you may wish to change the designated beneficiary of these assets.

**Property ownership:** consider holding some of your assets in joint ownership. Doing so facilitates a transfer of assets and reduces probate exposure if a spouse dies. Check Chapters 1 and 2 on joint tenancy with right of survivorship.

**Powers of attorney:** marriage doesn't give you rights to make financial decisions for an incapacitated spouse. You'll want to review Chapters 21, "Protect Property Today," and 22, "Look down the Road," about powers of attorney for property and personal care. These documents should be in your essential estate tool kit, as we discussed in Chapter 1.

**Prenuptial agreement:** will you be signing an agreement? If you're not treated as married and in a common-law or same-sex relationship, have you contemplated a cohabitation agreement? Deal with support and property rights in the event of a separation. Remember to allow sufficient time prior to the wedding to negotiate an agreement. I suggest three months. Working out the details can be frustrating while you're preparing for the big day.

---

**Bulletin**

You must designate your spouse as beneficiary of your RRSP and RRIF to qualify for the spousal rollover. For example, what if your former spouse is still your designated beneficiary of these assets? He or she isn't a qualifying spouse, so no rollover applies. Your ex could walk away with these assets and leave the tax bill for your estate.

---

## Protecting a Spouse

Tonesha is a dentist with all the investment savvy in her family. She is going into the hospital for surgery and is nervous. She wants to make sure her estate plan is up to date. She contacts a lawyer to change her will. "My husband isn't a sophisticated person financially. I love and care for him. He can't handle my investments if something should happen to me, and I am afraid that his ex-wife will get more support from him if he inherits money from me."

Tonesha says she wants her entire estate to be held in trust for her husband. She doesn't want his wife and children from his first marriage to benefit from her money. She has a friend who would act as executor and handle the investments.

The lawyer gives Tonesha this assessment. Her home is owned just in her name. She can't transfer it to a trust before she dies because her husband's consent and signature are required. He must permit her to deal with the family home. If Tonesha were to die, the home would not pass by right of survivorship. She must use her will to deal with this asset.

**It's Been Said**
......................................................

"One half of the world cannot understand the pleasures of the other."
— Jane Austen, 1775–1817

Tonesha could consider placing her investments, which are only registered in her name, into a trust. However, her husband does not have to accept Tonesha's proposal to benefit him under her will. He could go to court and elect to claim his spousal entitlement under provincial law.

The husband is asked what he thinks of the proposal. "She is just panicking. According to her, she wants to control all the assets, including our house, and leave me to deal with her executor."

Tonesha is upset by her husband's suggestion.

But he says, "You're thinking only about your money and not me."

Tonesha thinks a professional executor would be a benefit for her husband; he wouldn't have to worry about the day-to-day fluctuations of the market. She's also concerned, however, that he would remarry. A new wife could clean him out in a divorce. He'd be left with no financial resources to provide for his later years.

## What Are the Options?

Tonesha could consider placing her substantial assets, such as her stock portfolio, in a qualified spousal trust. She could consider having her husband and a corporate trustee jointly manage the portfolio for more personal involvement and professional management of the stocks.

The couple could reregister the house so that they are joint owners with rights of survivorship. This approach eliminates the need for Tonesha's husband to probate her estate just to transfer their residence. It will save legal and estate court costs and give her husband more security. Tonesha could also set aside a fund to help her husband live in and repair the home.

Tonesha's husband could sign a marriage contract, which would confirm that he would accept the provisions of her will and estate plan. In this contract, he would agree not to apply in court to seek a larger share of her estate.

---

**Legal Lingo**

*Common-law spouses* under federal income tax laws are those of the opposite sex in a conjugal relationship, with cohabitation in the preceding twelve months, or those who have parented a child. New definitions were introduced in 2000 to give same-sex spouses the same benefits.

---

## Spousal Tax Treatments

Tax planning matters were dealt with generally in Chapter 5, and we covered *inter vivos* or living trusts in Chapter 6. Here we will talk specifically of spouses as beneficiaries. Can you get any tax savings on transfers of property at death? If everything that exists at death is taxed, how can you avoid the inevitable? The answer is to take advantage of the tax strategies that are available. You must use them, or your estate will pay more taxes than necessary.

Let's recap what you know. On the death of a taxpayer, all capital property is deemed disposed of at fair market value. The exception to this rule is a transfer to a qualifying spouse or a spousal trust. Such transfers receive special tax treatment. In these circumstances, the death of the taxpayer will not trigger a "deemed sale" of the property. Your executor doesn't report a capital gain when there is a rollover to a qualifying spouse or a spousal trust.

Any income-qualifying transaction involving spouses is entitled to the rollover. A deferral of any tax payable is thereby created until the surviving spouse disposes of the property. The asset is rolled over into the surviving spouse's name without payment of income tax. This is a favourable result since the surviving spouse inherits the property and avoids the deemed disposition rules.

## Who's Your Spouse?

The word *spouse* is defined for income tax purposes. Legislative changes in 2000 expanded this definition. For tax planning purposes, spouses now include those in a same-sex relationship. In the spousal category since January 1, 1993, are common-law spouses. In some cases, former spouses (those separating or divorcing) qualify when marital property rights are settled in an agreement or court order.

The conditions for qualifying as a spouse are new. You'll need to refer specifically to the federal government guidelines to plan.

### It's Been Said
· · · · · · · · · · · · · · · · · · · · · · · · · · · · · · · · · · · · · · · · · · · · · · · · · ·

"Keep your eyes wide open before marriage, half shut afterwards."
— Benjamin Franklin, *Poor Richard's Almanac* (1738)

## Qualifying for Special Spousal Treatment

Transfers at your adjusted cost base for income tax purposes qualify if you meet the following conditions.

- You and your spouse must be resident in Canada immediately before the spouse's death.
- Property must be transferred to your spouse or to a qualifying spousal trust.
- Property transfers must occur within thirty-six months of the death of a spouse.
- For spousal trusts only, the spouse can be entitled to all the trust's income and capital during the spouse's lifetime. No one else can benefit during that period.

These gifts to qualified spouses avoid the deemed disposition rules on death. An example will show how the rollover works.

- Frank is a spouse who dies. He has stocks with a fair market value of $110,000.
- He purchased the stocks for $10,000.
- His deemed capital gain is $100,000.
- Frank's terminal tax return reports one-half of his capital gain of $100,000.
- The taxable capital gain of $50,000 would normally be included as his taxable income. Since his spouse is his beneficiary, this amount is not included as income.
- If this rollover was not available, and assuming a fifty percent tax rate, $25,000 would be due to the government.

- As a result of the rollover, Frank's wife receives the stock at his cost base.
- She pays tax only when she sells the stocks or on her death.

Since the surviving spouse inherits the deceased spouse's adjusted cost base, no tax is paid until the surviving spouse disposes of it. The effect is that there is a tax deferral of the payment. The $25,000 of deferred tax payments can continue to grow in value.

## The Advantages of Income Tax Deferrals

What advantage is there to a tax deferral on Frank's stocks? The deferral allows his spouse to decide how and when to sell the stocks. Timing is everything in the investment world. If the market rises, the stocks increase in value. Postponing the payment of a large tax bill has added benefits because your estate doesn't have to liquidate assets to pay the taxes. You'll avoid an immediate income tax bill of $25,000.

Here's an example for those without stocks. Lucy is the designated beneficiary of her husband's RRSP. Her husband died, and she paid no tax until she cashed in the RRSP. By deferring the tax, her RRSP continued to grow on a compounded basis.

### It's Been Said
...............................................

"Saw a wedding in the church; and strange to see what delight we married people have to see these poor fools decoyed into our condition."
— Samuel Pepys, December 25, 1665

## Should You Leave It to a Spouse or a Spousal Trust?

Refresh your memory about trusts by reading Chapter 6. In the meantime, I'll give you a quick review. Testamentary trusts are created in a will and are another way of gifting the trust's income and capital to a specified beneficiary. Spousal trusts can control a gift for a surviving spouse and income-split as well. Typically, when your surviving spouse passes on, the remaining trust funds go to your children or an alternative beneficiary. Spousal trusts provide for the surviving spouse while trustees control the assets.

Rollovers apply to assets transferred to a qualifying spousal trust. In comparison, if your will makes an outright gift to your spouse, you lose all control over the asset on death.

The nature and size of your assets will help you decide if a spousal trust is useful. You will need to consider the costs of creating a separate trust. These costs include accounting and legal expenses, annual tax filings, and compensation for the trustees. If you create a spousal trust, you must deal with a possible spousal election under provincial family law. You may need your spouse to sign a marriage contract to prevent these claims. The surviving spouse would agree to accept the trust terms.

One other condition applies for the spousal trust to obtain the tax rollover advantage. Spousal trusts must "qualify" by meeting certain rules. For example, only the spouse is entitled to all the income from a spousal trust during that surviving spouse's lifetime. Another rule is that no other person can use any capital from the trust during the spouse's lifetime. Only the spouse can use the trust assets. No sharing of income or capital from the trust to benefit children is possible. You'd have to create separate trusts or set aside assets for other beneficiaries.

## Marriage Contracts

Domestic or prenuptial contracts may allow you to avoid some restrictions of family law in your province. With such a contract, you can agree to waive your respective rights to make an election on the death of your spouse. You may agree to accept less for the sake of an estate plan designed to minimize the tax consequences of death. This may be a matter of serious negotiation if spouses have unequal incomes or assets. In many cases, both spouses want the security of knowing that neither spouse's beneficiaries will be disappointed. A sample contract is included in Chapter 18.

## Five Separate Spousal Situations

We will look at the options for each of the following types of spouses since each category has special issues to review:

1. Spouses planning to separate;
2. Separated spouses;
3. Divorced spouses;
4. Common-law spouses; and
5. Same-sex spouses.

## 1. Spouses Planning to Separate

While you're separating, you may want to leave everything you own to anyone but your spouse. Although the thought may be tempting, don't rush out to do this. Remember that, good or bad, spouses treated as married are protected by law. You can't just cut him or her out of your will. Especially if you have no final settlement on support and property issues, your freedom to give to others is restricted.

You can change your executor and powers of attorney, though, and perhaps the beneficiaries of any life insurance policy or pension. Consider setting up an *inter vivos* trust. Consult your family lawyer before proceeding, though.

Change your will so your spouse won't be the one handling any minor children's money. Review your choice of guardian for the children. Do you have real reasons why your separating spouse is unfit to have custody? Note them in a letter to your executor and lawyer.

## 2. Separated Spouses

Married spouses must release their claims to your estate through a court order or a negotiated separation agreement. Only then can their property claims be ignored in your will. Support payments, however, can still be binding on your estate. It may be wise to arrange life insurance policies to cover these obligations or to set up a separate trust. Support can be a first charge against your estate's assets. Ensure that your obligations are satisfied before you make any other gifts.

What happens if you have separated from your spouse but are not divorced? If you have children with a new partner, your first spouse may still have a claim to share in the estate on an intestacy. Plans to provide for the new twins' education can be cancelled by your first spouse's rights. Your married spouse's property or support rights should be covered or released in a separation agreement pending a divorce.

What if you don't have a signed and valid separation agreement? Your spouse is separated (but not divorced), so you are considered married spouses if you die without a will. In this intestacy, your separated spouse could become your sole beneficiary if you have no children. Separated spouses can still handle your estate, and they may have the right to apply to administer your estate.

Make sure you have designated new executors and beneficiaries in your will. Check with a lawyer to determine what restrictions (if any) exist regarding your ability to ignore your separated spouse.

"At the touch of love everyone becomes a poet."

— Plato, 427–347 B.C.

### 3. Divorced Spouses

Divorce terminates gifts to a spouse in your will unless there is specific language to the contrary. This also means your spouse cannot be executor of your estate, and your alternative trustee would be appointed if you named one.

You'll be bound by the terms of your divorce and separation agreements, which may affect your estate. Subject to these restrictions, you'll be free to deal with your estate. So you may legally ignore a divorced spouse.

### 4. Common-Law Spouses

As of January 1993, the word *spouse* includes a common-law spouse for income tax purposes. So now estate planning can include transfers to common-law spouses. But remember that, depending on your province's law, only spouses treated as married can make spousal elections.

A lasting relationship between two individuals of the opposite sex is often described as a common-law relationship. The income tax laws include common-law spouses. Basically, the tax statutes recognize you if you have been in a conjugal relationship for at least twelve months or if you are in such a relationship and have a child together.

The confusion, however, revolves around other provincial laws. It's true that common law is like married for income tax considerations but not for intestacy rules or the division of property in many provinces. New provincial legislation and court decisions can change this overnight. Make sure you update your situation with a lawyer to understand your obligations to a common-law spouse.

Common-law spouses need estate plans and wills to protect each other. But what if you have lived together for years like Doris and Lee? They never bothered to designate each other as common-law spouses and maintained separate residences. When Lee died, Doris wanted to know if she could claim support even though they had no "common-law" spousal label.

Lee was a retired professor and paid for all of Doris's vacations and entertainment. Doris, on the other hand, nursed Lee through several bouts of cancer. Lee promised he would provide for her in his will. Alas, he never got around to revising it.

Doris may have legal claims to support as a dependant under provincial law even though no formal designation of their relationship exists. Because Lee broke his promise, she could also sue his estate for services for which she was never compensated.

## 5. Same-Sex Spouses

Recent changes in provincial and federal laws give same-sex spouses rights to marry. If not married, they benefit from the same support and survivorship rights as common-law spouses. You can't deny a spouse his or her rights to support. Your estate would only end up in a court case that would upset your estate plan.

Now we've completed Step 5, "Benefit Your Beneficiaries." Let's move on to the last step, "Protect Yourself Now." First you'll learn about powers of attorney that protect your estate today. You'll also learn how to stay out of a nursing home.

## The Least You Need to Know

- Married spouses have specific estate, property, and support rights given by each province's family law.
- Each province's family law allows spouses to enter into prenuptial, domestic, or marriage contracts to exclude the operation of parts of the province's family law.
- If you marry, you should review the designated beneficiaries of all your assets, including insurance and RRSPs, and prepare a new will.
- Marriage contracts can also be used to ensure that your estate plan is not challenged.

# Protect Yourself Now

So far, you have taken five steps in your estate planning. Here is where you get to do something for yourself. With powers of attorney, you decide who will manage your money and health care while you're still alive.

Powers of attorney for property are loaded guns; be careful how you use them — they can backfire. I'll show you how you can protect your estate plan today. Prepare powers of attorney in case you become incapacitated. I'll explain why a living will may not be as important as you thought.

I'll give you ten commandments so you'll know when to revise your will. Treat your original will like gold — it's irreplaceable. I'll wrap up with ways to keep your estate plan up to date. You'll use a checklist for a before-and-after review of your estate planning needs. You'll see how far you've travelled and how much you've learned.

# Chapter 21

# Protect
# Property Today

In this chapter:

- Powers of attorney can be loaded guns.
- Who'll take over?
- Understand the dangers and abuses of incapacity.
- Review legal formalities and a sample power of attorney.

Powers of attorney documents are like loaded guns. They can be used to protect or abuse you. When they're turned on you, they can be fatal. Remember that both are powerful weapons — put them in the hands of the right people.

Incapacity comes in many forms. Strokes, old age, or disease can render you unable to handle your finances. Whatever the cause, the results are the same; someone must be appointed as your substitute to handle your legal affairs.

Appointments can occur in two ways. One way is expensive through a slow court appointment process. Someone, not you, must apply to be appointed as your financial guardian to handle your affairs. The other way is inexpensive and quick. You designate someone to handle your affairs by signing a power of attorney before you become incapable. Let's look at powers of attorney for property. I'll show you the dangers they can avoid.

## Help Line

**Q:** Can't I name an attorney in my will?

**A:** No. Wills become effective only on death. Provincial laws have separate requirements for powers of attorney. These documents are examined by the public as they are used before your death.

## You've Got to Be Ready

"Aren't I too young to need a power of attorney?" That's a question a lot of clients ask me. My answer is usually the same; I tell them about Stuart.

His car left the road as it skidded out of control. The police couldn't explain how the accident happened. Stuart couldn't explain it either. He was in a coma.

Lilly, Stuart's wife, was in shock. She hadn't been involved in any of the family finances. Instead, she had been responsible for their three children, all under the age of ten. Now she would have to take care of them and Stuart. At first, the only thing that mattered was Stuart's needs. Then gradually friends and family asked her the same questions. "Do you have enough money to pay your bills?" "Did Stuart give you a power of attorney for his financial matters?"

Weeks passed, with some gradual improvement in Stuart's condition. Lilly considered refinancing their home or even selling it to be closer to Stuart's rehabilitation clinic. She approached their family lawyer and learned the horrible truth: the house was registered in both their names. They were joint owners, but she couldn't sell or refinance it without permission from a court. Lilly was upset. She and Stuart had prepared wills; why wouldn't they help? The lawyer told her that Stuart's will would become effective only after his death. In the meantime, she couldn't sign papers for Stuart.

The lawyer explained that she and Stuart should have made a power of attorney for property. Now Lilly had to apply through the courts to get the relief she needed. She was appointed Stuart's guardian for his property to make his financial decisions.

## Powers of Attorney Protect like Insurance

I know, I know. I hear you saying a will is all the planning you can muster. Besides, powers of attorney are just for the elderly. But reality can surprise you. Stuart was only thirty-seven when it surprised him. Incapacity doesn't discriminate, and it can strike anyone at any age. Car accidents like Stuart's are daily reminders of how short and precious our lives are.

You don't expect to have a fire in your home. Yet you buy fire insurance on your apartment contents or home every year. You should consider powers of attorney like having insurance — just in case. Besides, they're much cheaper than the alternative.

Most people expect the law will let them act on behalf of a spouse who has had a stroke. But just try to get money out of a bank account that's not a joint account. No one can sell or mortgage your home to raise money without powers of attorney. You can't help your own parents unless they give you a power of attorney. Only then are you authorized to deal with someone else's assets.

> **Bulletin**
>
> A power of attorney doesn't mean you need a lawyer to act as your attorney. *Attorney-at-law* is an American term for lawyers. In Canada, the words *lawyer*, *barrister*, and *solicitor* are used. An attorney in this context is a substitute, agent, or proxy.

## What's an Attorney to Do?

An attorney is a person whom you select as your agent or substitute decision maker. A power of attorney is a legal written document, which you sign, appointing your attorney. It meets the legal requirements in your province. I set out a sample document below. You need to know that there are two common types of powers of attorney. In this chapter, we'll look at ones for property. Chapter 22, "Look down the Road," will deal with powers of attorney for personal care issues.

Your attorney can do anything authorized by provincial law except make a will. You can restrict attorneys with further conditions in the documents used to appoint them. Attorneys can represent you for all financial matters or just for a particular purpose. While you are out of the country, you can appoint your brother as an attorney to sell a house or stocks. Attorneys can handle banking for housebound relatives who no longer drive.

The real benefit comes from your attorney's ability to act in the event of your incapacity. Documents should state that attorneys can operate in the event of your incapacity. Some provincial laws require you to use words such as "enduring," "durable," or "continuing" in the document to confirm this. You need a provision to state that your attorney can act even after you become incapacitated.

This is the key to understanding the importance of preparing a power of attorney as an estate planning instrument. You can make one only while you are competent. If your mind is affected, it may be too late. Dementia, for instance, can affect your ability to understand the consequences of your financial decisions. If that's the case, you can't authorize a legal agent or attorney.

## Attorneys and Executors: A Comparison

Attorneys serve different functions than executors. Executors sell assets, pay off debts, and distribute property to your will's beneficiaries. Attorneys, on the other hand, manage and protect your property for your benefit. They can't distribute your assets. Attorneys' powers are restricted in law or by the power of attorney document itself. An attorney's power ceases upon your death. Executors, on the other hand, are authorized to act only after your death.

Help Line

**Q:** My mother is paranoid. She is accusing me of stealing her bank books and money. Can I have her declared incapable so I can take control of her money?

**A:** Not without a court order. Even a medical opinion won't be enough. But if you have an unrestricted power of attorney, you can take appropriate legal measures.

Attorneys can act under a continuing power of attorney while you are incapable. They can protect, manage, and preserve your property for the benefit of you and your loved ones. They can pay your bills or sell your house. Without an attorney, your family or the government may have to apply to become your guardian. Private solutions are always preferable to the costs and delays of court intervention.

If you want to limit what your attorney can do, it's easy to put these restrictions into the document when it is prepared. The people you choose as executors may also be suitable attorneys.

## The Alternative: A Court-Appointed Guardian

If you fail to designate an attorney, and you become incompetent, what happens? Your family, like Lilly, must ask a court to be appointed as your guardian. A government guardian may take over if no next of kin applies. This appointment process probably isn't the best means to protect your wealth.

To get a guardian appointed, you'll likely need a lawyer to prepare the court documents. Evidence is required to confirm your inability to handle your property, and your capacity to manage your finances must be assessed. This could require two independent assessments by professionals. The cost of the assessments can vary, but it's safe to budget $500 to $1,000. This amount doesn't include the cost of lawyers to handle the papers and court work.

## How Does the Court Process Start?

Major illnesses can make you unable to understand the consequences of your financial decisions. For example, you may refuse to pay your utility bills or start giving your money away. If you have no power of attorney for property, someone may start the court process.

Family members, friends, or, as a last resort, public government trustees can file papers to become your court-appointed guardian. As the incapable person, you'd get notice, as would your next of kin, who could oppose or support the cause. Can you imagine anything worse than your family fighting over control of your money while you are still alive? If your relatives oppose the appointment, there could be a trial to decide the issues. Of course, disputes can also arise when the guardian must determine the best course to take with your assets.

Courts can insist that a guardian, even if it is your spouse, still file a detailed management plan and a security bond. Guardians act only according to the terms of reference given by the court. They may reapply to the court for advice whenever unexpected events occur. These procedures, delays, and costs alone justify investing in a power of attorney.

"An ounce of prevention and a power of attorney are worth a ton of cures."
— Ed Olkovich

## What's a Court-Appointed Guardian to Do?

Guardians must account to the court, which audits and supervises their activities. Going to court to obtain a guardian appointment with court audit is expensive. Thousands of dollars of court and legal expenses can be just the start. Compare them to the cost of a few hundred dollars for a lawyer to prepare a power of attorney.

Court-appointed guardians usually file annual management and financial reports. They must explain what they have done with your property. If your home must be sold to pay for your care or because you can no longer reside in it, court approval may be required. The court audits financial records and, where requested, permits your attorney a small compensation fee.

Surprised and stunned. That's the reaction people have when I review these incapacity laws. I have to explain that a will operates only after death. It offers no assistance to protect you while you're alive. You need powers of attorney if you become incapable of handling your financial affairs. You must prepare these documents to protect your property and loved ones from your incapacity.

## Effectiveness of Powers of Attorney

Choosing a person to act as your attorney is a lot like choosing a person to handle your estate. The trustworthiness of the individual you select is paramount. Attorneys can abuse and mismanage your property. If you have any concerns, put safeguards in the power of attorney document.

Married people usually appoint their spouses as attorneys. Unless, that is, they're just starting a second or third marriage. But many people neglect to name an alternative attorney. What happens if a spouse or first-choice attorney dies or becomes incapacitated? In a car accident, you, the person giving the power of attorney (the donor), may be incapacitated. Your attorney can die in the same accident. Without an alternative, you are back to the court appointment process.

If you are a single parent, who will provide for the financial needs of your children? Think how much more secure you will feel if a trusted friend has power of attorney over your money.

# Standards of Conduct for Attorneys

Each province has a Powers of Attorney Act and some related statutes. These laws control how attorneys operate. Special care must be taken if you wish your attorney to sell or deal with real estate. Don't assume a power of attorney prepared in Nova Scotia will let you sell real estate in Florida or British Columbia. Check with your estate lawyer.

You must know the duties and obligations of an attorney before you name one. If you consent to act as a friend's attorney, here are some of your responsibilities.

**Accountability:** attorneys must be able to explain their financial dealings with another person's property. You are not an accountant; simple record keeping of all financial transactions is what is required. Records must be kept during disability, which can last years. Attorneys are obligated to account to your estate trustee and beneficiaries if you die or to you if you recover. The standards of care imposed on attorneys by the law vary.

The law requires a higher standard of care for an attorney who claims compensation. If no payment is received for their services, attorneys need only act reasonably. Attorney compensation can be specified in your document. If you don't do so, fees can be set if the attorney wants payment. Usually, this is done by a judge or without protest by a government fee schedule.

**Fiduciary obligations:** as fiduciaries, attorneys cannot profit from acting as such. Compensation for their services, however, is considered legal when approved or authorized. Attorneys can't make a hidden or secret profit at your expense. This is strictly enforced.

For example, an attorney can't purchase your car for two dollars because you can no longer drive it. As part of your estate plan prior to death, authorize attorneys to make gifts that can assist your beneficiaries. Doing so can especially benefit an attorney, who may be your only child, who needs support from you.

**Honesty and fraud:** attorneys are not above the law. Don't kid yourself — it can happen. Even family members can be charged with theft of your property when they convert it to their own use. You must realize that they are only human and subject to temptations. By appointing strangers, you may be putting yourself in unnecessary danger. Get legal advice on how you can protect yourself.

Choose your attorneys wisely to avoid abuse. An executor's duties begin when an attorney's work ceases at your death. That's one reason why it's not uncommon to see the same individual performing both tasks.

## Dangers to Avoid with Powers of Attorney

As I mentioned at the beginning of the chapter, a power of attorney is a loaded gun. It can be used to save and protect, or it can be turned on you to cause serious damage. If you are afraid of misuse by your attorney, include written restrictions in the document. You can specify that the attorney can act only if you are incapacitated (requiring an expert opinion).

Require your attorney to deliver annual financial statements to relatives, or have your attorney's dealings monitored by your accountant. This approach is reassuring for people who do not have close relationships with their attorneys. Also consider having more than one attorney so they can police each other.

> **Time Machine**
>
> Remember in those old movies the legal term everyone used? It was *non compos mentis* or "not of sound mind." Today we talk in terms of *capacity*, a key question that courts have to decide. Do you have the mental capacity to understand the consequences of your financial decisions? If so, usually you can sign a power of attorney.

You must name an alternative attorney. Conditional powers of attorney can also be considered. They are signed but not effective until an event occurs. You can request that your lawyer hold these documents for you. They won't be released, for example, until a certificate of incapacity is produced. Your lawyer must advise you of the pros and cons of these options.

**It's Been Said**

"Love all, trust a few."

– Shakespeare, *All's Well that Ends Well*, Act 1, Scene 1

## Watch out for Elder Abuse

It's called financial exploitation, criminal fraud, or elder abuse. Here's how it can start.

- Elderly persons become ill or housebound.
- They may be isolated or have no relatives.
- A new best friend or caregiver offers to help and even pay bills.
- The victim becomes dependent on that person.
- The new friend's or caregiver's behaviour changes to exploitation.
- Abusers may withhold care or medication to force their schemes.
- Abusers may obtain a power of attorney, a licence to access money.
- The victim may not know about the financial abuse.
- The victim may have difficulty getting proper legal advice.

Sometimes the victim dies with a depleted estate. Sometimes abusers just walk away after helping themselves to whatever they want. If you see any of the above happening, call a lawyer. Have the person revoke the power of attorney. This is a simple office procedure and not a court procedure. Counselling may be necessary to have the victim take action.

### Help Line

**Q:** My parents don't trust me to have their power of attorney. What can I do?

**A:** Recommend that they see their own lawyer independently to learn about their alternatives. Suggest another attorney to work with you. If necessary, a trust company can act as an independent attorney. They can also consider setting up a living trust.

In many cases, the elderly are too weak or embarrassed to go public or to the police. They don't wish to prosecute abusers, who are often family members. Prevention is always a cheaper cure. If your own family member is susceptible to this type of abuse, consider these steps.

- Consult a lawyer who handles capacity matters to learn about your rights.
- Have a specialist assess your family member for financial competence.
- Get a court-approved guardian to replace an attorney if necessary.
- Review the relative's financial records and question unusual transactions.

## Remember, Be Safe

At a minimum, you must understand that

- once you sign a power of attorney, unless it has restrictions, it's fully loaded;
- attorneys, with unrestricted powers, can do anything but change your will;
- your attorney cannot be in a conflict;
- your finances can be mismanaged, and abuses can occur;
- you can revoke a power of attorney if you still have legal capacity;
- you can have multiple powers of attorney for different purposes;
- you may need different powers of attorney where you own real estate; and
- you should get legal advice to avoid possible abuse and understand your options.

A medical opinion to demonstrate your competence to make a power of attorney may be required in doubtful cases. Witnesses who sign the document can't really prove your capacity. Witnesses must confirm that you, while not incapacitated, signed documents in their presence. Usually, witnesses can't be your attorney or your attorney's spouse. This is one more reason you should have professional advice — to ensure that you meet your province's requirements for witnesses.

## Legal Formalities for a Power of Attorney

Each province has a power of attorney law that must be followed when documents are prepared. Noncompliance with the legislative requirements can invalidate your documents. The more assets you have, the more you need proper protection. Use the services of a lawyer to prepare your power of attorney. I can't believe how many store-bought forms I have seen that are improperly completed. Document kits seldom deal with all contingencies or high-risk situations and don't give you advice.

Lawyers will ensure that your documents comply with all legal requirements. What if a person or bank, for instance, questions your documents? A lawyer who made them can attest to your competence to designate powers of attorney. Lawyers can also advise you of the risks and dangers of abuse. Develop a relationship with a lawyer for a few hundred dollars. It's a good investment to prevent problems. If you are elderly and have health problems, advice is essential.

Here's a sample of a power of attorney for property. It gives you an illustration of certain conditions and contents. Because all provincial laws are different, don't use this form since it may not be valid, especially in Quebec.

## Property Power of Attorney

1. I, Frank Donor, hereby appoint Rob Donor to serve as my Attorney to exercise the powers set forth below. If Rob Donor is unable or unwilling to serve, then I appoint Pat Tomkins as my Attorney.

2. I authorize my said Attorney to take all actions and perform all acts in my name concerning my affairs as my Attorney may deem advisable or necessary in his [her] absolute discretion. I give to my Attorney full power to act in the management and disposition of my property with the authority that I might exercise were I present, including, but not by way of limitation, any or all of the following:

(a) to manage my affairs, handle my investments, arrange for the investment and disposition of funds, exercise all rights with respect to my investments, establish, use, and terminate brokerage accounts, collect amounts owed or payable to me, open bank accounts in my name, enter my safe deposit box, and add to or remove from there any or all contents;

(b) to exercise all rights to securities and bonds, including the right to buy, sell, transfer, encumber, pledge, and vote and to establish, use, and terminate brokerage accounts;

(c) to buy, sell, transfer, lease, subdivide, alter boundaries, mortgage, encumber, pledge, manage, improve, and maintain real property, including the power to erect, repair, or demolish buildings;

(d) to buy, sell, transfer, lease, mortgage, encumber, pledge, manage, improve, maintain, repair, or alter personal property;

(e) to pay claims and debts, borrow money, and create security interests for the repayment;

(f) to disclaim any interest in property, renounce fiduciary positions, claim an elective share of the estate of my deceased spouse, make gifts, create trusts, and make additional gifts to trusts;

(g) to exercise all rights of mine under insurance and annuity policies, including the right to change beneficiaries, to borrow, to assign, to change owners, and to surrender the policies;

(h) to expend and to distribute income or principal for the benefit of my spouse and dependants;

(i) to file tax returns, obtain access to confidential files, and deal with the tax department;

(j) to engage and dismiss agents;

(k) to pay my bills and to pay for all things necessary for my physical care, protection, and well-being and for that of my property.

3. In making this Power of Attorney, I acknowledge that

(a) I am at least eighteen, and I may, while capable, revoke this Power of Attorney;

(b) the value of my property administered by my attorney may decline unless my Attorney manages it prudently;

(c) my Attorney could misuse the authority given by this Power of Attorney.

4. This Power of Attorney shall not be affected by my incapacity.

5. Alternative clause 4 (for a standby Power of Attorney). This Power of Attorney shall become effective only upon my incapacity. My incapacity shall be deemed to exist if I have been declared incapable upon a notarized affidavit signed by a licensed physician confirming that I am mentally incapable of managing my financial affairs. This Power of Attorney shall become effective on the date of the said notarized affidavit signed by a licensed physician.

6. Further alternative clause 4 (restricted). This Power of Attorney shall be restricted so that my Attorneys allow me to continue to reside in my home as long as possible. I hereby authorize them to use all my financial resources for my care regardless of how this might impact my estate beneficiaries.

7. SIGNED BY: _____
DONOR

on the _____ day of _____ , 2005 in the presence of the witnesses whose names appear below and who signed on the same date.

8. We have signed this Power of Attorney in the presence of the person whose name appears above and in the presence of each other.

Witness: _____    Witness: _____

Name: _____    Name: _____

Address: _____    Address: _____

## Help Line

**Q:** What if a caregiver or relative is abusing my financial power of attorney?

**A:** Unless you are incapacitated, you can revoke the power of attorney without going to court. Lawyers can explain what papers must be signed and which dangers to avoid.

### Ensure that Your Attorney Will Serve

You'd probably want to know if you are someone's attorney, but just because you're named in a document doesn't mean you have to take on the job. If you are consulted before the documents are prepared, ask if you will receive compensation. You and the donor can work it out in advance.

Decisions by attorneys can dramatically impact the value of your estate. You may wish to excuse them from honest mistakes that adversely affect the value of your property.

If you can no longer reside in your home, should your attorney sell it? What about those priceless treasures you have spent a lifetime accumulating? Will your attorney respect your wishes as set out in your will for distributing these assets when the house is sold? Do your province's laws require your attorney to do so?

Are you better off picking a professional such as your accountant to be your attorney? Not likely. Professionals may not have the time to attend to details. Selling or storing every knick-knack you have collected is time-consuming. Although the power of attorney can allow for delegation, such decisions must be made by the person you selected.

### Final Word

OK, you've selected a trustworthy attorney to handle your financial affairs if you become incapacitated. Every estate plan must plan for incapacity due to old age or mental or medical problems. You need the protection that a power of attorney can provide. Make sure you properly execute and store extra copies of your power of attorney documents. They are valuable, and misplacing them makes them useless.

Powers of attorney can be given to banks or brokers for specific times or purposes. While on vacation, you can give a power of attorney to someone you trust that you can revoke or automatically terminate when you return. You normally make a revocation in writing with witnesses. Make sure the attorney acknowledges the cancellation.

Consider using multiple powers of attorney for different purposes. Record who receives copies of documents if you must replace your attorney. Keep this loaded gun locked up if necessary. You can sign it, but arrange to deliver it or release it to your attorney only when it's needed.

· · · · · · · · · · · · · · · · · · · · · · · · · · · · · · · · · · · · · · · · · · · · · · · · · · · · · · · · · · · ·

## The Least You Need to Know

- You need a power of attorney for property as part of your estate plan.
- You can limit your attorney's authorization once you become incapacitated.
- You can revoke your power of attorney without a court order if you are competent.
- Store power of attorney documents safely like your will.

# Chapter 22

# Look down the Road

In this chapter:

- Who will speak for you?
- Choose a decision maker.
- Avoid dangerous options.
- Make it legal.

Do you wish to prolong your life indefinitely? Before you answer that question, consider another one. Are you prepared to live with a level of disability or dependency? If your answer is yes, but with certain stipulations, whom do you trust to ensure your conditions are met if you are unable to communicate? These questions can torment your family, but you can ensure they won't agonize over them. Designate an attorney to express your wishes when you can't.

You can express your preferences for personal and health care matters in advance, and I'll show you how in this chapter. If you are unable to make your own decisions, you can choose a person to speak for you. A power of attorney document authorizes and instructs your attorney as your substitute decision maker. Much has been said about living wills and medical directives. The information is often confusing. I'll also set the record straight to benefit you and your elderly family members.

## Searching for Answers

Isaac was desperately calling all the lawyers in his neighbourhood. He had to take his wife into the hospital for emergency surgery on Monday, and she wanted him to get her a living will. Isaac didn't know if he should call a doctor or a lawyer. He searched the Internet for answers. Finally, he bought a kit, but he thought it better to see a lawyer to make it legal.

Isaac and his wife were preparing to deal with some of the most difficult decisions individuals and family members have to make. They had read about advance medical directives, powers of attorney for care, and living wills. These things were now something more than reading material — they were necessities.

If you're baffled by all of this, you're not alone. Every jurisdiction has a different set of rules for proxies, attorneys, and directives. So let's try to distinguish each of these documents.

---

**Legal Lingo**

---

*Power of attorney for personal care* is a legal document you sign. It must comply with provincial, legal, and witness formalities. *Agents*, *proxies*, or *attorneys* are given power to make decisions. These powers of attorney are restricted to personal or health care decisions and are usually separate documents from a power of attorney for property.

---

## Some Important Terms

Let's consider your options and define the important terms I am talking about. This discussion should help you decide which documents you should have in your estate tool kit.

- Powers of attorney for health or personal care legally designate who is to make decisions for you.
- Living wills are for those "pull the plug" type of health decisions.
- Medical directives express your treatment choices in advance.

Let's try to clear up some misconceptions by looking at Ontario as an example. People sixteen years of age or older can sign documents called powers of attorney for personal care. Attorneys are designated in advance in a signed legal document properly witnessed. Your agent makes decisions only when you can't and respects your wishes expressed in "writing or otherwise."

"In writing" means those wishes can be set out in the power of attorney document, a living will, a medical directive, or a note you attach. For example, you can express your religious belief on treatment or blood transfusions, and this belief binds your attorney. The "otherwise" portion means your attorney is also bound by your oral wishes, if any. If you express no preferences, attorneys determine what is in your best interests. You don't need a great deal of detail if you trust a family member.

So, indirectly, living wills and directives are recognized by your attorney. Here's where the confusion exists. People may create living wills or directives without also authorizing a person to act as their substitute decision maker. They do not comply with witness requirements to make their document a legal power of attorney. How is that a problem?

### Help Line

**Q:** What are personal care decisions?

**A:** Each province has definitions to cover health care decisions. They include safety, hygiene, shelter, medical care, and treatment.

### It's Been Said
. . . . . . . . . . . . . . . . . . . . . . . . . . . . . . . . . . . . . . . . . . . .

"Every man desires to live long but no man would be old."

— Jonathan Swift, 1667–1745

## Legally, Who's Going to Decide?

If you are unconscious, can anyone authorize medical procedures? Can doctors treat you without instructions? Having a personal or health care power of attorney is like having a spare tire: you hope you never need it, but it's there just in case. It protects you and makes you feel safe and secure.

You just don't have the right to tell your doctors what to do. Don't assume your scribbled notes in your kitchen carry any legal weight. Informal documents, unless they comply with the legislative requirements in your province, may be useless.

Decisions relating to health or personal care are ultimately legal decisions. Your province's laws must be considered. Some provinces recognize proxies, mandates, or powers of attorney for health issues. It's only when you are incapacitated and can't decide that your attorney, a proxy, or a substitute decision maker steps in. That's usually not the same for the power of attorney for property. Those loaded guns become weapons effective immediately unless you restrict them.

## What Are the Important Issues?

Here are some of the factors your caregivers may be concerned about.

- Will they be charged with assault if unwanted medical procedures are performed?
- Are they assisting in an unlawful attempted suicide with risk of prosecution?
- How can they identify a patient's capacity to make health care decisions?
- When documents are presented with questionable legality, how should they act?
- When medical treatment and legal issues overlap, which takes priority?
- How should they interpret an out-of-date medical directive?

Here's what you are likely concerned about.

- Will my life be unnecessarily prolonged?
- How can I make sure I receive the treatment I want?
- When I can't decide, who will make decisions for me?
- Will my family be powerless to tell my caregivers what to do?
- Who is going to decide what pain or financial costs I can bear?
- Will I keep my dignity?

Attorney documents must meet legal requirements. No specific form is usually prescribed, nor are you required to see a lawyer to prepare one. Have you properly designated a decision maker? Have you met your province's statutory requirements?

To be sure, check with your lawyer. There's no substitute for proper legal advice. A lawyer's duty is to confirm your capacity to sign the power of attorney. That way your decisions or directives likely won't be challenged because you were mentally incapable at the time.

# What's a Power of Attorney for Personal Care?

- It is a written document you sign in the presence of two qualified witnesses.
- You name a person, your attorney, as your substitute decision maker.
- Personal or health care decisions can then be made by your attorney if you are incapacitated.
- Personal care decisions include health care, nutrition, shelter, or safety arrangements.
- It is different from a power of attorney for property, which deals only with your financial affairs.
- It allows you to give directions verbally or in writing to your personal care attorney.
- Instructions can be in a living will or medical directive given to an attorney.

I have included a sample of a power of attorney so you can see what it looks like. Don't use this form. It's for demonstration only and may not be valid in your province.

---

### SAMPLE — NOT TO BE USED

## Power of Attorney for Personal or Health Care

1. I, Rachel Donor, name Francine Nightingale as my attorney to act for me in matters affecting my personal care, in particular to
    (a) consent to or refuse health care for me;
    (b) employ or contract with servants, companions, or health care providers;
    (c) admit or release me from a hospital or health care facility;
    (d) have access to my records, including medical records;
    (e) prepare anatomical gifts on my behalf;
    (f) make decisions regarding my shelter, nutrition, clothing, hygiene, or safety; and
    (g) make plans for the disposition of my body.
2. I authorize my attorney to make decisions in my best interest concerning the withdrawal or withholding of health care. If at any time, based on my previously expressed preferences and diagnosis and prognosis, my attorney is satisfied that certain health care is not or would not be beneficial, or

---

that such health care is or would be excessively burdensome, then the attorney may express my will that such health care be withheld or withdrawn and may consent on my behalf that any or all health care be discontinued or not instituted even if death is the result.

3. If I am incompetent or incapable, my attorney may make such a decision for me, after consultation with my physician or physicians and other relevant health care providers. To the extent appropriate, my attorney may also discuss this decision with my family and others, to the extent they are available.

4. If the above-appointed attorney is unable to act for any reason, I substitute and appoint Darlene Barber to act as my attorney for personal care.

5. My attorney shall attempt to follow my wishes, which I may set out in a living will or other separate documents attached to and forming a part of this document.

Date: _____, 2001

Donor of Power of Attorney _____

As witnesses, we believe the donor to be of legal age and capable of making decisions regarding his or her health care.

I am competent and at least eighteen years of age.

Date: _____     Date: _____

Witness _____     Witness _____

## What's a Living Will?

Living wills are different from a power of attorney for personal care. They may not be legally recognized in every province. You can't appoint an attorney in a living will unless you comply with the power of attorney requirements. You can give your attorney directions through a living will.

## Living wills

- are not really wills since they deal with your health, not property after your death;
- are suggested, but not legally recognized, in all jurisdictions;
- are used when you cannot communicate your medical treatment wishes;
- are personal statements that may not have been witnessed;
- may not comply with legal requirements to be a personal care power of attorney;
- are not wills because they may not comply with the legal formalities for wills;
- do not always appoint a person to make treatment decisions;
- have limited use, usually for terminal illnesses and your "right-to-die wishes";
- may be useless unless combined with a power of attorney; and
- have drawbacks when they are overly specific or ambiguous.

Here's a sample of a living will for you to review.

---

### SAMPLE — NOT TO BE USED

### Living Will Declaration

Declaration made this 5th day of March, 2005.

I, _____, being of sound mind, wilfully and voluntarily make known my desires that my dying shall not be artificially prolonged under the circumstances set forth below, and I declare:

If at any time my attending physician certifies in writing that (1) I have an incurable injury, disease, or illness; (2) my death will occur within a short time; and (3) the use of life-prolonging procedures would serve only to artificially prolong the dying process, I direct that such procedures be withheld or withdrawn and that I be permitted to die naturally with only the performance or provision of any medical procedure or medication necessary to provide me with comfort care or to alleviate pain and, if I have so indicated below, the provision of artificially supplied nutrition and hydration. [Indicate your choice of a, b, or c by initialling or making your mark before signing this declaration.]

---

(a) I wish to receive artificially supplied nutrition and hydration, even if the effort to sustain life is futile or excessively burdensome to me;

(b) I do not wish to receive artificially supplied nutrition and hydration, if the effort to sustain life is futile or excessively burdensome to me; or

(c) I intentionally make no decision concerning artificially supplied nutrition and hydration, leaving the decision to my health care representative appointed under my power of attorney for health care.

In the absence of my ability to give directions regarding the use of life-prolonging procedures, it is my intention that this declaration be honoured by my family and physician as the final expression of my legal right to refuse medical or surgical treatment and accept the consequences of the refusal.

I understand the full import of this declaration.

Signed _____
Name of Declarant


The declarant has been personally known to me, and I believe him or her to be of sound mind. I did not sign the declarant's signature above for or at the direction of the declarant. I am not a parent, spouse, or child of the declarant. I am not entitled to any part of the declarant's estate or directly financially responsible for the declarant's medical care. I am competent and at least eighteen (18) years of age.

Witness_____     Date:_____

Witness_____     Date:_____

## Advance Medical Directives

These directives can be detailed or general to describe illnesses and treatment methods. They cover a range, from pain relief, to blood transfusions, to tube feedings, to life-saving surgery. Your thinking about treatment may change if you are in a coma, have suffered a stroke, or are fighting a terminal illness. It's hard to believe that these documents can cover all future situations without confusion or ambiguity. Documents you sign today may not be relevant in the future unless you keep them up to date. That's why it is preferable to have an attorney designated to communicate your wishes for you.

Advance medical directives

- are written documents prepared in advance of your incapacity;
- may combine personal care powers of attorney and living will principles;
- may request your physicians to provide certain medical treatment options;
- may not legally be valid unless incorporated by reference or attachment to a power of attorney; and
- are limited in their use because all variables and contingencies are not covered.

**It's Been Said**
● ● ● ● ● ● ● ● ● ● ● ● ● ● ● ● ● ● ● ● ● ● ● ● ● ● ● ● ● ● ● ● ● ● ● ● ● ● ● ● ● ● ● ● ● ● ● ● ● ●

"Nature abhors a vacuum."

– Benedict Spinoza, 1623–77

## Help Line

**Q:** Should I have more than one attorney for personal care?

**A:** Yes, always have a backup attorney named in the documents. You can also have more than one attorney. Attorneys can be authorized to act jointly or not.

## Consider These Requirements

Living wills can be too vague or too specific to be effective by themselves. A living will becomes meaningless if you use undefined terms. In an emergency, phrases such as "use no heroic measures to keep me alive" may not be understood by your medical team. What about the phrase "no artificial means"? Modern medicine has made the "artificial means" of providing food and water ordinary. Another drawback is that you must keep up with medical advances. If you have a particular medical condition, then a living will may be too rigid to cope with the miracle of medical advancement.

You cannot predict which medical problems will be resolved in the future. You don't have to spell out what is to happen in every circumstance;

you need to give your attorneys necessary flexibility. How can you define which heroic measures to keep you alive may become mandatory? Doctors will not risk withholding treatment that falls below the minimum standards of their specialty. As these treatments evolve, a living will must be amended. Don't risk having an out-of-date living will. Instead, rely on a person you trust to act as your designated attorney.

Your attorney can share this responsibility with another attorney. You may want your personal care attorney to consult with your attorney for property. Doing so would be useful if your home must be sold to pay for long-term chronic care. Your attorneys may need to consult or make joint decisions. Similarly, you can limit the circumstances under which your attorney can intervene on your behalf.

## Who Should Be an Attorney?

Location is critical. If your attorney is located outside your province, availability becomes an issue. How can life-threatening decisions be made during a long-distance telephone call? Select someone who lives close to you or is willing to travel. If you are hospitalized for a long time, your attorney may need to communicate frequently with medical staff. You should choose a friend or relative who will respect your wishes and instructions along with your values and beliefs.

### Help Line

**Q:** What's a proxy?

**A:** A proxy is a legally authorized agent in corporate law who can attend a meeting and vote for another. In personal care decisions, it's a pinch-hitter — someone designated to bat for you if you can't step up to the plate.

Always appoint an alternative attorney in your documents. Review and revise your paperwork regularly since forms can become outdated. Your instructions should be current. Medical circumstances and options change. Give a copy of the power of attorney document to your attorney, and discuss your wishes with him or her. Unlike most powers of attorney for property, this document has no value until you become incapacitated as you authorize all care. Keep track of who has received a copy in case you wish to revise the document or attached instructions.

## What Are the Legal Requirements?

Most provinces regulate the following particulars.

- Caregivers are disqualified by legislation from acting as attorneys or witnesses.
- The age of a donor is sixteen in Ontario and other provinces.
- You must know the consequences that flow from any personal care decision.
- Certain persons, including attorneys, spouses, and partners, can't be witnesses.
- Compensation for an attorney can be specified.

## Dealing with Your Doctor

Many medical practitioners are uncomfortable with discussing the subject of living wills. They don't wish to be seen withholding medical treatment. They may wish, however, to be consulted about your choices of treatment for a medical directive. They may welcome the opportunity to educate you about your personal care choices. Your attorney need not have medical experience but should understand your medical condition. Tell him or her your choices for long-term treatment measures.

What if you are having a surgical procedure? Make your doctor and hospital aware that you have an attorney and documents. Your attorney should be notified of the surgery. Discuss with your medical practitioner your options and concerns, and inform your attorney of your preferences based on the factors discussed. Take this precaution to ensure your instructions, in written directives, are not ambiguous. Any conflicts between your right to self-determination and your doctor's obligations should be discussed.

## How to Compose Directives for Treatment

Flexibility is important because you cannot spell out what you want done in every contingency. If you are unconscious, you can't indicate you do not want to be tube-fed. Even if you have specified which procedures and treatments are to be avoided or provided, difficult decisions remain, and they can be painful for family and friends to resolve. By designating an attorney, you ease the burden and guide them on the following questions.

- When exactly is treatment to stop?
- Should pain medication continue?
- Is surgery to be avoided if it can't reverse your condition?
- Can ventilators for breathing be used if you are permanently unconscious?

Generally, I advise my clients to leave specific instructions in a separate document. That way the power of attorney doesn't need to be updated each time an instruction is changed. If the document doesn't mention specific instructions, your agent will rely on any legal provisions that control which factors must be considered. Your best interests are considered, including the beliefs you expressed while you were capable.

If you provide specific instructions, you must realize that it may be impossible to carry them out. Avoid terms that aren't defined, such as "dying with dignity" and "recovery." I encourage clients with any serious illness to discuss various treatment scenarios with their physicians. Consider keeping a card in your wallet that summarizes your preferences. Let people know where the documents can be located. There is no need to file these documents with any central registry.

## Guardianship of a Person

In some provinces, when you haven't appointed an attorney for personal care, a statute will apply. It can set out that a government guardian will be your decision maker for health care. Family members can apply to become your guardian for personal care decisions.

Medical assessments may be required by the court to substantiate your incapacity to make personal care decisions. This capacity is a lower standard than one needed to make a will or a financial power of attorney. You should discuss the issue with elderly parents before they become incapable of executing documents.

The consequences and costs outweigh the discomfort that many clients have talking about dying. Even those without current medical problems should consider a power of attorney. It's an alternative to the appointment of a guardian. Otherwise, you can be kept alive with unbearable consequences for you and family members. In many provinces, you can prepare such documents at the age of sixteen. Doesn't that suggest everyone needs one?

## Your Gift of Life

You may wish to instruct your attorney before death to donate your organs. You can also, in many provinces, register your consent to be an organ or tissue donor. Health Canada sponsors a national organ donation site at www.organandtissue.ca. The site explains that you need to discuss organ and tissue donation in advance with your family.

Most doctors still require your family's permission even if you have registered your wishes as a donor. Each province has different laws and forms. Some provinces provide an organ donor card with a driver's licence. Here is what a sample organ donor document looks like.

---

### SAMPLE — NOT TO BE USED

### Organ Donor Declaration

This is to inform you that I want to be an organ and tissue donor if the occasion ever arises. Please see that my wishes are carried out by informing the attending medical personnel that I am a donor. My desires are indicated below.

In the hope that I may help others, I hereby make this gift for the purpose of transplant, medical study, or education, to take effect upon my death. I donate

(       )   any needed organs/tissues;

(       )   only the following organs/tissues: [specify the organ(s)/tissue(s)].

Limitations or special wishes, if any:


This is signed by the donor and the following two witnesses in the presence of each other.

Date _____

Donor _____

Donor's date of birth _____

City and province _____


Witness _____  Date _____

Witness _____  Date _____

Next of kin _____  Telephone _____

---

## What Should You Do?

Self-help kits do exist for powers of attorney, but they are a lot like aspirins; after you take one, the symptoms may be gone but not the problem. You may have a false sense of security that everything has been resolved.

You can avoid talking about the painful choices Isaac and his wife needed to discuss. If you have a chronic illness, cancer, or HIV, you'll need to start care discussions. Most importantly, see a lawyer to ensure that your wishes and choices will be legally enforceable. The best advice I can give you is to appoint a decision maker or attorney. This person will be authorized to make decisions with the necessary legal authority.

No form can guarantee that your wishes will be followed. You can't cover every type of treatment decision. You want your attorney to be your advocate when life or death decisions are on the line.

## One Last Celebration: Or, What's a Funeral For?

You may prefer to leave funeral arrangements to your family or executor. Or you may wish to arrange them in advance. Will it be a public or a private service? If you're over fifty-five, you're entering the funeral director's ideal target market for prearranged funerals.

Prearrangements allow you to make important decisions in advance, decisions that won't be a burden on your family and friends. Some arrangement plans allow you to protect your estate from the cost of inflation through instalments that may actually save your estate money.

Investigate whether your province guarantees the security of funds delivered to the funeral home. That's just in case there are any difficulties with the funeral home operator in the future. Your funds may be insured in case the funeral home declares bankruptcy.

Read on, and I'll give you ten commandments to keep your will and estate plan current.

## The Least You Need to Know

- Health care decisions will impact your financial and estate plans, so prepare for your incapacity prior to death.
- Name an attorney in a power of attorney for personal or health care as your advocate to make decisions when you can't.
- Living wills and advance medical directives may be recognized when coupled with a legally valid power of attorney, depending on your province's requirements.
- Select an attorney or proxy and alternatives who will be able to travel to deal with any long-term care or hospitalization.

# Chapter 23

# Keep Your Gold Safe

In this chapter:

- Keep your plan current.
- Learn the ten commandments for changes.
- Make small changes in codicils.
- Properly store your gold.

I tell all clients to treat their signed original wills like gold. All your hard work creating an estate plan is worthless if your original documents can't be found. If they are lost, they must be replaced. That's assuming you can still make a new one. In this chapter, you can take a quiz and learn how to get your affairs in order. I'll give you some ideas for storing and changing documents, and I'll present some shocking tales that I hope won't happen to you.

## Jack and the Missing Will

Jack was an elderly dairy farmer. He and Laura, his young common-law wife, just had a baby daughter. He never got around to changing his will when the baby was born. This is what happened to his family.

In his last will, Jack left his farm to Robert, his son from a previous marriage, and his bonds to Laura. But he'd already sold the bonds and given the money to Robert. Jack said he was going to rewrite his will, leaving everything else to Laura and the baby. But when he died, no one could find a new will.

Laura was the first to point out that Jack had already sold the bonds left to her in the will. Robert had received those proceeds, and the will now also left him the dairy farm. That's where the problems started.

## Keep It Current — or Else

"How can it be fair?" a despondent Laura asked. "Jack and I had a daughter, and he left us nothing!" Her lawyer reassured her that she had certain rights, as did the child. The lawyer explained how he could refer Laura to a lawyer who handled estate lawsuits and could make a claim for support against Jack's estate. But first she should search for a new will in case Jack had made one.

Laura called Jack's real estate lawyer and asked if his will had been updated. The lawyer had only a photocopy of a new will leaving everything to Laura. He told her that Jack had taken the original will home.

"Can a court accept the photocopied will as an original?" asked Laura.

"Only in special cases," the lawyer explained. First, the court would have to be satisfied that the original hadn't been destroyed by Jack. Second, Laura would have to explain to a judge how it had been misplaced. Third, no other interested parties or beneficiaries could object. The court could then accept a copy as an original.

"That will never happen," Laura said. "Jack's son, Robert, will never give up what he's got, never."

## Storing Your Original Document

What happened to the original of Jack's will? Laura will likely continue to ask herself that question. Only the original is valid, so where should you keep it?

Some lawyers who prepare wills routinely store originals for clients. It's an added-value service that helps build client loyalty. At the appropriate time, the family executor calls for the will. But current legal practice varies widely. Many lawyers no longer retain their clients' original wills for safekeeping.

Some law firms retain their own safe deposit boxes or vaults and store all clients' wills indefinitely.

If banks are closed, accessing safe deposit boxes is impossible. However, I have had no negative experiences with banks and the retrieval of clients' wills. If a trust company is your executor, it may store your will without charge.

> **Legal Lingo**
>
> *Revocation* of a will means revoking or cancelling it. Revocation may be done by the testator when he or she makes a new will or marries.

Do you want to keep the details of your estate plan confidential until your death? If so, the name of the lawyer who prepared the will and the location of your bank box may be all the information you give to your executors. Some people give their executors photocopies of their wills. Be careful, though, if you change your executor. Some family members or friends may be offended by your request to return documents.

If you make your own will, the original must be produced on death since a copy is of no value. In the future, who knows what will be accepted? Long-term storage of data produced by inkjet printers on inexpensive paper may become problematic. The letters may literally fall off the page if the papers are not properly stored. Wills prepared on paper that is not acid-free may not survive the lifetimes of their makers.

Photocopied versions of your will are of no value if you don't have the original. The same holds true for your powers of attorney. They are all worthless if nobody can find the originals. Store these documents in your estate essentials toolkit.

## Revoking a Will

Each new will automatically revokes the previous one you made unless you specify a contrary intention. Wills are revocable unless a contractual arrangement such as a marriage contract exists to negate this option. The ability to cancel a will is one important reason wills are made in the first place. If you could never correct a mistake of judgment in a will, who would use one? That's why wills are never cut in stone. You'll find them easier to change that way.

If you wish to revoke a will, you can do so in the same manner as you make one. Have two witnesses watch you sign a written revocation. Where holographic instruments are allowed, a simple handwritten revocation would also suffice. To be valid, it must be 100 percent in your own handwriting, signed, and dated.

You can also revoke a will by tearing, burning, or otherwise destroying the original document. The law also assumes your will has been cancelled if the original in your possession cannot be located. Ensure that your will is properly stored in a location known to your executor to avoid problems.

Destruction of a will can be done by someone else, but it must be in the testator's presence and with the maker's direction. Courts have had to interpret the partial tearing or burning of a will. Don't take a chance; get rid of it all yourself. Leave no doubt about your intention to destroy it.

### When Should You Change Your Will?

Keep your will up to date. Wills must reflect major changes in your life. A regular review of your will can help keep it current. Below are the factors to consider in revising your will. Use them as a checklist.

### Ten Commandments for Will Changes

Perhaps I got carried away with this. But a commandment is a good way of explaining how important these rules are. Follow them to keep your plan up to date. Change your will whenever one or more of the following occurs.

**1. When persons named in your will die:** when a person who dies is an executor or beneficiary, change your will. Ensure that an alternative person is designated in your will for every major gift in case this sort of situation occurs. As well, you may never know during your lifetime that a distant beneficiary has died.

**2. When major assets are purchased or sold:** review your estate plan whenever there's a major change in assets. An increase or decrease in the size of your distributable estate will affect cash and percentage gifts. After-tax calculations must be made to ensure that sufficient cash reserves exist. Insurance policies may need to be purchased to cover contingent liabilities or taxes.

Specific provisions to deal with tax matters may need to be considered. If gifted property no longer exists, your will must be revised. If you start a business or purchase real estate, review your will. For that matter, don't forget a power of attorney to run the business, just in case. Remember, in Step 1, I showed you how you own property can make a difference to your estate plan. Refresh your understanding of joint ownership, how assets are designated and controlled by your will. It's as simple as reviewing Chapter 2.

**3. When you remarry, separate, divorce, or cohabit:** a change of spousal status can raise matrimonial claims, which take priority over existing wills. Separated spouses should be removed as executors unless there are good reasons not to do so. New marriages revoke all wills. Divorce voids all gifts and appointments to a former spouse. Unless your province treats common-law spouses as married, they or same-sex couples must be specifically provided for whenever a relationship begins or ends.

**4. When tax laws change:** any significant tax changes warrant an automatic review. No one wants to pay too much tax. Take advantage of any tax deferrals and deductions. Preview your estate for tax impact. The federal budget changes in February 2000, for example, dramatically changed charitable gift strategies. New developments in *inter vivos* trusts for those over sixty-five have created opportunities. Before 1999, you couldn't create an alter-ego or joint partner trust, which may be a valid will substitute for high-income individuals.

**5. When you move to a new jurisdiction:** moving to a new province or country means your will is valid only if it complies with the local formalities. Holograph wills, for example, are not recognized in some jurisdictions. Spousal property rights and tax laws also vary from one jurisdiction to another. Avoid having your spouse make a claim against your estate by ensuring that your will is revised.

**6. When executors no longer wish to serve:** to be effective, your executor must be close at hand. Executors living in California cannot do the job unless you live in California. If a person says he or she can no longer act as the guardian for your children, use a simple codicil to make this change.

**7. When children are born or adopted:** children should be individually named in your will. A death, birth, or adoption of a child necessitates a review of your will.

**8. When any person named in the will becomes ill:** what happens if your friend becomes terminally ill? If he or she has a role to play in the administration of your estate, change your will. Persons who become incapacitated need to be replaced, and any gifts to them can be placed in trust. The advanced age of a beneficiary or executor may also cause you to revise your will.

**9. When your children reach the age of majority:** you cannot appoint minors to handle their own money or your estate. As they reach the age of majority, though, they can act as executors. You can avoid the cost of using nonfamily executors for your business by appointing children if you consider them appropriate for the tasks.

**10. When beneficiaries are changed:** changing your mind about what a beneficiary will get means changing your will. If debts are paid or forgiven, this should be reflected in the will. Because your will is the cornerstone of your estate plan, keep it in good repair.

## Help Line

**Q:** What does a codicil cost to prepare?

**A:** Shop around. Sometimes it will be less than the cost of a new will. If your original will is lost, a codicil is of no use. Sometimes in the long run it's a better idea to make a new will.

## Codicils as Amendments

Marks on a will when you try to change it yourself can lead to a legal dispute. Someone could argue that you intended to revoke the will by marking it for cancellation. Be careful; never make any marks, alterations, or handwritten changes on your original will.

Don't try to scratch out your brother's name after you've had a falling out with him. It won't work except to possibly cancel your will and start a court fight.

A codicil states, "I revoke the gift in paragraph 4 of my will dated February 4, 2000." The change to a portion of the will may affect the rest of the will, which can have unexpected consequences. To avoid future uncertainty, codicils should be prepared by lawyers. Use them sparingly and only to make minor changes.

### It's Been Said

"A man's friendships are, like his will, invalidated by marriage — but they are also no less invalidated by the marriage of his friends."

— Samuel Butler, 1835–1902

**SAMPLE — NOT TO BE USED**

## A Sample Codicil

THIS IS A CODICIL to the last Will and Testament of me, Mary Swan, of the City of Vancouver, in the Province of British Columbia, which last Will and Testament bears the date the __14th__ day of ____February____, 20 _05_.

1. I REVOKE the appointment of Verna S. as an Executor and Trustee contained in paragraph 3 of my said last Will and Testament, and I appoint Chester S. as an Executor and Trustee of my said last Will and Testament in the place and stead of the said Verna S.

2. I REVOKE paragraph 5(b)(ii) of my said last Will and Testament.

3. In all other respects, I CONFIRM my said Will.

4. IN TESTIMONY WHEREOF I have, to this Codicil to my last Will and Testament, written upon this single page of paper, subscribed by [name] this _____ day of _____, 20____.

WITNESSES:

This is signed by __Mary Swan_____
and by us, all in the presence of each other.

_____          _____
        Signature of Witness                              Mary Swan

Name: _____
Address: _____

_____

_____
        Signature of Witness

Name: _____
Address:_____

## Papers Everywhere

Life insurance, deeds to property, and appraisals may be difficult to replace. Some people purchase a fireproof and waterproof box to keep these documents at home. Others rely on a bank's safe deposit box. You do have to be concerned about a possible fire at home destroying everything. Let people you trust know where you store "your gold," because the original will and powers of attorney are irreplaceable.

. . . . . . . . . . . . . . . . . . . . . . . . . . . . . . . . . . . . . . . . . . . . . . . . . . .

## Your Information Quiz

| | Not Sure | Yes | No |
|---|---|---|---|
| 1. Can you locate your life insurance policies? | ❏ | ❏ | ❏ |
| 2. Can you confirm who the beneficiaries are for your | | | |
| (a) life insurance; | ❏ | ❏ | ❏ |
| (b) RRSPs | ❏ | ❏ | ❏ |
| (c) RRIFs; | ❏ | ❏ | ❏ |
| (d) pension; | ❏ | ❏ | ❏ |
| (e) segregated funds? | ❏ | ❏ | ❏ |
| 3. Is the title to your home registered | | | |
| (a) in your name alone; | ❏ | ❏ | ❏ |
| (b) jointly with survivorship rights; | ❏ | ❏ | ❏ |
| (c) as tenants-in-common? | ❏ | ❏ | ❏ |
| 4. Do you know where your birth, marriage, divorce, citizenship, and banking papers are located? | ❏ | ❏ | ❏ |
| 5. Will your executor find all the information needed to prepare and file your income tax returns, including information to calculate capital gains? | ❏ | ❏ | ❏ |
| 6. Does your executor/attorney know where to find your original will/power of attorney? | ❏ | ❏ | ❏ |
| 7. Do you know if the witnesses to your will and powers of attorney are alive and where to locate them? | ❏ | ❏ | ❏ |
| 8. Have you got a plan to transfer your business? | ❏ | ❏ | ❏ |
| 9. Have you prearranged your wishes for funeral, religious service, and cemetery arrangements? | ❏ | ❏ | ❏ |

## Get Your Affairs in Order

That's exactly what you can do if you have the time. Sometimes you never get a chance for one more day or hour. So now is the time to get organized. Here's how you can do it.

Don't assume your partner or executor will be able to locate anything important you've been handling. Here's a list of information you should organize. Record the information here or on a photocopy or computer to make it easier to update.

### 1. Estate Asset Inventory

|  | Asset | Joint Asset | Designated Asset | Will Asset |
|---|---|---|---|---|
| 1. Personal property (cars, boats, art) | ❑ | ❑ | ❑ | ❑ |
| 2. Life insurance | ❑ | ❑ | ❑ | ❑ |
| 3. Private and government pensions | ❑ | ❑ | ❑ | ❑ |
| 4. RRIFs, RRSPs, and annuities | ❑ | ❑ | ❑ | ❑ |
| 5. Home or real estate | ❑ | ❑ | ❑ | ❑ |
| 6. Bonds, stocks, and mutual funds | ❑ | ❑ | ❑ | ❑ |
| 7. Bank accounts and certificates | ❑ | ❑ | ❑ | ❑ |
| 8. Business interests | ❑ | ❑ | ❑ | ❑ |

Record where these assets can be located on your list of assets. Now do the same for your debts.

### 2. Estate Debt Inventory

Here is where you list your liabilities or photocopy particulars for

1. Bank loans: _____

2. Personal loans: _____

3. Credit cards: _____

4. Mortgage/other loans: _____

## 3. Location of Estate Inventory

Ensure that your executor knows

- the location of the safe deposit box;
- its contents; and
- the location of the key and necessary documents for access.

## 4. Insurance Inventory

Type of Insurance                                  Agent/Broker

    1. Life insurance            _____

    2. Home insurance           _____

    3. Car insurance            _____

    4. Business insurance       _____

**It's Been Said**

Thomas Jefferson's Ten Commandments

1. Never put off till tomorrow what you can do today.
2. Never trouble another for what you can do yourself.
3. Never spend your money before you have earned it.
4. Never buy what you do not want just because it is cheap.
5. Pride costs more than hunger, thirst, or cold.
6. We seldom report of having eaten too little.
7. Nothing is troublesome that we do willingly.
8. How much pain evils have cost us that have never happened.
9. Take things always by the smooth handle.
10. When angry, count ten before you speak; if very angry, count a hundred.

## 5. Professional Advisors

1. Name of my estate lawyer: _____

Firm: _____

Address: _____

Telephone: _____

2. Name of my accountant: _____

Firm: _____

Address: _____

Telephone: _____


3. Name of my financial advisor:

Firm: _____

Address: _____

Telephone: _____


4. Name of my life insurance agent: _____

Firm: _____

Address: _____

Telephone: _____


5. Name of my business lawyer: _____

Firm: _____

Address: _____

Telephone: _____


6. Name of my investment/stock broker: _____

Firm: _____

Address: _____

Telephone: _____

# 6. Document Inventory

## Wills

Dates of will and codicils: —————————————————

Original stored at: —————————————————————

Executor: ————————————————————————————

Address: ————————————————————————————

Telephone: ——————————————————————————

## Dates of spouse's will and codicils: ——————————————

Original stored at: —————————————————————

Executor: ————————————————————————————

## Powers of Attorney for Property

Date of document: ————————————————————

Original stored at: —————————————————————

Attorney: ————————————————————————————

Address: ————————————————————————————

Telephone: ——————————————————————————

## Date of spouse's original: ——————————————————

Original stored at: —————————————————————

Attorney: ————————————————————————————

Address: ————————————————————————————

Telephone: ——————————————————————————

## Powers of Attorney for Personal Care

Date of document: ———————————————————

Original stored at: ——————————————————

Attorney: —————————————————————

Address: —————————————————————

Telephone: ————————————————————

## Date of spouse's original: ————————————

Original stored at: ——————————————————

Attorney: —————————————————————

Address: —————————————————————

Telephone: ————————————————————

## 7. Other Important Documents

Ensure that your executor knows the locations of your original

- birth certificate;
- marriage certificate;
- citizenship and government documents;
- separation agreements;
- divorce judgments;
- marriage contracts;
- memo for distribution of personal assets;
- deeds/titles to property;
- passwords with PIN numbers;
- pension records; and
- foreign records.

Attach copies of documents.

## Funeral Arrangements

I would like to be buried _____ or cremated _____.

I would like to use this funeral home.

Name _____

Address: _____

Telephone: _____

Contact: _____

I have the following prearrangements in place:

_____

_____

## Religious Services

Clergymen: _____

Music: _____

Flowers: _____

Memorials: _____

Pallbearers: _____

Other requests: _____

## Cemetery Arrangements

Name of Cemetery: _____

Address: _____

Telephone: _____

Location of deed: _____

Plot in name of: _____

Section: _____ Plot number: _____

You have covered the six essential steps to estate planning, but don't stop now. Let's review what you need to remember in the next chapter as we wrap it all up. Get ready for my top ten tips.

## The Least You Need to Know

- Never alter or write on an original will, or it could be considered revoked.
- You can revoke a will by marrying, by tearing or otherwise destroying it, or by making a new one.
- Update your will if major changes occur in spousal status or jurisdiction.
- Always let your executor know where the signed original will is stored.

# Chapter 24

# Wrap It All Up

In this chapter:

- Check off your goals.
- Learn the top ten tips.
- Create a lifetime plan.

Here's a before-and-after story with a happy ending. Before you read this book, you may not have taken the first step toward estate planning. Perhaps you were confused and had no sense of direction. Now that you've finished reading it, you have a simple save-and-protect system. That's the happy ending.

You have to identify and implement your goals and develop an estate plan. The government's approach toward income tax, incapacity, and intestacy is what you'll get if you don't plan. This will impose a financial burden on your heirs and become a nightmare to untangle.

**It's Been Said**
. . . . . . . . . . . . . . . . . . . . . . . . . . . . . . . . . . . . . . . . . . . . . . . .

"The truth is, I do indulge myself a little more in pleasure. . . . [M]ost men that do thrive in the world do forget to take pleasure during the time that they are getting their estate, but reserve that till they have got one, and then it's too late for them to enjoy it."

— Samuel Pepys, March 10, 1666

## Six Simple Steps: A Foolproof Way to Create and Maintain Your Estate Plan

Here's a final review of all you've learned.

### Step 1: Get Started

You created your own personal wish list of rewarding goals. You examined how the law controls what you can do with your estate pie. You analyzed an asset list, including your investments, and then subtracted your estate liabilities. This process allowed you to preview your estate. Assets from your business, investments, right through to knick-knacks were covered.

### Step 2: Avoid the Big Tax Bite

You learned how to save income and probate taxes. These savings maximize what will be left for those you love. You also learned how probate costs can be reduced and the dangers of trying too hard to do that. Charitable gifts were shown to be exceptionally rewarding through the tax credits they generate.

### Step 3: Make Your Will

Nothing is more fundamentally important than your will. You learned the ins and outs of making one. We looked at a sample will and its clauses, and you learned how to bulletproof your will to avoid a costly court case.

### Step 4: Choose Your Executors

I outlined the key decisions relating to executors and estate administration. The right executors can save money and protect your beneficiaries. You will continue to review your choices to ensure they're appropriate. Analyzing all your alternatives is easy with the executor's checklist.

### Step 5: Benefit Your Beneficiaries

You learned that your beneficiaries have rights and can take your estate to court. Cutting them out of your estate needs certain precautions. The best way to take care of children is to treat them equally. Don't forget that minors need trusts and guardians. Remember those spousal tax benefits and how marriage contracts work.

### Step 6: Protect Yourself Now

Protect yourself today. Use powers of attorney for property and for personal care. They'll keep you in control. We talked about how to treat your documents like gold. Keep your will current with ten commandments. Review my six simple steps of estate planning regularly.

## Your Estate Planning Checklist

Here's a chapter-by-chapter review. Check off what you have done and the current status for each chapter to see how far you have come.

| You've Learned To . . . | Yes | No | Comments |
|---|---|---|---|
| 1. Benefit from an estate plan wish list. | ❑ | ❑ | _____ _____ |
| 2. Divide your estate pie into designated, joint, or will assets. | ❑ | ❑ | _____ _____ |
| 3. Check your investment inventory and have a buy/sell agreement. | ❑ | ❑ | _____ _____ |
| 4. Preview your estate to estimate what's available to distribute. | ❑ | ❑ | _____ _____ |
| 5. Understand taxes at death, including deemed dispositions, exemptions, and rollovers. | ❑ | ❑ | _____ _____ |
| 6. Use tax tips in planning for gifts, trusts, and tax exemptions. | ❑ | ❑ | _____ _____ |
| 7. Plan rewarding charitable gifts for tax credits and generous feelings. | ❑ | ❑ | _____ _____ |
| 8. Avoid probate problems plus the Five Terrible D's. | ❑ | ❑ | _____ _____ |
| 9. Remember the twenty-four reasons to make a will so you don't die intestate. | ❑ | ❑ | _____ _____ |
| 10. Understand the ten will fundamentals. | ❑ | ❑ | _____ _____ |
| 11. Avoid the top ten will mistakes. | ❑ | ❑ | _____ |

| You've Learned To . . . | Yes | No | Comments |
|---|---|---|---|
| 12. Keep your will out of court and bulletproof your wishes. | ❏ | ❏ | _____ |
| 13. Know what an executor does through Estate Administration 101. | ❏ | ❏ | _____ |
| 14. Review executors' obligations and duties. | ❏ | ❏ | _____ |
| 15. Use trustees and trusts. | ❏ | ❏ | _____ |
| 16. Review a checklist to analyze available executor choices. | ❏ | ❏ | _____ |
| 17. Follow good guidelines to give away your estate. | ❏ | ❏ | _____ |
| 18. Keep your estate out of court by recognizing that beneficiaries have rights. | ❏ | ❏ | _____ |
| 19. Plan for children with trusts, guardians, and equal treatment. | ❏ | ❏ | _____ |
| 20. Define spouses, family law, and wills and variations for newlyweds and couples. | ❏ | ❏ | _____ |
| 21. Use property powers of attorney to help with finances if you're incapacitated. | ❏ | ❏ | _____ |
| 22. Create living wills and personal care powers of attorney. | ❏ | ❏ | _____ |
| 23. Safeguard your will with ten commandments for changes and prepare an estate inventory. | ❏ | ❏ | _____ |
| 24. Regularly review this checklist for your six simple steps in estate planning. | ❏ | ❏ | _____ |

## Top Ten Tips

After finishing this book, keep in mind my top ten tips.

1. Jointly owned assets do not eliminate the need to make a will.
2. Arrange life insurance to be paid tax free to beneficiaries to avoid probate.
3. Choose the right persons as executors and guardians for your children.
4. Update your will to reflect a change in your marital status.
5. Prepare a financial affairs power of attorney for property.
6. Arrange donations with charity and tax credits in mind.
7. Prepare a power of attorney or proxy for personal or health care issues.
8. Reduce your estate's income tax liability with tax rollovers and planning.
9. Have a buy/sell agreement and will to protect your business investments.
10. Take command of your estate planning goals and tools.

### It's Been Said

"It requires a great deal of boldness and a great deal of caution to make a fortune, and when you have it, it requires ten times as much wit to keep it."
— Ralph Waldo Emerson, 1803–82

### It's Been Said

"The beginning of wisdom is the definition of terms."
— Socrates, 469–399 B.C.

## Final Words of Caution

Can self-help kits replace the need for advice? The short answer is no. Kits contain disclaimers and waivers of liability. All kits basically state that no guidebook, reference text, or form will suit everyone's circumstances. Individual needs may be unique and beyond the scope of a sample self-help form.

Only a trained professional can advise and properly assist you. Remember that American Internet sources rarely apply to Canada. Canadians do not have the same laws for living wills and estate, probate, income, or gift taxes as Americans.

Using a kit is no substitute for proper legal advice. Nor is this book, for that matter. Because laws are so complex and the expense terrifying, people have turned away from professional help to self-help. Any approach that keeps you out of the court system may seem worthwhile but may carry dangers that surface after you're gone. Don't forsake good advice and rely on amateurs to protect your loved ones.

**It's Been Said**

· · · · · · · · · · · · · · · · · · · · · · · · · · · · · · · · · · · · · · · · · · · · · · · · · ·

"Believe one who has proved it. Believe an expert."

— Virgil, 70–19 B.C.

## Conclusion

Estate planning includes having relationships with qualified professionals. There's no substitute for help from experienced lawyers, tax advisors, trustees, life underwriters, and financial planners.

Remember that getting started is half the battle. You'll achieve peace of mind just by knowing that you've done the right thing for those closest to you.

Now you know the essential six steps in my save-and-protect system for your loved ones. Review this book every time there is a change in your assets or relationships. That way you'll prevent another town scandal and have your affairs in order.

**It's Been Said**

· · · · · · · · · · · · · · · · · · · · · · · · · · · · · · · · · · · · · · · · · · · · · · · · ·

"I'll tell you that virtue does not come from money, but that from virtue comes money and every other good of man, public as well as private."

— Plato, *Socrates' Apology*

· · · · · · · · · · · · · · · · · · · · · · · · · · · · · · · · · · · · · · · · · · · · · · · · · · · · · · · · · · · · · ·

## The Least You Need to Know

- No kit can explain estate planning like the six simple steps do.
- Once you have an estate plan, use the six simple steps to review and revise it.
- Planning your estate is a lifelong process, but once it's in place it's easy to update.
- On your birthday each year, look at your before-and-after estate planning picture.

# Glossary of Terms

**Adjusted cost base.** This is the original price of the property you acquire adjusted as permitted by the tax laws for allowable capital improvements.

**Administrators.** Persons appointed by the court to handle your estate if you die without a will. In Ontario, administrators are also called "estate trustees without a will." Administrators must be appointed by a court. Executors or estate trustees with a will are confirmed by a court.

**Affidavit.** A written statement signed by the person who wrote it. This person swears under oath that the contents of the affidavit are true from his or her personal knowledge. Affidavits can be affirmed and accepted by the courts.

**Agent.** A person authorized to act on behalf of another person. Agents can also be attorneys when authorized under the appropriate provincial laws.

**Alter-ego trust.** This *inter vivos* trust, like a partner trust, is a living trust for those over sixty-five years of age. It allows for assets to be transferred into the trust without a deemed disposition. Assets can then be transferred on death without probate.

**Assets.** Property an executor takes control of on your death. Real assets are real property or real estate. Personal assets are personal property, which includes all other kinds of property.

**Attorney.** Generally an agent or substitute decision maker you designate in a signed and witnessed legal document. Attorneys are also called proxies. They are authorized to act in the place of another. Each province has legal requirements for appointing attorneys or proxies.

**Beneficiary.** One who receives or enjoys benefit, advantage, profit, or fruit under a trust, insurance policy, or will.

**Buy/sell agreements.** Partners and shareholders need these legal contracts. These agreements ensure that a deceased's interest is bought out by the surviving party. A fixed price or formula is used to establish the price.

**Capital gain.** Capital property has a fair market value (FMV) on death. The difference between the proceeds of disposition of property and its adjusted cost for tax purposes may be a gain. A portion of this gain or loss is included on a taxpayer's return.

**Child.** Every province has laws that define the word *child*. Each law may have a specific definition. For example, "child" has a different meaning for divorce, support, or dependant's claims.

**Co-executor.** Anyone who is a joint executor with one or more other executors.

**Cohabitation agreements.** These contracts have been used traditionally by common-law or same-sex couples not treated as "married." These contracts can specify your rights during cohabitation and after separation. Legal changes have been introduced for same-sex couples and common-law couples. Your existing cohabitation agreements may need to be revised to deal with support and other property claims.

**Common-law spouses.** Under federal income tax laws, this term means that you were of the opposite sex in a conjugal relationship, with cohabitation in the preceding twelve months, or that you parented the same child. New definitions were introduced in 2000 to give same-sex spouses the same benefits.

**Confidentiality.** One of the hallmarks of the legal profession that separates it from some others. When you see a lawyer, whatever you discuss will remain confidential. If your will is challenged, experts say that access to the lawyer's notes can be obtained to defend the will.

**Court orders.** Sometimes you don't need to contest a will but simply need to get information, which could be an inventory of estate assets if you have a financial interest in the estate. Cite or summon the executor to file the material you're entitled to. Ask the court for a citation or court order for information to compel the executor to comply.

**Deemed disposition.** You're considered at death to have received the fair market value (FMV) for all capital property. Yes, even if you give it away without getting any money in return. This deemed sale triggers tax liabilities for a deceased's estate. Capital assets include real estate, stocks, and art but not cash investments.

**Distributable estate.** What's available in your estate after all expenses and taxes are paid. What's left of your assets is what gets distributed to your beneficiaries.

**Domicile.** From the Latin *domus*, a "home" or "dwelling house." Domicile can be fixed by birth or designated by choice or law. You can have numerous residences but always return to one fixed place of domicile.

**Encroachments.** In real estate law, these are unlawful gains on the property of another. But in estate law, an encroachment is an early payment from income or capital. The early payment goes to the beneficiary.

**Estate.** Everyone has one. Definitions vary, but for this book consider an estate as everything you own or control that must be delivered or dealt with on your death. It includes your assets (cash to real estate) and liabilities.

**Estate residue.** What's left over in your estate after expenses and specific gifts are made. In your will, it reads as what is left, as in "the residue of my estate goes to my spouse."

**Even hand rule.** Your estate's legal representative must manage the assets in a manner fair to all beneficiaries. An encroachment of all the capital for a life tenant may not be justifiable, especially to the remainderman, who would receive nothing. That's why beneficiaries are treated evenly.

**Executor.** The person you appoint by will. The executor or estate trustee pays your estate expenses, the Big Four bills (funeral, liabilities, expenses, and taxes), before distributing assets to beneficiaries.

**Fiduciary.** A person in a relationship who is bound to exercise rights and powers for the benefit of another. Fiduciaries must act without personal gain or advantage and are accountable for their actions.

**Gift *inter vivos*.** This gift is made during your lifetime and is voluntary, without strings attached. A testamentary gift is made by your will and is revocable until you die.

**Gifts.** Voluntary transfers of property, without payment, between the living.

**Guardians.** They are not executors, but executors can be guardians. Executors have the larger responsibility of handling your entire estate for all beneficiaries. Guardians handle the needs of those without full legal capacity, such as your minor children.

**In ventre sa mere.** This means "in his mother's womb." It's used to describe unborn children. In some provinces, the law recognizes unborn children as capable of inheriting an estate or needing a guardian.

**Income attribution rules.** These tax rules generally attribute any income or taxable capital gains realized from the gifted property back to the donor. There are exceptions if there is consideration equal to the fair market value of the property. If minors receive gifts, a subsequent taxable capital gain does not attribute.

**Inter vivos trusts.** You'll recognize the terms "private," "family," or "personal trust," which are forms of *inter vivos*, or living, trusts.

**Intestacy.** You've died without a will. Your estate is distributed by the intestate laws in your province. The government writes a will for you that may not be to your liking. Jointly owned or designated assets are not affected by an intestacy.

**Joint tenancy.** A way you can own property with a record of ownership like a deed or bank account. You're really the owner, not a "tenant." Joint tenants own things with a survivorship right. The share of the first to die goes to the survivors, even without a will.

**Jointly owned property.** A legally recognized form of ownership. All joint owners have an equal right to deal with the asset while they're alive. If one joint owner dies, that person's interest is automatically inherited by the other joint owner under what's called right of survivorship.

**Lapsed gifts.** These gifts disappear because the beneficiary has died before you. Ademption is when the gift is gone and no longer exists by the time you die.

**Legacy.** A transfer of personalty (as opposed to realty) by will. So leaving a legacy, strictly speaking, does not include a testamentary gift of real estate.

**Letters probate.** Refers to the court certificate attached to the original will. It confirms that the court is satisfied that the will has complied with the formalities of proof.

**Litigation.** A contest in a law court to enforce rights. To litigate is to carry on a lawsuit.

**Living will.** Sets out your medical treatment wishes. Living wills can't deal with property and are not really valid wills. Don't be fooled thinking you are protected with just a living will. You must have a legally valid will so you won't die intestate.

**Marriage contracts.** Also called domestic or prenuptial agreements, they can be entered into once spouses are already married. If you are going into business, your spouse may be required to sign a marriage contract as part of a partnership or shareholders' agreement. It may list what rights a spouse may have to the business in a divorce.

**Matrimonial home.** This definition varies in each province. The home could be called family or marital property. Usually, it is the dwelling place ordinarily used by a married couple as their residence. Ontario laws allow couples to designate which property this is for purposes of the Family Law Act, which gives spouses special rights to the matrimonial home. You can have a number of matrimonial homes.

**Mediation.** A way for people in a dispute to meet with a neutral person (the mediator) to find a solution to their dispute. Unlike a trial, with its winner-take-all approach, mediation starts with the idea that persons in the dispute wish to reach some out-of-court settlement. Mediation allows everyone to make a deal without the complex process of going to trial.

**Mediator.** In most mediations, a lawyer or retired judge with estate experience is a preferred mediator. Unlike a trial judge, a mediator can help steer the parties to a satisfactory resolution.

**No contest clause.** This wording in a will is designed to disinherit any beneficiary who contests the will. In some jurisdictions, these clauses are not enforced. If you leave only a token amount to the beneficiary, he or she may have no financial incentive not to challenge your will.

**Planned giving.** A charitable gift that maximizes tax and estate planning advantages. It can be made while you're alive or when you're gone through your will as a deferred gift.

**Power of attorney.** A legal document signed and witnessed to appoint an agent, proxy, or attorney. You can choose attorneys to make decisions when you can't.

**Power of attorney for personal care.** A legal document you sign. It must comply with provincial, legal, and witness formalities. Agents, proxies, or attorneys are given power to make decisions. These powers of attorney are restricted to personal or health care decisions and are usually separate documents from a power of attorney for property.

**Power of attorney for property.** A legal document signed and witnessed according to provincial law to designate an agent, proxy, or substitute decision maker to handle your financial affairs. You can place restrictions or conditions on when your attorney can act. Generally, you must specify that your attorney can act even if you are found to be incapable. If these documents contain no restrictions, they are valid upon being signed and are like loaded guns.

**Prenuptial agreement.** A marriage contract that can be used to deal with support and property rights between spouses. You can sign agreements before or during a marriage.

**Probate.** Relates to all matters over which estate or probate courts have jurisdiction. Probate taxes are levied on estates administered through the courts with or without a will.

**Probate taxes.** These are also estate administration taxes and are paid to provincial governments through the estate court. You'll pay probate taxes (except in Quebec) whenever assets are passed through your estate whether you have a will or not.

**Remainderman.** The person who gets the balance of the funds not used during the beneficiaries' lifetimes.

**Revocable or irrevocable personal trusts.** If you create a revocable trust, you're probably one of the trust's trustees. You can cancel a revocable trust. Irrevocable trusts don't let you collapse the trust and regain the trust property. These are forms of living trusts.

**Revocation of a will.** Revoking or cancelling it. Revocation may be done when a person marries, destroys an older will, or makes a new will.

**Spousal elections.** Spouses receive property rights when they marry. You can't ignore these rights when you plan your estate; they take precedence over your will. Your married spouse can elect to take his or her entitlement under family property laws instead of the will.

**Spousal preferential share.** In some provinces, those treated as "married" receive the first portion of the estate. This comes off the top; in Ontario only, a married spouse gets the first $200,000 of your intestate estate.

**Spousal rollovers.** Important tax advantages. They are the main exception to the deemed disposition rule. Rollovers allow a postponement or deferral of capital gains. These are available to qualifying spouses, common-law or same-sex spouses, spousal trusts, and financially dependent children or grandchildren.

**Spouse.** The definition of this term varies from province to province and in each piece of provincial legislation. Terms such as "spouse," "child," or "dependant" are often defined differently in specific laws.

**Succession laws.** Provincial laws that decide who shares in your estate if you die intestate.

**Tenants-in-common.** Another way of describing property ownership. Even though the law refers to it as "tenancy," it's the opposite of joint tenancy, with no automatic rights of survivorship. Tenants-in-common can have unequal interests, such as a sixty/forty split. This type of property must be dealt with by will.

**Terminal return.** "Terminal" means the end of a series. For tax purposes, it's the last personal return, which is filed for all income to the date of a person's death.

**Testamentary.** A paper, document, or appointment is "testamentary" when it's made to be effective only after the death of the person making it. Testamentary means it must be revocable. The maker of the testamentary document keeps control over the property until death.

**Testamentary trustees.** Appointed by a will to carry out the trust terms. Trustees are not necessarily executors or estate administrators or guardians. You can, though, give an executor the additional role of a trustee.

**Testator.** A male writing a will.

**Testatrix.** A female writing a will.

**Trusts.** Legal relationships, usually put in writing, where trustees manage assets for the benefit of trust beneficiaries, such as minors. Can be created by your will as a testamentary trust or during your lifetime as an *inter vivos* or living trust.

**Will.** A revocable written and signed document effective after your death. You set out your last wishes for your property after your death. Your will names beneficiaries, persons you trust to be executors, and guardians for minors. Wills must comply with each province's legal requirements to be valid.

# Index

## About the Author

Edward Olkovich is a nationally recognized expert on estate planning. He is one of the first lawyers certified as a specialist in Estates and Trusts Law in Ontario and sits on the committee that certifies other specialists. Author of three other books on estate planning (available at www.estatetips.com), Edward has written for the American Bar Association, is quoted in national publications, and guests on television and radio.

Edward has instructed new lawyers since 1990 in the Ontario Bar Admissions course. He has chaired various programs, committees, and sections for the Ontario Bar Association including General Practice and Law Practice Management. A past executive member of the Trusts and Estates Section, he is founding chair of Ontario's Make a Will project.

Edward is a member of The Canadian Association of Professional Speakers (C.A.P.S.) and is available for your education programs and client seminars. He can be reached at www.mrwills.com or by telephone at 416-769-9800 or 1-800-679-4557. Oh yes, he makes whole wheat bread for his wife Krystyna and his two sons, Nick and Adam.